In Memory of

Emma Moore
from the
Class of '65

DATE DUE

Y0-CAZ-009

COOKING WITH TEXAS HIGHWAYS

COOKING WITH
Texas Highways

EDITED BY NOLA MCKEY

FOREWORD BY JACK LOWRY

Food Photography by J. Griffis Smith

Food Styling by Fran DeCoux Gerling
and Quincy Adams Erickson

UNIVERSITY OF TEXAS PRESS
AUSTIN

Second printing, 2007

Requests for permission to reproduce material from this
work should be sent to Permissions, University of Texas
Press, Box 7819, Austin, TX 78713-7819.
www.utexas.edu/utpress/about/bpermission.html

∞ The paper used in this book meets the minimum
requirements of ANSI/NISO Z39.48-1992 (R1997)
(Permanence of Paper).

LIBRARY OF CONGRESS
CATALOGING-IN-PUBLICATION DATA

Cooking with Texas highways / edited by Nola McKey ;
foreword by Jack Lowry ; food photography by J. Griffis
Smith.—1st ed.
          p.   cm.
Includes index.
ISBN-13: 978-0-292-70629-3 (cloth : alk. paper)
ISBN-10: 0-292-70629-4
1. Cookery, American—Southwestern style. I. McKey,
Nola, 1946– II. Texas highways.
TX715.2.S69C665 2005
641.5979—dc22   2004020259

To all the loyal readers of Texas Highways,
who make publishing the magazine a labor of love.

Contents

Acknowledgments

Cookbooks usually represent the contributions of many individuals, and this one is no exception. Most of the tantalizing food shots on these pages, for example, are the result of a longtime collaboration between staff photographer J. Griffis Smith and food stylist Fran DeCoux Gerling. Between Griff's superb photographic skills and Fran's culinary genius, this team produced many a masterpiece. Fran, who also tested the majority of the recipes and even provided some of her own, retired in late 2002. Griff continues shooting food for the magazine, aided by food stylist Quincy Adams Erickson, and her fine work also appears in the book.

Photography editor Michael A. Murphy deserves special recognition. He not only provided direction regarding photography but supplied invaluable computer expertise on this project as well. And as our resident Dutch-oven expert, Mike tested recipes and wrote copy for the Dutch-Oven Dishes section.

Other *Texas Highways* editorial staff—namely Jack Lowry, Jill Lawless, Ann Gallaway, Lori Moffatt, Marty Lange, Jane Wu Knapp, Jane Sharpe, Kirsti Harms, and Nora Baldwin—also contributed immeasurably to the cookbook. From coordinating, editing, and designing the food stories where most of the recipes originated to picking up the slack on the magazine when cookbook deadlines loomed, their respective talents and support were crucial to this project. Thanks, gang. Special appreciation goes to Jack Lowry, Jill Lawless, Ann Gallaway, and Lori Moffatt for their help in editing cookbook copy and recipes.

Members of the Texas Department of Transportation's Travel Division, which publishes *Texas Highways,* were also supportive. Not only was this group always ready to taste-test, they were willing to cook! When the word went out that we needed recipe testers for some of the older recipes, a number of people volunteered to try them at home. In addition to editorial folks, *TH* circulation manager Cynthia Kosel and *TH* administrative assistant Lupe Valdez, along with Travel Division staffers Lois Rodriguez, Alice Sedberry, Julie Welsh, and Mary Lynn Mathews, also tested recipes on their own time. As a result of these collective efforts, we eliminated several recipes outright and updated or improved many others.

Thanks also go to *TH* publisher Kathy Murphy and ancillary products manager Julie Jacob for championing the cookbook. Julie's initial entry of more than three hundred recipes on the magazine's Web site (www.texashighways.com) laid the digital foundation for this project. (As the magazine's recipe archives grow, more recipes will be added to the Web site.)

And finally, our thanks go to all the chefs, restaurant owners, and others who furnished recipes over the years (check out the credits at the end of each recipe), and to the *Texas Highways* readers who gave us enthusiastic feedback. We appreciate your contributions to what we hope is a mouth-watering, can't-put-it-down guide to Texas cooking.

NOLA McKEY ∼ ASSOCIATE EDITOR, *TEXAS HIGHWAYS*

Foreword

Cooking with *Texas Highways*. Sounds like fun.

Since *Texas Highways* became a travel publication in 1974, we have published hundreds of recipes and restaurant reviews, and we have let readers know about savory foods at Texas' great festivals and celebrations. Texas has a rich culinary heritage, and the readers of *Texas Highways* have come to expect a variety of food features and tips on where to eat all across the Lone Star State. And our readers have been generous in sharing their recipes and favorite dining spots, as well.

One thing I have learned over more than two decades as a *Texas Highways* editor is that Texas food is about fun, fellowship, and flavor. Texans know that good eating involves deep-down enjoyment—from selecting the right ingredients to preparing them in myriad ways, to sharing the finished product with friends, family, and strangers, too.

Associate editor Nola McKey spent months compiling, testing, and improving the recipes in this book. She talked to food experts and colleagues about their preferences, and picked their brains for suggestions on how to make the recipes as clear, concise, and appetizing as could be. We think she has succeeded admirably.

Along the way, Nola has been assisted by the talented staff of *Texas Highways* (see Acknowledgments), and in great part by photography editor Michael A. Murphy, longtime *Texas Highways* food stylist Fran De-Coux Gerling, and staff photographer J. Griffis Smith, who has been photographing food for the magazine for more than twenty years.

This book itself reflects three decades of Texas cooking. The University of Texas Press published the first *Texas Highways Cookbook* in 1986. Since then, Texas cuisine has evolved in numerous ways that you'll find reflected throughout these pages: We have seen a gradual move toward lighter, healthier ingredients; ethnic cuisines have multiplied in the state; and

Texans are willing to try a greater variety of foods and methods of preparation. At the same time, Texans are reluctant to let go of their culinary traditions. And why should they? Classic Texas fare attracts foodies from all walks of life, and old standbys like Tex-Mex and barbecue are known around the globe. So here you have it: Welcome to the latest *Texas Highways* cookbook. We think you'll relish cooking with *Texas Highways*.

What more can we say? *Bon appétit! Guten appetit! ¡Buen provecho!* And happy cooking.

JACK LOWRY — EDITOR, *TEXAS HIGHWAYS*

State Fare:
AN INTRODUCTION

As a travel magazine, *Texas Highways* has never claimed to be in the same culinary league as *Gourmet* or *Bon Appétit*, but you can't travel the state for more than three decades, as we have, without picking up a few good recipes. Texas abounds with great cooks, from Dutch-oven masters to trend-setting restaurateurs, and over the years, many of them have shared their favorite recipes with us. Now, we'd like to share our collection with you.

The roundup includes Lone Star classics like chicken-fried steak and chili, as well as exotic fare like tabouli and Thai Pesto. The mixture is as diverse as Texas, and just as flavorful. Many of our recipes rely on the state's wealth of fruits and vegetables, meats, freshwater fish, and seafood. Others take their cues from the cultural traditions of other lands— Texas has representatives from scores of ethnic groups. As you might expect, the combining of such varied resources makes for some exciting concoctions.

Looking for a new spin on beef stew? We've got it. How about a recipe for blackened catfish? We've got that, too. Tex-Mex? You know it. Vegetables? The list includes traditional favorites like fried green tomatoes, as well as entrées like Spinach-Mushroom Lasagna and Grilled Portobellos. Desserts? Whatever suits your fancy, from kolaches to Nopalito Pie. (Turn to page 189, if you want dessert first.)

No, we can't offer you the only cookbook you'll ever need, but we can offer you a gastronomic tour of the state. Along the way, you can enjoy our signature photography—magnificent scenes of fields and forests, roadsides and rivers, and more, from the Panhandle to the Gulf Coast. So come on, roll up your sleeves, find an apron, and start cooking with *Texas Highways*.

COOKING WITH TEXAS HIGHWAYS

Snacks & Beverages

Whether it's kicking back with a few friends and watching a football game on TV, hosting a family get-together, or visiting with a neighbor who just dropped by, Texans are known for their hearty hospitality. When company comes, food and drink are never far behind.

Snacks and appetizers run the gamut of possibilities, but tops on any Lone Star list of tasty openers has to be chips and salsa (followed closely by chips and queso). Of course, Texans also use salsa as a condiment, ladling it on everything from scrambled eggs to black-eyed peas. Our versions of this perennial favorite begin on page 3, followed by other culinary icebreakers like Vietnamese Egg Rolls, Goat Cheese Kisses, and Cactus Fries.

Recipes for liquid refreshment range from Apple Cooler and Watermelon Smoothie to holiday favorites like wassail and glögg. And while we can't give you the recipe for Dr Pepper, which originated in a Waco drugstore in 1885, we do include tips for making another Texas standard—iced tea. Offered morning, noon, and night, summer or winter, it remains the (nonalcoholic) beverage of choice from Amarillo to Zapata.

Laura's Salsa

A basic red salsa, this recipe calls for both fresh and canned tomatoes. For variety, add mashed avocado or black-eyed peas. You can also mix equal amounts of chopped mango (fresh or bottled) and this basic recipe to make a tropical-flavored sauce you can dip with tortilla chips or use on meat or fish.

3 (14.5-oz.) cans tomatoes	juice of 1 to 2 limes
1 large tomato, quartered	1 tsp. sugar
1 jumbo or 2 small red onions, quartered	1 tsp. red wine vinegar
1 T. chopped garlic	½ tsp. salt, or to taste
1 bunch fresh cilantro, stems removed	½ tsp. pepper, or to taste
½ c. pickled jalapeño slices, drained	¼ tsp. granulated garlic, or to taste

In a food processor, pulse canned and fresh tomatoes until finely chopped (may need to pulse half at a time). Remove tomatoes and pulse onion, garlic, cilantro, and jalapeño until finely chopped.

Combine the processed mixtures and remaining ingredients; refrigerate overnight before serving. Store in sterilized jars in refrigerator (will keep at least 2 weeks). **Yield: About 9 cups.**

LAURA PATTERSON ~ JANUARY 1998

How hot is too hot? The answer varies from one salsa aficionado to another. For a milder salsa, devein and seed the chiles in the recipe, or simply use fewer chiles.

Opposite page (clockwise, from top): Salsa Verde, Matt's Smoked Salsa, Laura's Salsa (this variation with chopped mango), and Avocado Salsa

Matt's Smoked Salsa

This recipe is adapted from one that appears in Matt Martinez's Culinary Frontier:
A Real Texas Cookbook *by Matt Martinez Jr. and Steve Pate (1997).*
It's great with chips, but it's heavenly with barbecue, steaks, and scrambled eggs.
If you don't have a smoker, a barbecue pit works fine.

3 whole medium tomatoes	¾ tsp. salt, or to taste
½ medium sweet white onion, cut in chunks	1 tsp. red wine vinegar
3 whole jalapeños *or* 6 whole serranos (use the latter for a hotter salsa)	2 tsp. vegetable oil
3 cloves garlic	½ c. water

Combine ingredients in a heavy pot and place the pot (uncovered) in a smoker for 1½ to 2 hours or until the vegetables are soft. (Do not allow the vegetables to become dry; add more water if needed.) Remove pot from smoker.

Mash (do not blend) the vegetables, taking care to mash one chile at a time until salsa tastes hot enough; discard any extra chiles. (Salsa will be chunky.) Adjust the salt to taste. Store in an airtight container in refrigerator (will keep about 2 weeks). **Yield: 2 cups.**

NOTE: For a thicker salsa, combine 1 T. cornstarch with 2 T. water and drizzle the mixture into the salsa while it's still hot, stirring constantly. Simmer on low heat 5 to 10 minutes, stirring occasionally, until salsa reaches the desired thickness. If it becomes too thick, simply add a bit more water.

MATT MARTINEZ ~ JANUARY 1998

Salsa Verde

As the name suggests, this salsa is bright green, thanks to a flavorful combination of
tomatillos, serranos, and cilantro.

7 medium tomatillos, husks and stems removed	1 large bunch cilantro, stems removed
½ white onion, quartered	½ tsp. salt
4 serranos (use fewer for a milder taste)	1 T. fresh lime juice
1 clove garlic	

Place tomatillos in a saucepan, cover with water, and bring to a boil. Simmer gently, uncovered, about 15 minutes or until tomatillos are soft. Turn off heat and allow tomatillos to cool in the cooking water.

Combine remaining ingredients in a food processor or blender and purée. Drain tomatillos, add to mixture, and purée. Store in refrigerator (will keep about a week). **Yield: 2½ cups.**

JANUARY 1998

Texas alone produces more than 100 commercial brands of hot sauce, picante sauce, and salsa, with pepper power varying from the mildly hot to the "Help, I'm on fire!" variety.

Avocado Salsa

This chopped-not-blended concoction blurs the lines between salsa and pico de gallo.

2 avocados, peeled and chopped	1 T. minced serranos (about 3 serranos)
2 tomatoes, chopped	1 T. minced cilantro
1 T. fresh lime juice	1 tsp. ground cumin
1 T. fresh lemon juice	½ tsp. salt
2 tsp. minced garlic (about 3 cloves)	

Combine ingredients and refrigerate for at least 1 hour. Yield: 2 cups.

JANUARY 1998

Fresh Watermelon Salsa

A good addition to summertime meals, this unusual salsa is delicious served with grilled chicken. For a hotter version, add 1 to 4 seeded and diced jalapeños.

2 c. seeded and coarsely chopped watermelon	1 T. balsamic vinegar
2 T. chopped onion	¼ tsp. garlic salt
2 T. water chestnuts	additional balsamic vinegar
2 to 4 T. chopped Anaheim chiles	

Combine first 6 ingredients; mix well. Refrigerate for 2 hours. Add more balsamic vinegar to taste. Yield: 2½ cups.

JUNE 1993

Guacamole

*Ever-popular guacamole works as a dip, as a salad atop a bed of lettuce,
or as an addition to fajitas or tostados.*

3 large or 4 small ripe avocados, peeled and mashed	2 to 3 T. picante sauce (optional)
1 ripe tomato, diced	2 T. minced onion
salt to taste	4 green onions with tops, chopped
¼ tsp. garlic powder	juice of 1 lime

Combine all ingredients in a medium-size mixing bowl and blend well. Serve with fajitas or tostados. **Yield: About 4 cups.**

FEBRUARY 1987

Lone Star Caviar

*We first printed this recipe in December 1982, and it's been around longer than that.
Even so, it's still a favorite for New Year's Eve parties. You can substitute 5 cups of
canned and drained black-eyed peas (buy three 15-oz. cans) for the cooked peas
in this recipe.*

1 lb. dried black-eyed peas	½ c. finely chopped jalapeño
2 c. Italian salad dressing	1 (3-oz.) jar diced pimiento, drained
2 c. diced green pepper	1 T. finely chopped garlic
1½ c. diced onion	salt to taste
1 c. finely chopped green onion	hot pepper sauce to taste

Soak peas in enough water to cover for 6 hours or overnight; drain well. Transfer peas to a saucepan, add enough water to cover, and bring to a boil over high heat. Reduce heat and cook until tender, about 45 minutes. Do not overcook. Drain well and place peas in a large bowl. Blend in dressing and let cool. Add remaining ingredients, mix well, and chill. **Yield: 7½ cups.**

DECEMBER 1982 AND JULY 1994

Ro-Tel Forever

A small entrepreneur in Elsa, Texas, developed one of the mainstays of Tex-Mex cooking—Ro-Tel Tomatoes & Green Chilies—in the early 1940s. One item in a line of vegetable products that Carl Roettele produced in his family canning business, it quickly became a favorite with Carl's customers.

At first, the zesty tomatoes were shipped only as far away as San Antonio, Houston, and Dallas. But by 1956, cooks could buy them elsewhere in the state, as well as in Oklahoma and Arkansas. According to legend, demand for the product skyrocketed in 1963 when the wife of a Washington politician revealed to a national magazine that Ro-Tel was the secret ingredient in her chili recipe.

Since then, Ro-Tel has found its way into many traditional Texas recipes, including King Ranch Casserole and the ubiquitous, oh-so-delicious cheese dip that bears its name. No one knows when the spicy dip, which pairs Ro-Tel with Velveeta, was first created, but the dish's popularity is surely responsible for moving mountains of both products off supermarket shelves.

Despite its sale to an out-of-state company in 1992, Ro-Tel remains a staple in Texas pantries and no doubt will always be identified with Tex-Mex cuisine.

Here's the recipe for the quintessential Texas version of chile con queso, followed by a couple of variations.

FAMOUS RO-TEL CHEESE DIP

The easiest way to prepare this dish is to microwave it. However, if a microwave isn't available, just combine the first 2 ingredients in a saucepan and stir over very low heat until the cheese spread is melted.

1 lb. Velveeta or other pasteurized, processed cheese loaf, cut into 1-inch cubes	1 (10-oz.) can Ro-Tel Diced Tomatoes & Green Chilies
	tortilla chips

Place first 2 ingredients in a casserole dish; cover and microwave on HIGH for about 5 minutes or until cheese spread is melted, stirring once. Serve warm with chips. Yield: About 3½ cups.

NOTE: Variations of this simple recipe abound. For a meaty version, prepare the original recipe, then stir in ½ to 1 lb. cooked and drained lean hamburger meat or sausage. For fewer calories, combine ⅓ to 1 lb. Velveeta Light, 1 (10-oz.) can Ro-Tel Diced Tomatoes & Green Chilies, and 1 (4.5-oz.) can diced green chiles. The resulting dip will be slightly soupier than the original recipe, but still mighty tasty. Consider serving it with a platter of celery sticks or other raw vegetables instead of chips.

2003

Stuffed Jalapeños

Texas Highways *photo editor Mike Murphy is a member of the Hamilton Pool Jalapeño Squeezers, a group of friends who enjoy competing in barbecue cook-offs. The group agreed to share one of its award-winning recipes; however, Mike cautions: "You might want to wear some disposable food-service gloves when preparing these appetizers, and don't rub your eyes or anything else!" He adds, "These are fun to serve at parties— they tend to separate the real Texans from the wannabes!"*

18 to 24 large, fresh jalapeños	½ tsp. salt
1 smoked chicken breast (precooked), finely chopped	½ tsp. pepper
1 onion, finely chopped	juice of 1 lime
1 bunch cilantro, finely chopped	½ c. chopped pecans (optional)
1 (8-oz.) pkg. cream cheese, softened	1 lb. bacon (either thin- or thick-sliced)
2 tsp. Tony Chachere's Original Seasoning	sturdy round toothpicks

Slice each jalapeño lengthwise, from tip of pepper to below stem, *almost* in half, so that you can open it like a clam. Remove seeds and veins, using a small melon scooper or spoon. Rinse jalapeños, making sure to wash away any remaining seeds.

Combine chopped chicken breast, onion, and cilantro in a medium-size bowl. Add cream cheese, seasonings, and lime juice (and pecans, if desired) and mix well; set aside.

Remove 9 to 12 slices of bacon from package, cut slices in half, and set aside. (Reserve remaining bacon for another use.)

Using a spoon, fill each jalapeño with stuffing and squeeze the pepper closed. Scrape off excess stuffing, then wrap a length of bacon around pepper and secure it by inserting a toothpick all the way through. (Any remaining stuffing makes an excellent dip.) Refrigerate peppers (overnight, if necessary) until ready to cook.

Prepare charcoal fire. (Peppers may also be deep-fried, if you prefer.) Grill peppers over medium-hot coals, turning often, about 10 minutes or until bacon looks done, then serve. **Yield: 18 to 24 appetizers.**

HAMILTON POOL JALAPEÑO SQUEEZERS ⁓ 2003

Vietnamese Fried Egg Rolls

If you haven't made egg rolls before, you may need to practice a few times to get the procedure down; hence the extra wrappers. (This recipe is adapted from one that calls for rice-paper wrappers, which are more delicate than conventional egg-roll wrappers. After you become proficient with this version, you may want to try the recipe again using rice-paper wrappers.)

1 lb. ground pork or ground chicken

½ c. crabmeat or small shrimp, mashed

¾ c. chopped onion

⅓ c. finely chopped wood ears or other mushrooms

1 tsp. salt

¼ tsp. black pepper

10 (8½-inch-square) egg-roll wrappers, cut in half diagonally

2 egg whites, beaten slightly

vegetable oil

Bibb or romaine lettuce leaves (optional)

Nước Chấm (optional) (recipe follows)

Combine first 6 ingredients; set aside.

Lay wrapper triangle with right angle pointing away from you. Place 2 T. stuffing in a 3-inch-long strip across wrapper about 2 inches from bottom in the center. Roll up wrapper halfway (toward the point) into a cylinder. Fold both sides of wrapper inward, enclosing filling, and continue to roll up. Brush edges with a little egg white to seal. Repeat procedure, using remaining stuffing. (You may have leftover wrappers.)

In a 3- to 4-qt. pan, pour oil to a depth of at least 2 inches and heat to 350° to 375°. Fry egg rolls, a few at a time, until crisp and light golden (about 6 minutes). Drain on paper towels. Serve alone or wrapped in lettuce and dipped in *Nước Chấm*. **Yield: About 14 large rolls.**

NƯỚC CHẤM

This delicious dipping sauce is the universal condiment of Vietnam.

2 garlic cloves

½ to 1 tsp. crushed red pepper

1 T. sugar

¼ c. plus 2 T. *nước mắm* (fish sauce)

¼ c. plus 1 T. fresh lime juice or rice wine vinegar

¼ c. water

Using a mortar and pestle, mash garlic with red pepper. Add sugar and pound to a glossy paste. Add remaining ingredients and stir well. **Yield: About ¾ cup.**

ANH CHI DINH ～ JUNE 1996

Fresh Vietnamese Spring Rolls and Vietnamese Fried Egg Rolls

Fresh Vietnamese Spring Rolls

*Once you get the hang of handling the rice-paper wrappers,
these delicious rolls are easy to make.*

2 oz. thin rice vermicelli	1 c. fresh bean sprouts
12 oz. boneless pork loin or chops, pounded thin	½ c. fresh mint leaves
1 large carrot, shredded	8 medium shrimp, cooked, peeled, deveined, and sliced in half lengthwise
1 tsp. sugar	½ c. fresh cilantro leaves
8 rice-paper wrappers, about 8½ inches square	Peanut Sauce (recipe follows)
4 large red leaf or Boston lettuce leaves, cut in half	

Prepare noodles according to package directions; set aside.

Cook pork in boiling, lightly salted water 20 minutes. Chill in cold water, drain, and thinly slice into 1 x 2-inch pieces. In a bowl, combine shredded carrot with sugar; let stand 10 minutes.

Have a basin of warm water ready for moistening wrappers. Work with one sheet at a time, keeping remaining sheets covered with a barely damp cloth. Immerse each sheet in water, remove, and spread on a dry, smooth kitchen towel.

Lay one piece of lettuce on bottom third of wrapper. On lettuce, place 1 T. noodles, 1 T. shredded carrot-sugar mixture, a few pieces of pork, and a sprinkling of bean sprouts and mint leaves. Roll up paper halfway into a cylinder. Fold both sides of paper inward, enclosing filling. Lay two shrimp halves along crease. Place several cilantro leaves next to shrimp. Keep rolling wrapper into a cylinder to seal. Cover finished rolls with damp towel while you fill remaining wrappers. Serve with Peanut Sauce. **Yield: 8 rolls (4 servings).**

PEANUT SAUCE

¼ c. hoisin sauce (available at Asian import stores and at many grocery stores)	1 T. soy sauce
¼ c. chicken broth or water	2 T. dry-roasted unsalted peanuts, crushed
	1 fresh red chile, seeded and thinly sliced

Combine first 3 ingredients; stir in peanuts and chile pepper. **Yield: About ½ cup.**

JUNE 1996

Native Americans prized popcorn not only as a dietary staple but also for its use in headdresses, necklaces, and corsage-like decorations.

Tex-Mex Popcorn

Looking for something to spice up a TV evening? This zesty popcorn will do the trick.

2 tsp. chili powder	2 tsp. ground cumin
2 tsp. paprika	2 qt. freshly made oil-popped popcorn

Mix seasonings together in a large bowl and toss with popcorn. Serve warm. **Yield: 2 quarts.**

JUNE 1999

Chili Peanuts

The combination of chili powder, cayenne, and garlic makes this snack addictive. Some people say it reminds them of Corn Nuts.

2 lb. (about 7 c.) unsalted roasted peanuts	3 T. peanut oil, canola oil, or vegetable oil
1½ T. kosher salt	12 large cloves garlic, peeled, *or* 2 T. dried, chopped garlic
1 T. chili powder	
1 T. cayenne	1 T. lemon juice

Place peanuts in a large bowl. Combine salt, chili powder, and cayenne in a small bowl. Sprinkle over peanuts and toss to coat; set aside.

Heat oil in a large skillet until hot; add garlic and cook over medium heat until garlic begins to turn golden. Add lemon juice and peanut mixture and cook, stirring frequently, for 2 minutes. **Yield: About 7 cups.**

AUGUST 1994

Salted Pecans

If you have pecan trees in your backyard, you'll want to make lots of this tasty snack. Don't have a handy source? Then look for pecans at fruit stands in the fall, and be sure to buy enough to freeze for later use.

2 T. butter or stick margarine, melted	salt to taste
2 c. pecans	⅛ to ¼ tsp. cayenne (optional)

Place melted butter in a shallow pan, stir in nuts, and spread evenly in a single layer. Sprinkle with salt and cayenne and bake at 300° for 15 to 20 minutes or just until browned. Watch carefully and stir occasionally. Drain well on paper towels before storing. **Yield: 2 cups.**

DECEMBER 1982

Roasted Sunflower Seeds

This recipe is easy to increase or decrease: Just use 1 tsp. melted butter per cup of raw kernels.

2 c. raw sunflower kernels	2 tsp. melted butter or stick margarine
	salt

Spread a single layer of raw kernels in a shallow pan and roast in a 300° oven 30 to 40 minutes, depending on the degree of brownness and crispness desired.

Remove pan from oven. Stir in melted butter until kernels are coated; drain well on paper towels. Salt to taste. Store in a tightly covered container. **Yield: 2 cups.**

AUGUST 1995

Americans consume about a billion pounds of fiber-rich popcorn each year.

When preparing cactus, remember that tunas (prickly pear fruits) and even spineless nopalitos (tender, young prickly pear pads) can have tiny, painful stickers. Wear heavy gloves or use tongs to avoid barbs.

Cactus Fries

Dubbed the "Cactus King" by some prickly-pear promoters, Texas chef Jay McCarthy contributed this recipe (pictured on page 68) for our March 1998 story on prickly pear. Jay suggests serving this unusual dish as an appetizer with habanero-laced ketchup, or pairing it with shrimp or scallops.

2 lb. nopalitos	1 tsp. baking powder
3 T. cornstarch	1 egg white
2 T. achiote paste (look for it in the Mexican specialty-foods section of your supermarket)	about ¾ c. ice water
⅔ c. all-purpose flour	peanut oil

Remove thorns (if any) and "eyes" from cactus and trim edges of pads. Cook cactus, covered, 2 minutes in enough boiling salted water to cover; drain. Cut cactus in 3- to 4-inch strips similar to French fries; set aside.

Combine cornstarch and achiote paste in a blender or food processor and pulse until smooth. In a medium-size bowl, combine flour and baking powder, add cornstarch-achiote mixture, and blend well.

In another bowl, beat egg white until stiff peaks form. Fold into flour mixture, alternating with enough ice water to make batter the consistency of unbeaten egg white. Chill batter.

Dredge cactus strips in batter and fry in deep hot oil (375°) 2 to 3 minutes or until crisp and golden. Drain well. **Yield: 3 to 5 servings.**

JAY MCCARTHY ～ MARCH 1998

Hummus Bi Tahini (Chickpea Dip)

You can start with dried garbanzos, but most Lebanese cooks use canned beans to make hummus these days. Look for tahini in Middle Eastern specialty grocery stores or health food stores.

1 (15½-oz.) can garbanzos (chickpeas) *or* 1½ c. cooked dried garbanzos plus 3 to 4 T. cooking liquid

⅓ c. tahini (sesame seed paste)

⅓ c. fresh lemon juice (juice of 3 medium lemons)

1 tsp. salt

1 large clove garlic, crushed

pocket bread (pita bread), soft or toasted

Drain canned garbanzos, reserving 3 to 4 T. liquid; set aside. Place 1½ c. garbanzos in blender or food processor. Stir tahini thoroughly, then add to garbanzos. Turn on blender and very slowly add 3 T. garbanzo liquid, blending well. Add lemon juice, mixing slowly. Add salt and garlic; mix well. (Add additional garbanzo liquid for a thinner consistency.) Serve with pocket bread. **Yield: About 6 servings.**

JO ANN ANDERA 〜 AUGUST 1996

Tabouli (left) and Hummus Bi Tahini (Chickpea Dip)

Brie en Croûte

This appetizer takes a while to make, and it's anything but light.
Nonetheless, it's a classic for holiday buffets.

1 (3-oz.) pkg. cream cheese, softened	1 (4½-oz.) round Brie, with skin intact
¼ c. butter or stick margarine, softened	1 egg yolk
¾ c. all-purpose flour	½ tsp. sesame seeds

Combine cream cheese and butter in a medium-size bowl and blend well. Add flour and cut in with a pastry blender or two knives until particles are size of small peas. Form pastry into a ball; wrap in plastic wrap and refrigerate at least 1 hour.

Divide dough into 2 pieces, one slightly larger than the other. On a lightly floured surface, roll each piece to about ⅛-inch thickness. Cut out one 6-inch round and another slightly larger round, reserving scraps for decoration. Place smaller round on a cookie sheet and center Brie on top of it. Fit larger round of dough over top of Brie, and press edges of both rounds together, crimping all the way around to seal.

Roll out pastry scraps and use cookie cutter to make desired shapes (flower, star, etc.); place on top for decoration. Combine egg yolk with 1 T. water and brush mixture over entire pastry. Sprinkle sesame seeds over top and refrigerate until just before serving time. Bake at 400° about 20 minutes or until golden brown. Let stand a few minutes. To serve, slice into small wedges (cheese will be soft inside). **Yield: 12 to 16 appetizer servings.**

DUSTY McGUIRE ⌒ DECEMBER 1982

Cheese Straws

These old-fashioned appetizers were prepared in most fashionable Southern homes before the holidays and stored in tins for serving to guests who dropped in unexpectedly.

¾ lb. sharp cheddar cheese, grated	¾ tsp. salt
¾ c. butter or stick margarine, softened	½ to 1 tsp. cayenne
2½ c. all-purpose flour	

Combine cheese and butter in a large mixing bowl; beat well at medium speed of an electric mixer. Combine dry ingredients and gradually add to cheese mixture, mixing until dough is no longer crumbly.

Flatten dough to ¼-inch thick on a sheet of waxed paper (you may want to divide dough into 3 or 4 parts). Cut into thin strips about 2 inches long and twist gently. Bake at 375° about 10 minutes or until very lightly browned. When cool, store in an airtight container, placing waxed paper between layers. **Yield: About 10 dozen.**

SAM BELL MAXEY HOUSE ∾ DECEMBER 1982

Chili-Cheese Log

Pair this spicy concoction with a variety of party crackers and you've got an easy-to-make appetizer.

1 (3-oz.) pkg. cream cheese (let stand at room temperature to soften)	¼ c. pecans, finely chopped
2 c. shredded American cheese	1 tsp. chili powder
1 T. lemon juice	1 tsp. paprika
¼ tsp. garlic powder	assorted crackers

Combine cheeses, lemon juice, and garlic powder in the bowl of a heavy-duty mixer or food processor and blend well. Stir in pecans. Using a rubber spatula, scrape mixture onto a piece of waxed paper. Shape cheese mixture into a roll about 1½ inches in diameter.

Combine chili powder and paprika. Unwrap cheese log and sprinkle mixture on waxed paper, turning roll as needed to coat. Rewrap roll using same waxed paper and refrigerate several hours or overnight. Let stand at room temperature 10 minutes before serving with crackers. **Yield: 1 cheese log.**

BETSY SIMPSON & CAROLYN SCRAFFORD ∾ DECEMBER 1982

Texas' first commercial goat cheese operations sprang up in the Hill Country in the late 1980s. Today, goat cheese takes shape inside small dairies statewide. The most widely produced variety is chèvre, a smooth, soft cheese with a slightly salty kick. It resembles cream cheese but has fewer calories and less fat.

One of the state's best-known goat cheese producers, Pure Luck Organic Farms in Dripping Springs, offers not only chèvre, but a wide variety of other cheeses as well, reflecting Americans' growing interest in artisanal, or specialty, cheeses.

Goat Cheese Kisses

You can prepare these elegant hors d'oeuvres ahead and freeze them until you need them. Keep in mind that frozen kisses take slightly longer to bake.

¾ c. olive oil	8 sheets phyllo dough
1 T. dried herbs (any kind you like)	6 oz. chèvre (goat cheese)
1 clove garlic, crushed	

Heat olive oil with herbs and garlic until warm (don't boil). Remove from heat and let steep 15 minutes. Strain and cool.

Stack 4 phyllo sheets and cut into a 12-inch square. (Freeze the remainder for another use.) Cut square into thirds vertically and horizontally to form 9 four-inch squares. For each kiss, place one square (one layer) of phyllo on a flat surface. (Cover the rest of the phyllo with a damp cloth as you work.) Brush with oil, then add three more phyllo layers, brushing each layer with oil. Place about 2 tsp. cheese in the center and pull all corners together, pinching to enclose cheese. Repeat procedure with remaining 4 sheets phyllo dough. Bake on a greased cookie sheet or in greased mini-muffin pans at 400° for 10 to 12 minutes. **Yield: 18 kisses.**

MAY 1998

Look for another appetizer, Brie with Toasted Pecans, in the Dutch-Oven Dishes section (page 223). A creative cook can easily adapt the recipe for stovetop cooking.

Opposite page (counter-clockwise, from top): Mixed Greens–Feta Salad, Goat Cheese Kisses, and Warm Goat Cheese–Potato Cakes

Now-and-Later Lemonade

This recipe makes enough simple syrup for several pitchers of lemonade.
After you mix up one, just store the rest of the syrup in the refrigerator until you have
a yen for more of the tart stuff.

3 c. sugar	1 qt. sparkling water
3 c. water	ice
juice of 4 to 6 lemons	

In a medium saucepan over medium heat, dissolve sugar in 3 c. water; cool. Pour 1 c. cooled syrup into a pitcher (store remainder in a covered container in refrigerator); combine with lemon juice and sparkling water. Serve over ice. **Yield: About 1½ quarts.**

LORI MOFFATT ∼ JULY 2003

Apple Cooler

Adapted from a recipe that appears in Love Creek Orchards' Adams Apple Cookbook
(1994 and 2001), this beverage is perfect for summertime sipping.

1 qt. apple cider	juice of 6 limes
1 c. apricot nectar	club soda

Combine apple cider, apricot nectar, and lime juice. Pour over ice into 6 tall glasses, dividing mixture equally. Fill glasses with club soda. **Yield: 6 servings.**

LOVE CREEK ORCHARDS ∼ JUNE 1995

Watermelon Smoothie

If you have fresh ginger on hand, try adding ½ tsp. freshly squeezed ginger juice to this
mixture for extra zip (extract juice using a garlic press).

2 c. seeded watermelon chunks	1 to 2 T. sugar
1 c. cracked ice	½ tsp. ground ginger
½ c. plain yogurt	⅛ tsp. almond extract

Place all ingredients in a blender; blend until smooth. Serve in tall glasses. **Yield: 2 smoothies.**

JUNE 1993

Iced Tea

Anyone can throw a few tea bags into a pot of boiling water and come up with the base for a decent iced tea. But making a perfect pitcher of the amber-colored beverage time after time requires a bit more finesse. First of all, forget the boiling water. If you heat a pot of water for tea and it boils, throw the water out and start over. Remember sun tea? One of the reasons it was so good was that the water never boiled. Today, the tea industry discourages making sun tea because of concerns about bacterial growth during the long brewing period. Assuming you don't have half a day to make tea anyway, here's a method that works just as well.

Place 3 tea bags in a saucepan, add a small amount of water, heat until you see steam rising, and then *turn off the heat*. Cover and let steep about 10 minutes.

Meanwhile, put a cup or two of cold water in a 2-quart glass pitcher (to prevent the pitcher from breaking when you add the hot liquid later). If you want sweet tea, this is when you add the sugar. A cup of sugar per pitcher was once the norm for many Texans, but these days, most folks think that's excessive and use somewhere between one-fourth and one-half cup.

After the tea has steeped, remove the tea bags and pour the liquid into the pitcher, stirring until the sugar has dissolved. Stir in additional water until the tea reaches the desired strength. Serve over ice—lots of ice—in tall glasses. Lemon slices and fresh mint optional.

The refreshing, fruit-flavored drinks called aguas frescas that are common in Mexico (street vendors ladle them from huge glass jars) are now showing up in many Mexican-food restaurants in Texas. In their purest form, aguas frescas are simply drinks made of fresh fruit, sugar, and water, served over ice. Associate editor Lori Moffatt, who likes to play in the kitchen, shares these recipes for her favorite summertime drink.

Cantaloupe Agua Fresca

This drink is great to serve from July to September, when Pecos cantaloupes are plentiful.

1 cantaloupe	juice of 4 Mexican limes
water	¼ c. sugar, or more to taste

Peel, seed, and coarsely chop cantaloupe. (You should have about 4 c. melon.) Place 2 c. melon in a blender, add water to cover, and blend well. Strain through a piece of cheesecloth or fine strainer, reserving liquid. Place cantaloupe liquid in a 2-qt. pitcher and discard solids. Repeat procedure with other half of cantaloupe.

Add lime juice and sugar to pitcher and stir well. Serve over ice. **Yield: About 2 quarts.**

LORI MOFFATT ～ 2003

Lime-Cucumber Agua Fresca

If you like cucumbers, here's another way to enjoy them. Although unusual, the lime-cucumber flavor combination proves quite refreshing.

3 peeled cucumbers, cut into pieces	½ c. sugar, or more to taste
1 gal. water	pinch of salt (optional)
juice of 10 Mexican limes	pinch of chili powder (optional)

Place cucumbers and 2 c. water in a blender and blend well. Strain through a piece of cheesecloth or fine strainer, reserving liquid. Place cucumber liquid in an extra-large pitcher or other container and discard solids.

Add lime juice, sugar, and remaining water to pitcher. Add salt and chili powder, if desired, and stir well. Serve over ice. **Yield: About 1 gallon.**

LORI MOFFATT ～ 2003

Horchata

Texas Highways editor Jack Lowry has fond memories of drinking this rice-flavored agua fresca while growing up in Venezuela. Some recipes call for coconut or almonds to be ground up along with the rice, and some omit milk altogether.

3 c. uncooked rice	⅓ c. sugar, or more to taste
3 (3-inch-long) cinnamon sticks	½ gal. skim milk
hot water	1 tsp. vanilla
1 (14-oz.) can sweetened condensed milk	

Place rice and cinnamon sticks in a large bowl and add hot water to cover. Allow to soften 20 minutes.

Place mixture in blender and pulverize rice and cinnamon sticks. Strain through a piece of cheesecloth or fine strainer, reserving liquid. Put solids back into the blender, add more water, blend, and strain again. You should have about 2 qt. liquid. Discard remaining solids.

Place rice liquid in an extra-large pitcher or other container and add sweetened condensed milk, sugar, skim milk, and vanilla. Stir well and serve over ice. **Yield: About 1 gallon.**

LORI MOFFATT ✑ 2003

Frank Lively's 2-1-1 Margaritas

Frank Lively, editor of Texas Highways *from 1962 to 1990, is famous for his margaritas, among other things. He says using the small, juicy Mexican limes is crucial. Frank adds that the name of this recipe makes it easy to remember the proportions of the main ingredients, but cautions, "If you have to ask what the 2 is for, you shouldn't be drinking them."*

salt	½ c. freshly squeezed lime juice (you'll need about 12 Mexican limes)
1 c. tequila (Frank likes Cuervo Silver)	
½ c. Triple Sec	ice

Rim 4 glasses with salt. Combine tequila, Triple Sec, lime juice, and ice in a cocktail shaker. Shake well and pour margaritas into glasses. Serve neat or on the rocks. *¡Delicioso! ¡Salud!* **Yield: 4 margaritas.**

FRANK LIVELY ✑ 2003

Mexican-Style Hot Chocolate

Mexican-American cooks often make hot chocolate with cakes of prepared Mexican chocolate, which is already flavored with sugar and cinnamon. Although that product isn't available in some areas, this recipe makes a similar drink.

2 c. milk	½ tsp. cinnamon
1 oz. unsweetened chocolate	pinch of salt
2 T. sugar	

Combine ingredients in the top of a double boiler. Cook over low heat until chocolate melts, stirring frequently. Beat until foamy and serve in cups. **Yield: 2 servings.**

MAGGI STEWART ∼ DECEMBER 1981

Glögg

Senior editor Ann Gallaway offers this recipe for the traditional Swedish Christmas punch. She warns that it's powerful stuff (but delicious), and adds, "It'll warm every inch of a body on a cold night!"

1 c. water	a sprinkling of raisins
2 cinnamon sticks	a handful of whole raw almonds
6 whole cloves	2 c. port wine
3 whole cardamom pods	1 c. brandy
peel of 1 orange	½ c. sugar

Combine all but last 3 ingredients in a small saucepan; simmer 30 minutes and set aside.

Bring remaining ingredients *almost* to a boil in a large pot; stir in spice mixture and serve warm, reserving seasonings in the pot. **Yield: About 4 cups.**

2002

Holiday Wassail

When serving wassail, some hosts like to add a cinnamon stick to each guest's cup.

2 to 3 qt. apple cider	1 cinnamon stick
3 c. orange juice	whole cloves
1 c. fresh lemon juice	honey to taste
1 c. pineapple juice	rum to taste

Mix all ingredients together in a large pot and simmer 2 minutes. Serve hot, reserving spices in the pot. **Yield: 3½ to 4½ quarts.**

THE FORMER BRENT HOUSE IN DALLAS ⌁ DECEMBER 1980 & DECEMBER 1994

Breads

Despite their penchant for Mexican food, Texans do not live by tortillas alone. They also consume their share of the Southern staff of life, cornbread. Myriad versions reside in recipe files across the state, more than a few titled simply "Mama's Cornbread." Of course, many cooks no longer need a recipe, having committed theirs to memory years ago.

Served with everything from stuffed peppers to spaghetti, the golden wedges also star in a favorite Texas twosome, pinto beans and cornbread. Longtime Texans consider this not only a complete meal, but a great meal. No salad, no meat, just beans and cornbread (the latter preferably hot from the oven and moist with butter). Condiments might include chow-chow (a sweet, spicy cabbage relish) and hot pepper sauce.

Another bread that finds its way onto Texas tables on a regular basis is biscuits. We're not talking about the canned variety here, but soft, fluffy, layered rounds made from scratch. They're a natural with chicken-fried steak, or fried chicken, for that matter. As with cornbread, cooks often use recipes that have been handed down from one generation to the next.

Our recipe for biscuits is both traditional and unusual. It comes from the 1912 Hotel Limpia in Fort Davis, but it includes honey, which gives the biscuits a hint of sweetness. Try it; we promise you'll hear "pass the biscuits" more than once.

Of course, special occasions call for special breads, and there's no scarcity of either in Texas. Having a fish fry? Don't forget the hush puppies. Planning a Saturday brunch? The choices range from beignets to *kartoffelpuffer* (potato pancakes). Looking for something distinctive for an afternoon reception? Consider Cardamom Braid, a subtly flavored Swedish bread that doubles as a dessert. Other dessert candidates range from cinnamon rolls to intriguing concoctions like Peach-Pecan Bread and Blueberry–Sweet Potato Bread. In Texas, even the bread-and-butter choices are far from ordinary.

Cafe Cornbread

Stone-ground cornmeal adds an interesting flavor and texture to that most Southern of breads, cornbread. This recipe is adapted from one that appears in the Wunsche Bros. Cafe Cookbook *(1993). For a crispier cornbread, use 1 T. less oil and put all of the oil in the bottom of the skillet before pouring in the batter.*

5 T. vegetable oil, divided	½ tsp. baking soda
2 c. cornmeal (preferably stone-ground)	1 tsp. salt
1 c. all-purpose flour	2 eggs, slightly beaten
2 T. sugar	2 c. buttermilk
1 T. baking powder	1 c. fresh or frozen corn (optional)

Place 2 T. oil in a 10-inch cast-iron skillet and swirl to coat bottom and sides. Put skillet in a 425° oven to heat while preparing batter.

Combine next 6 ingredients in a bowl and set aside. Combine eggs, buttermilk, and remaining 3 T. oil and add to dry ingredients, blending well. Stir in corn, pour mixture into heated skillet, and bake at 425° for 15 to 25 minutes. Slice into wedges and serve hot. **Yield: 6 to 8 servings.**

BRENDA GREENE MITCHELL ∼ JULY 1996

Easy Jalapeño Cornbread

Texans like to put their own stamp on things. Take this cornbread recipe, for example—it's a sure bet it didn't originate in Georgia.

1½ c. cornbread mix	1 large onion, chopped
1¼ c. milk	1 c. drained canned corn
⅓ c. vegetable oil	¼ c. pickled jalapeños, minced
2 eggs, beaten	¾ c. grated cheddar cheese
1 tsp. sugar	

Combine all ingredients, stirring just until dry ingredients are moistened. Pour batter into a greased 11 x 7 x 1½–inch pan. Bake at 375° for 30 minutes or until lightly browned. **Yield: 8 to 10 servings.**

FRAN DeCOUX GERLING ～ NOVEMBER 1988

Green Chile Cornbread

This cornbread is so good you'll eat it hot or cold, with or without butter.

3 (6-oz.) pkg. Corn-Kits cornbread mix	1 (5-oz.) can diced green chiles, undrained
2½ c. milk	2½ c. grated sharp cheddar cheese
3 eggs, beaten	1 large onion, grated
1 (15¼-oz.) can whole kernel corn, drained	½ c. vegetable oil

Empty packages of Corn-Kits in mixing bowl. Stir in milk and eggs, then add corn, chiles, cheese, and onions.

Heat oil and stir into mixture. Pour into a greased 9 x 13–inch pan and bake at 375° for 45 minutes or until edges pull away from pan. Cool briefly; slice into squares. **Yield: 12 to 16 servings.**

LUPE VALDEZ ～ 2004

Opposite page: Cafe Cornbread

Flour Power

Possibly the oldest continuously operated family-owned milling company in the United States, San Antonio–based C. H. Guenther & Son celebrated its 150th anniversary in 2001. Carl Hilmar Guenther, an ambitious young German immigrant, founded the company in Fredericksburg in 1851 and moved it to San Antonio in 1859. Around the end of the nineteenth century, the company began calling itself Pioneer Flour Mills to stress its heritage. The twenty-story Pioneer grain elevator on the San Antonio River, in the King William District, is a longtime Texas landmark.

Today the company produces a variety of mixes and other convenience foods under several brand names, but C. H. Guenther & Son remains a working flour mill.

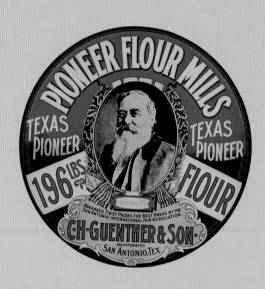

Hotel Limpia Buttermilk-and-Honey Biscuits

At the Hotel Limpia Dining Room in Fort Davis, the baker offers hot pans of these delectable biscuits to diners periodically. Sometimes he doesn't even make it to the back of the room before they're all gone. This recipe is adapted from one that appears in The Hotel Limpia Cookbook *(1998).*

2 c. all-purpose flour	¼ c. Crisco shortening
1 tsp. salt	2 T. honey
1 tsp. baking soda	¾ c. buttermilk
½ tsp. baking powder	

Combine dry ingredients in a large bowl. Cut in shortening with a fork or pastry blender until mixture resembles coarse meal. Add honey, mixing well. Add buttermilk and stir until mixture forms a soft ball that will roll easily. Turn biscuit dough out onto a floured board and roll dough to 1-inch thickness. Cut with biscuit cutter and place biscuits on a greased baking pan. Bake at 450° for 10 to 12 minutes or until browned. Serve hot. **Yield: 12 to 14 biscuits.**

LANNA DUNCAN ∼ 2003

Beer Bread

With only four ingredients and no kneading, this bread is ready for the oven in a jiffy.

3 c. self-rising flour	1 (12-oz.) bottle cold beer (the colder the better)
¼ c. sugar	¼ c. butter or stick margarine, cut into pats

Combine first 3 ingredients in a large mixing bowl and mix with a fork just until flour is thoroughly moistened. (Batter will be lumpy.) Scrape batter into a greased and floured loaf pan, spreading into corners. Dot top with pats of butter. Bake at 350° for 1 hour. Best when served hot. **Yield: 1 loaf.**

ANN GALLAWAY ∼ AUGUST 1995

Flour Tortillas

Most cooks will tell you that the best tortillas are made with lard; however, Mexican-cookbook author Jim Peyton encourages folks to experiment with both the type and amount of fat called for in this recipe. For example, health-conscious cooks may want to use canola oil—as little as one tablespoon. "The tortillas will lack some of the taste and texture of the original version," says Jim, "but the results are still excellent."

2 c. all-purpose flour	3 T. lard, shortening, or canola oil
1 tsp. salt	(*or* 1½ T. each of lard and butter)
	⅔ c. water

Combine flour and salt in a large bowl (or combine in the bowl of a food processor fitted with a steel blade).

Heat lard and water in a large saucepan over low heat until lard has just melted (*do not* allow to boil). Allow mixture to cool for a minute or two, then gradually stir it into the flour mixture. Form into a dough by hand (or pour mixture into the bowl of the food processor with the motor running). The result should be a dough that is neither wet nor dry and crumbly. If too wet, add a little more flour; if too dry, add a little more water. Knead dough briefly, then divide into 12 pieces. Roll the pieces of dough into little balls between the palms of your hands, place on a flat surface, cover with a slightly damp towel, and allow to rest for at least 10 minutes (up to 1½ hours).

Preheat a large, heavy skillet or griddle. Using a rolling pin, roll dough into rounds about 6 to 7 inches in diameter. Place a dough round on the cooking surface; within about 30 seconds the dough should start to bubble, and little brown spots should begin to form on the bottom. (Stove settings vary, so you'll have to experiment with the amount of heat.) Flip tortilla and cook another 30 seconds. By this time it should start to puff a little more, and the other side should develop light brown spots. Flip tortilla again; it should immediately begin to puff, sometimes into a large, nearly round ball. When tortilla has fully expanded, remove it from the heat and place it in a tortilla warmer or wrap it in a thick towel. Adjust heat as necessary as you cook remaining tortillas. **Yield:** 1 dozen.

JIM PEYTON ⌇ 2003

Hush Puppies

When we published our story on Texas catfish restaurants in July 1997, Scott McLean, the owner of Country Kitchen and Bakery in Lampasas, offered to share his hush puppies recipe with our readers. He notes that the restaurant uses a commercially available, hard-wheat flour and fine-ground cornmeal, which gives its hush puppies an unconventional texture. Your homemade version may not be exactly the same, but will still be mighty tasty.

1¾ lb. high-gluten flour (bread or baker's flour)	1 T. baking powder
1½ lb. cornmeal	1 medium onion, finely chopped
1 T. granulated garlic or garlic powder	4 green onions with tops, chopped
1 T. onion powder	about ⅓ c. whole milk
½ c. sugar	vegetable oil
2 tsp. salt	

Combine dry ingredients. Stir in onions. Add milk slowly until mixture holds together well (mixture should roll between fingers with little sticking).

Carefully drop batter by teaspoonfuls into deep hot oil (350°) and fry about 3 minutes on each side or until brown. Drain on paper towels. **Yield: 25 to 35 hush puppies.**

SCOTT MCLEAN ~ JULY 1997

Corn Fritters

Try these served with sausage or pork chops, or make them the center of a vegetarian menu.

1 large ear fresh corn, cooked and cooled	⅛ tsp. salt
2 eggs, separated	1 tsp. sugar
6 T. all-purpose flour	vegetable oil
½ tsp. baking powder	

Cut corn from cob, scraping cob well to remove all milk; set aside.

Beat egg whites with an electric mixer until stiff but not dry; set aside.

In another bowl, combine flour, baking powder, salt, and sugar. Add corn and egg yolks, mixing well. Fold in egg whites with a spatula. Refrigerate mixture 1 hour for best results.

Carefully drop batter by tablespoonfuls into oil heated to 350° in a deep fryer. Fry until golden brown and cooked through, turning once. Drain on paper towels. Serve with syrup or powdered sugar. **Yield: About 1 dozen.**

FRAN DECOUX GERLING ~ NOVEMBER 1988

Kartoffelpuffer
(POTATO PANCAKES)

This recipe is from Aunt Hank's Rock House Kitchen, *written in 1977 by Georgia Mae Smith Ericson, the granddaughter of Henry Clay Smith (Heinrich Schmitt) and Elizabeth Boyle Smith. Known affectionately as "Uncle Hank" and "Aunt Hank," they were early pioneers on Texas' High Plains.*

3 c. grated potatoes, drained well	½ c. vegetable oil
1 small onion, grated, drained well	sugar
2 eggs, well beaten	cranberry sauce or cinnamon-flavored applesauce (optional)
2 T. all-purpose flour	
⅛ tsp. salt	

Combine first 5 ingredients, mixing well. Form into patties and fry in hot oil in a shallow skillet until evenly browned, turning once. Drain well on paper towels and sprinkle with sugar. Serve with cranberry sauce or cinnamon-flavored applesauce, if desired. **Yield: 6 to 8 pancakes.**

MARCH 1996

Beignets

You probably don't want to indulge in beignets every day, but keep this recipe in mind for a weekend breakfast or special brunch.

2¼ c. all-purpose flour	1 tsp. vanilla
2 T. plus 1 tsp. sugar	vegetable oil
⅛ tsp. baking soda	powdered sugar
1¼ tsp. baking powder	butter or margarine (optional)
2 eggs, well beaten	syrup (optional)
1¼ c. milk	

Sift dry ingredients into a mixing bowl. Combine eggs, milk, and vanilla; stir into dry ingredients and mix well. Carefully drop batter by spoonfuls into deep hot oil and fry until golden brown; drain on absorbent paper. Sprinkle with powdered sugar while still warm. Serve with butter and syrup, if desired. **Yield: 15 to 20 beignets.**

MARCH 1981

Opposite page: Kartoffelpuffer (Potato Pancakes)

Name That Pan Dulce!

Thanks to the state's strong Hispanic heritage, many towns in Texas, especially South Texas, have Mexican bakeries, or *panaderías*. They provide Mexican-Americans and other aficionados of Mexican baked goods with *pan semita* and *bolillos*, and on special holidays, *pan de muerto* and *rosca de reyes*. In addition, there are more than 400 types of *pan dulce*, or sweet bread, many of which look more like cookies than breads.

One of the best places to see an assortment of Mexican breads and pastries is at the De Alba Tortilla Factory and Bakery, which has locations in McAllen and Mission. Another is at San Antonio's Mi Tierra Café y Panadería, next to Market Square. The colorful arrays can prove a bit overwhelming to first-time buyers. The names for the various baked goods can also be confusing; some are derived from their shape or from some connection to social rituals. Descriptions of some of the more common panadería items follow.

bolillo (bo-LEE-yo): A small, white, oval French bread.

cochino: A thick, cookie-like bread shaped like a pig. It comes in two versions—soft and hard.

concha or *mollete* (mo-YEH-teh): A round, soft bread with a thick, sugary topping. The first name comes from the similarity of the bread's shape to that of a conch shell. The word *mollete* means simply "rounded loaf." If you're traveling in Mexico, you ask for a *concha*; in Texas, you ask for a *mollete*. Either way, it's the same bread.

cuernito ("little horn"): There are two types—a larger, soft-textured bread that's usually dipped in coffee as it's eaten, and a smaller, hard bread that's sugar-coated.

empanada: A fruit-, vegetable-, or meat-filled bread similar to a turnover. The most common fillings are pumpkin and pineapple.

pan de muerto ("bread of the dead"): A special yeast bread offered to the departed on *El Día de los Muertos*, the Day of the Dead (known also as All Souls' Day), November 2 (and also on All Saints' Day, November 1). It may be round or oval with a cross in the center, or shaped like long bones, skulls, or the human figure.

pan de polvo: A cinnamon-and-sugar-coated cookie-like bread that's always served at weddings, *quinceañeras* and *quinceañeros* (girls' and boys' fifteenth-birthday parties), and other special events, as well as at Christmas.

pan dulce ("sweet bread"): Includes most items in a panadería.

pan semita: A rounded, anise-flavored bread often made with yeast.

piedras: Small, sugar-coated hard breads that look like small rocks.

rosca de reyes: A large, round, braided bread containing a doll that represents the baby Jesus. Available only during the Christmas season, this pan dulce commemorates the gifts brought to the baby Jesus by the three kings (*reyes*).

tres leches: A cake made from "three milks" (regular milk, evaporated milk, and sweetened condensed milk).

Whole Wheat–Pecan Muffins

Sure, these muffins offer the healthful benefits of whole wheat, but what's more, they're just plain delicious.

1 c. all-purpose flour	1 c. coarsely chopped pecans
1 c. whole wheat flour	¾ c. milk
½ c. firmly packed brown sugar	½ c. vegetable oil
2½ tsp. baking powder	1 egg
½ tsp. salt	Pineapple–Cream Cheese Spread (recipe follows)

Combine flours, brown sugar, baking powder, and salt; stir in pecans. In a small bowl, combine milk, oil, and egg. Add to dry ingredients and stir just until moistened. Spoon mixture into a greased or paper-lined 12-cup muffin pan, filling each cup two-thirds full. Bake at 350° for about 20 minutes or until lightly browned. Serve with Pineapple–Cream Cheese Spread. **Yield: 1 dozen.**

PINEAPPLE–CREAM CHEESE SPREAD

½ c. (4 oz.) pineapple-flavored cream cheese, at room temperature	¼ c. sifted powdered sugar
	2 to 3 T. milk

Combine cream cheese with powdered sugar and beat until light and fluffy. Blend in just enough milk until frosting reaches spreading consistency. **Yield: About 1 cup.**

DECEMBER 1993

Blueberry-Oatmeal Muffins

Oatmeal, honey, and blueberries prove a winning combination in these easy muffins.

1¼ c. uncooked oats	1 c. milk
1 c. all-purpose flour	¼ c. vegetable oil
1 T. baking powder	¼ c. honey
½ tsp. salt	¾ c. fresh blueberries
1 egg, beaten	

Combine first 4 ingredients in a bowl; make a well in the center of mixture. Combine egg, milk, oil, and honey; add to dry ingredients, stirring just until moistened. Fold in blueberries. Spoon into greased muffin pans, filling two-thirds full. Bake at 400° for 20 to 25 minutes. **Yield: 1 dozen.**

MAY 1992

Blueberry–Sweet Potato Bread

You can substitute canned or baked sweet potatoes in this recipe. If using the latter, substitute ¼ c. water for the sweet potato liquid.

2 to 3 large sweet potatoes, unpeeled	2 c. sugar
4 c. all-purpose flour	5 eggs, beaten
2 T. baking powder	½ c. vegetable oil
½ tsp. baking soda	2 c. frozen blueberries, unthawed, but separated with a fork
1 T. plus 2 tsp. cinnamon	
½ tsp. nutmeg	

Scrub sweet potatoes and cook in boiling water for 20 minutes or until soft. Drain, reserving ¼ c. liquid; set aside. Peel and mash enough sweet potatoes to measure 2 cups; set aside to cool completely.

Sift together next 5 ingredients in a large bowl; set aside.

In another large bowl, combine by hand the mashed sweet potatoes, ¼ c. liquid, sugar, eggs, and oil. (Batter will be lumpy.) Add flour mixture to sweet potato mixture; stir just until moistened. (Batter will be stiff.) Fold in blueberries. Spoon mixture into 2 greased 11 x 7 x 4–inch loaf pans. Bake at 350° for 50 to 60 minutes or until wooden toothpick inserted in center comes out clean. Cool in pans for 10 minutes. Remove bread from pans and let cool on wire racks. **Yield: 2 loaves.**

FAYE PORTER ⁓ OCTOBER 1997

Texas Peach-Pecan Bread

Two Texas favorites star in this unusual bread.

2 c. unsifted all-purpose flour	1½ c. sugar
2 tsp. baking powder	2 eggs
½ tsp. ground nutmeg	¼ c. sour cream
½ tsp. salt	1 c. peeled, mashed fresh peaches
⅔ c. butter or stick margarine	1 c. chopped pecans

In a small bowl, stir together flour, baking powder, nutmeg, and salt. In a large mixing bowl, cream butter and sugar. Add eggs and sour cream; beat 1 to 2 minutes or until light. Stir in flour mixture alternately with peaches. Stir in pecans. Pour into a greased 9 x 5 x 3–inch loaf pan and bake at 350° for 50 to 60 minutes or until knife inserted in center comes out clean. Cool 10 minutes in pan. Remove from pan to wire rack and cool completely. **Yield: 1 loaf.**

JULY 1994

Czech It Out

Unless you've had the pleasure of eating a kolache, you might find it hard to understand why Texas boasts not one, but *three* annual kolache festivals.

For the uninitiated, a kolache is a soft, sweet yeast roll that's either topped or filled with a variety of ingredients. Fruit fillings are the most typical—cherry, pineapple, prune, apple, and apricot—but cream cheese and poppy seed are common, too. (Sausage-filled rolls are called *klobasniky*, or pigs-in-the-blanket.) Other fillings include cabbage (a traditional ingredient in the Old Country, or what is now the Czech Republic) and such "Americanized" combinations as ham and cheese. In South Texas, meat-filled variations often come with jalapeños.

Kolaches are as delicious as they are difficult and time-consuming to make, but they're also a gastronomic symbol of Czech culture, which is alive and well in many parts of the state. Czech Texans celebrate their heritage at more than a dozen festivals from Praska to Pasadena. These events sometimes include parades, domino tournaments, and Czech craft demonstrations, but they all feature lively polka bands and plenty of kolaches.

As for the festivals dedicated to kolaches, mark your calendar: East Bernard's Czech Kolache-Klobase Festival takes place the second Saturday in June. Caldwell holds its Kolache Festival the second Saturday in September, and Hallettsville's Kolache Festival happens the last Saturday in September. And, oh, yes, make sure to go hungry.

Kolaches

Adapted from an award-winning recipe provided by Dorothy Kubena, a longtime participant in Caldwell's Kolache Festival, these kolaches feature sour cream in the dough for extra tenderness.

1 c. sour cream	2 eggs, beaten
½ c. sugar	4 c. all-purpose flour (maybe more)
1½ tsp. salt	Prune or Apricot Filling (recipes follow)
½ c. butter or stick margarine, softened	Streusel Topping (recipe follows)
2 pkg. dry yeast	⅓ c. additional butter or stick margarine, melted
½ c. warm water	

Heat sour cream until warm. Stir in sugar, salt, and softened butter; set aside to cool.

Sprinkle yeast over warm water; let stand until yeast dissolves. Add to sour cream mixture. Add eggs and flour; mix well (dough does not need kneading).

If necessary, work in enough additional flour to make dough spongy but not sticky. Put dough in a large greased bowl; cover and refrigerate overnight.

Remove dough from refrigerator. Shape into balls about 1½ inches in diameter and place on lightly greased baking sheets about an inch apart. Flatten balls to ½ inch thick and let rise for about 10 minutes.

Make indentations in the middle of each kolache by pressing down firmly with the first two fingers of both hands. Spoon about 1 T. Prune or Apricot Filling into each indentation. Sprinkle about ½ tsp. Streusel Topping over filling. Cover kolaches with a sheet of waxed paper and let rise until double in bulk. Remove waxed paper and bake at 350° for 15 to 20 minutes or until golden. Remove from oven and brush top edges and sides of kolaches with melted butter. **Yield: About 2 dozen.**

PRUNE FILLING

2 (12-oz.) pkg. dried, pitted prunes	¾ c. sugar
⅛ to ¼ tsp. cinnamon	additional sugar to taste (¼ to ⅓ c.)

Cover fruit with water and cook 12 to 15 minutes or until tender, stirring often; drain.

Purée fruit in food processor or blender. Immediately stir in cinnamon and ¾ c. sugar. Add more sugar to taste and mix well. **Yield: Enough filling for about 2 dozen kolaches.**

NOTE: For Apricot Filling, use 3 (6-oz.) pkg. dried apricots and follow the same recipe except cut apricots into pieces before cooking, omit cinnamon, start with 1 c. sugar instead of ¾ c., and add another ½ to ¾ c. sugar.

STREUSEL TOPPING

⅔ c. all-purpose flour	about ⅓ c. melted butter or stick margarine
1 c. sugar	

Blend flour and sugar in a bowl. Add just enough melted butter to moisten dry ingredients (mixture will be crumbly); mix well. **Yield: Enough topping for about 2 dozen kolaches.**

DOROTHY KUBENA ~ NOVEMBER 1996

Opposite page: Kolaches

Sunday Morning Cinnamon Rolls

This recipe is adapted from one that appears in Texas Morning Glory: Memorable Breakfast Recipes from Lone Star Bed and Breakfast Inns *by Barry Shlachter (Great Texas Line, 2002). The proprietor of the Lighthouse Bed and Breakfast in McGregor, where these rolls are often served, offers these tips: To save time in the morning, you can prepare these rolls the night before and refrigerate them. Just take them out of the refrigerator 30 minutes before baking and allow an extra 5 to 10 minutes in the oven.*

3 c. all-purpose flour	¾ c. butter or stick margarine, melted and cooled, divided
1 T. plus ½ tsp. baking powder	
¼ tsp. salt	½ c. sugar
½ c. sugar	2 T. cinnamon
⅔ c. milk	1½ c. sifted powdered sugar
2 eggs, lightly beaten	1 tsp. vanilla
	milk

Sift first 4 ingredients together in a bowl and set aside.

Combine ⅔ c. milk, eggs, and ½ c. melted and cooled butter in a separate bowl; stir into dry mixture. Turn dough out onto a lightly floured board and roll into a ½-inch-thick rectangle (about 12 x 16 inches). Using a pastry brush, spread remaining ¼ c. melted butter over dough. Sprinkle with ½ c. sugar and cinnamon. Roll as for jelly roll and seal edge. Cut into ¾-inch slices. Place slices flat, sides touching, in a greased 9 x 13–inch baking dish. Bake at 375° for 25 to 30 minutes or until golden.

Combine powdered sugar and vanilla in a small bowl; stir in enough milk to make a thin icing. Drizzle over hot rolls. **Yield: 18 rolls.**

BARRY SHLACHTER ∼ JULY 2003

Opposite page (clockwise, from left): Sunday Morning Cinnamon Rolls, Streusel-Filled Coffee Cake, and Rosemary–Cream Cheese Eggs

Company Challah

In Jewish families, challah is baked especially for the Sabbath and religious holidays. This version (pictured on page 62) is adapted from a recipe that appears in From Generation to Generation, *a cookbook compiled by the Sisterhood of Temple Emanu-El in Dallas (1993).*

3 pkg. dry yeast	4 eggs, beaten
2 c. warm water	1½ to 2 c. additional unbleached flour, if needed
8 c. unbleached flour, divided	1 egg, beaten (for glaze)
1½ c. sugar, divided	1 T. poppy seeds
1½ tsp. salt	1 T. sesame seeds
1 c. butter or stick margarine	

Dissolve yeast in 2 c. warm water in a large mixing bowl; let stand 5 minutes. Add 3 c. flour and 1 c. sugar. Stir with a fork, cover bowl, and let rise in a warm place for 30 minutes.

In another bowl, combine remaining flour, remaining sugar, and salt. Add butter and cut with a knife or pastry blender until mixture resembles coarse meal. Set aside.

After yeast mixture has risen for 30 minutes, add 4 beaten eggs and stir well. Add flour-butter mixture and work into yeast mixture with a sturdy wooden spoon. (If your mixer has a dough hook, you can use it for this step.) If sticky, add 1½ to 2 c. additional flour. Turn onto well-floured surface and knead until dough is smooth and elastic (about 10 minutes). Place in a large, well-greased bowl, turning to grease top. Cover and let rise in a warm place for 1 to 2 hours or until doubled in bulk.

Punch dough down, turn out onto a floured surface, and knead lightly for 1 to 2 minutes. Divide dough into 3 pieces and roll into strips about 1½ inches wide. Transfer strips to lightly greased baking sheet. Braid strips, tucking ends of strips under each end of loaf. (Braid may also be cut in half and placed in two lightly greased 9 x 5 x 3–inch loaf pans.) Cover and let rise in a warm place for 3 to 5 hours or until at least doubled in bulk.

Brush loaf with beaten egg and sprinkle with poppy seeds and sesame seeds. Bake at 350° for 20 to 25 minutes. Cool on wire rack. **Yield: 1 large loaf or 2 normal-size loaves.**

JANUARY 1997

Dinner Rolls

This dough keeps several days in the refrigerator after the first rising, so it's ideal for preparing one day and baking the next. After the second rising, you can shape a portion of the dough into rolls and save the rest to bake later. If you double the recipe, remember to allow a little extra time for rising.

1 package dry yeast	1 tsp. salt
¼ c. warm water (105° to 115°)	1 egg, beaten
¾ c. milk	3 to 4 c. all-purpose flour, divided
¼ c. sugar	3 T. butter or stick margarine, melted (optional)
3 T. shortening	

Dissolve yeast in ¼ c. warm water in a large bowl; let stand 5 minutes.

Combine milk, sugar, shortening, and salt in a saucepan; cook over low heat, stirring until shortening melts. Cool to 105° to 115° . Stir into yeast mixture; add beaten egg and 1 c. flour, beating well at medium speed with an electric mixer. Gradually stir in enough remaining flour to make a soft (but not sticky) dough.

Turn dough out onto a floured surface and let stand about 10 minutes.

Knead dough until smooth and elastic. Place in a well-greased bowl, turning to grease top. Cover with a damp cloth and let rise in a warm place (85°), free from drafts, about 1 hour or until doubled in bulk.

Punch dough down, cover bowl tightly, and place in refrigerator 8 to 10 hours.

Remove dough from refrigerator and punch down again. (If not using right away, replace cover and return to refrigerator until about 1½ hours before serving time.) Turn dough out onto a floured surface. Shape dough into 1½-inch balls and place in well-greased muffin pans. Cover and let rise in a warm place (85°), free from drafts, about 1 hour or until doubled in bulk. Bake at 425° for 10 to 15 minutes or until golden. If desired, brush rolls with melted butter. **Yield: About 16 rolls.**

N O T E : You can use this same dough to make cloverleaf or crescent rolls. To make cloverleaf rolls, follow the same procedure except shape dough into 1-inch balls and place 3 balls in each muffin cup.

To make crescent rolls, instead of shaping dough into balls, roll half of it out into a large circle (about 10 inches in diameter) on a lightly floured surface. Cut into 8 wedges; roll each wedge tightly, beginning at wide end. Seal points, shape into crescents, and place rolls on a greased baking sheet. Repeat procedure with remaining dough.

N O L A M c K E Y ~ 2 0 0 4

A Taste of Sweden

Many Swedish Texans celebrate Sankta Lucia Day, or St. Lucia Day (December 13), a beloved Swedish holiday that commemorates a young Sicilian saint, who in the fourth century chose martyrdom rather than renounce her faith. One of the most popular legends about St. Lucia is that she appeared on a ship on December 13 surrounded by light and bearing food for hungry people.

In many Swedish homes, it was once traditional for the eldest daughter, wearing a long, white robe with a red sash and a crown of lighted candles, to serve coffee and *lussekatter* ("Lucia cats," or Lucia buns) to family members before sunrise on St. Lucia Day.

Today, in most cases, the ceremony has moved from the home to the church. A girl is chosen from the congregation to be St. Lucia; wearing the candle crown, she proceeds slowly down the aisle from the front of the darkened church to the back, sometimes followed by "Lucia maidens" and "star boys," who carry wands with paper stars on the tips to symbolize the Christmas star.

The Sankta Lucia tradition has become a public affirmation of ethnicity with which most Swedish-Americans can identify. For Carrin Patman of Austin, it's a perfect way to express her Swedish heritage. For the past sixteen years, she has baked St. Lucia buns for family members and close Swedish friends who live out of town. She sends them by overnight mail, so her loved ones can enjoy them on the morning of December 13. "What could be more appropriate for the holidays," she says, "than a gift that symbolizes light and warmth?"

St. Lucia Buns

Many Swedes think St. Lucia Buns are more traditional when they have only saffron to flavor them; however, some cooks add nuts and fruit for extra color. Note that the already sticky dough is harder to shape with these additions.

1 tsp. saffron threads	2 eggs, divided
1 c. plus 1 T. sugar, divided	6½ to 7½ c. bread flour, divided
¼ c. boiling water	½ c. slivered almonds (optional)
1¾ c. milk	½ c. mixed candied orange and lemon peel, diced (optional)
⅓ c. butter	⅔ c. golden raisins (optional)
1 tsp. salt	2 to 4 T. raisins
2 pkg. active dry yeast	
½ c. lukewarm water	

Place saffron threads on a piece of aluminum foil and dry in a 200° oven for about 5 minutes (be careful not to burn the saffron). Grind dried saffron and 1 tsp. sugar into a powder in a mortar and pestle. Pour mixture into a small bowl; stir in ¼ c. boiling water and set aside.

Combine milk and butter in a saucepan; heat over low heat until very warm. Stir in 1 c. sugar and the salt. Cool to lukewarm.

Dissolve yeast and remaining 2 tsp. sugar in ½ c. lukewarm water; set aside.

Beat 1 egg in large bowl of electric mixer, add above 3 mixtures, and mix well. Gradually add 3½ c. flour. Beat 5 minutes. Gradually add another 3 c. flour and mix well. Turn dough out onto a lightly floured surface and knead for 8 to 10 minutes (or knead in mixer with dough hook), *adding only as much of the last cup of flour as needed to keep dough from being too sticky.* If using nuts and fruit in the dough, add them now (reserve dark raisins for later), gently working them into the dough until they're distributed evenly. Place dough in greased bowl, turning to grease top. Cover loosely with plastic wrap and a kitchen towel; let rise in a warm, draft-free place until doubled in bulk (about 2 hours).

Punch dough down, turn out onto a floured surface, and divide into 28 equal pieces, each about the size of a large lemon. Roll each piece of dough into a 10-inch-long strip. Form into S shapes or other traditional shapes (see photo on page 46). Place on greased baking sheets about 2 inches apart. Cover loosely with plastic wrap and let rise until doubled in bulk (about 1½ hours).

Beat remaining egg with 1 tsp. water and brush on buns. Press a dark raisin into the center of each coil. Bake at 400° for 10 to 15 minutes or until browned. Wrap buns lightly in a kitchen towel and cool on wire racks. **Yield: About 2 dozen.**

CARRIN PATMAN ∿ DECEMBER 2002

Cardamom Braid

The dough in this recipe is quite sticky—too sticky for a bread machine. A few kneading tips: Use a clean powder puff to dust flour on the kneading surface, the dough, and your hands. A steel scraper and a marble board also come in handy. Letting the dough rise in the refrigerator the first time makes it less sticky, though the process takes longer.

1 pkg. active dry yeast	4 c. bread flour
1 tsp. sugar	1 tsp. ground cardamom seed
¾ c. lukewarm water	1 tsp. water
3 eggs, divided	2 to 3 T. sugar
¾ c. sugar	additional sugar
1 tsp. salt	cinnamon
¼ c. butter, melted	

Dissolve yeast and 1 tsp. sugar in ¾ c. lukewarm water; set aside.

Beat 2 eggs in large bowl of electric mixer. Add ¾ c. sugar and beat well. Add salt and melted butter and beat well. Stir in yeast mixture. Combine flour with cardamom seed and gradually add to mixing bowl, mixing well. Turn dough out onto a lightly floured surface and knead 5 to 10 minutes or until smooth and elastic, adding only enough flour to the surface to keep the dough workable (or knead in mixer with dough hook).

Place dough in greased bowl, turning to grease top. Cover loosely with plastic wrap and a kitchen towel and let rise in a warm, draft-free place until doubled in bulk (about 1½ hours).

Grease a 7½ x 11½–inch Pyrex dish or two 4 x 8½–inch loaf pans, line them with parchment paper, and then grease paper; set aside.

Punch dough down, turn out onto a lightly floured surface, and knead again for 5 to 10 minutes. (Note: Dough will be very sticky. Dust the work surface, dough, and your hands with just a little flour at a time, and use a light touch to handle the dough.) Divide dough in half, then divide each half into 3 pieces. Hand-roll each piece of dough into a strip about 12 inches long. (As you roll and stretch the strips into the desired length, let them rest for a minute or two occasionally, so that the dough will relax enough to hold the lengthened shape.) Braid 3 dough strips, making 2 braided loaves, each about 11 inches long; place loaves side by side in prepared dish or separately in loaf pans. Cover with plastic wrap and let rise again about 1 hour or until almost doubled in bulk.

Beat remaining egg with 1 tsp. water. Place about ¼ of mixture in a small bowl, reserving the remainder for another use. Stir in 2 to 3 T. sugar to thicken. Using a pastry brush, paint egg mixture evenly on the tops of loaves, coating lightly (avoid letting mixture fill up the cracks made by braiding; stop painting just before separations). Sprinkle more sugar over the loaves, then sprinkle generously with cinnamon. Bake at 350° for about 30 minutes or until a toothpick inserted in center comes out clean. Remove from dish or loaf pans and let cool completely on a wire rack before serving or freezing. Slice, using a serrated knife. **Yield: 2 loaves.**

CARRIN PATMAN ～ DECEMBER 2002

Soups & Salads

In the broad spectrum of Texas cuisine, soups and salads have traditionally received little respect compared to their meat-and-potatoes counterparts. Where this prejudice came from is anyone's guess, but it may have stemmed, at least in part, from the cowboy mystique, embraced by Texans statewide. Back in the days of the cattle drives, cowboys had few opportunities to linger over bowls of hot soup or crunchy salad. Quick nourishment that stuck to your ribs—that was what mattered on the range.

Whatever the reason for their original lack of Lone Star status, soups and salads have come into their own. Witness the popularity of tortilla soup and spinach salad, to name just two examples.

On the soup front, in recent years, we've published recipes for savory French onion soup and Sun-Dried Tomato–Basil Soup, as well as recipes for ethnic favorites like matzo ball soup and gazpacho. The latter perks up summertime meals, as does Cream of Avocado Soup, a dish served at Paloma Blanca, a popular Mexican restaurant in San Antonio.

Salads have also gained ground on the Texas culinary scene. Sure, iceberg lettuce and chopped tomatoes topped with ranch dressing is still a favorite, but it's not the only blip on the radar. Our recipes reflect crunchy concoctions with such varied ingredients as cabbage, corn, cranberries, and cactus. (Yes, Texans really do eat cactus salad.)

First course or main course, winter or summer, soups and salads have found their place in the Texas sun, bringing with them new flavors, interesting combinations, and welcome diversity.

Mushroom Soup

A medley of mushrooms adds distinction to an old standby. The original recipe called for whites, creminis, lobsters, and shiitake, but other varieties will work, too.

¼ c. butter or stick margarine	¼ c. dry sherry
1 lb. mixed fresh mushrooms, cleaned and sliced	1 T. plus 2 tsp. cornstarch
1 c. peeled and sliced potatoes	1 tsp. salt
1 c. sliced carrots	¼ tsp. white pepper
½ c. chopped celery	1 c. whole milk
½ c. chopped onion	1 c. half-and-half
1 (14½-oz.) can chicken broth	fresh chives or parsley (optional)

Melt butter in a large, heavy saucepan. Stir in mushrooms, potatoes, carrots, celery, and onion. Cook over medium heat, stirring frequently, 6 to 10 minutes or until mushrooms are golden. Stir in chicken broth and bring to a boil. Reduce heat, stir in sherry, and simmer, covered, 15 minutes.

Meanwhile, in a small bowl, combine cornstarch, salt, and pepper with milk and half-and-half, blending well. Add slowly to mushroom mixture, stirring constantly, and cook over low heat until mixture comes to a boil. Cook about 1 minute longer or until slightly thickened, stirring constantly. Ladle into bowls and garnish with chives or parsley, if desired. **Yield: 6 servings.**

NOVEMBER 1998

Canadian Cheese Soup

Texas culinary legend Helen Corbitt (1906–1978) made this soup famous.

¼ c. butter or stick margarine	4 c. chicken broth
½ c. diced onions	4 c. milk
½ c. diced carrots	⅛ tsp. baking soda
½ c. diced celery	1 c. grated processed American cheese
¼ c. all-purpose flour	salt and pepper
1½ T. cornstarch	2 T. finely chopped fresh parsley

Melt butter in a large pot. Add onions, carrots, and celery; sauté over low heat until soft. Add flour and cornstarch; stir and cook until mixture bubbles. Stir in broth and milk to make a smooth sauce. Stir in baking soda and cheese. Season with salt and pepper. Cook over low heat until cheese melts; stir in parsley. **Yield: 8 servings.**

HELEN CORBITT ～ DECEMBER 1990

Opposite page: Mushroom Soup

French Onion Soup

This savory soup is a good choice on a cold winter day.

5 c. thinly sliced yellow onions (about 2 lb.)	3 (14½-oz.) cans water
¼ c. butter or stick margarine	½ c. white wine
1 T. olive oil	salt and pepper
1 T. salt	8 (¾-inch-thick) slices French bread, toasted
¼ c. all-purpose flour	4 oz. Swiss cheese, grated
3 (14½-oz.) cans beef broth	

Combine onions, butter, and olive oil in a heavy 4-qt. pot and simmer, covered, 15 minutes. Sprinkle with 1 T. salt and stir in flour to coat. Remove from heat and set aside.

In another large pot, combine beef broth and water and bring to a boil; gradually stir into onion mixture. Add wine and cook over low heat, covered, 30 to 45 minutes. Add salt and pepper to taste.

Place 8 ovenproof serving bowls on a baking sheet. Place 1 bread slice in each bowl; ladle soup into bowls and sprinkle Swiss cheese over top. Broil 6 inches from heat until cheese melts. **Yield: 8 to 10 servings.**

APRIL 1990

Potato-Parsley Soup

This vichyssoise-like soup can also be served hot.

1 large onion, sliced	½ c. chopped parsley (about half a bunch)
2 T. butter or stick margarine	1 tsp. salt
5 medium to large potatoes, peeled and thinly sliced	½ tsp. pepper
4½ c. chicken stock	additional parsley (optional)
1½ c. half-and-half	slivers of carrot (optional)

Sauté onion in butter until tender but not brown. Add potatoes and chicken stock and simmer, covered, about 15 minutes or until potatoes are done. Cool.

Gradually add half-and-half to cooled potato mixture, mixing well, and stir in parsley and seasonings. Purée half of mixture in an electric blender until smooth; repeat with remaining mixture. (A hand mixer works almost as well.) Taste, and adjust seasonings, if necessary; chill. Garnish with parsley and carrot slivers, if desired, and serve ice-cold. **Yield: About 10 cups.**

JANUARY 1984

Sun-Dried Tomato–Basil Soup

This soup is a particularly good choice in the summertime when fresh tomatoes and basil are plentiful.

8 Roma tomatoes	6 fresh basil leaves (or more to taste), cut into thin strips
1 red onion, diced	1 tsp. salt
3 cloves garlic, minced	¼ tsp. white pepper
1 T. olive oil	hot pepper sauce
12 oz. tomato juice	celery leaves (optional)
6 sun-dried tomatoes, diced	

Place Roma tomatoes in boiling water for about 20 seconds, then remove and place in a bowl of cold water; peel, halve, and seed when cool.

In a medium skillet, sauté onion and garlic in olive oil until soft. Purée onion mixture and Roma tomatoes with tomato juice in a food processor or blender. Combine mixture with sun-dried tomatoes, basil, salt, and white pepper in a medium saucepan; heat thoroughly. Add hot pepper sauce to taste. Ladle soup into bowls and garnish with celery leaves, if desired. **Yield: 4 servings.**

JIMMY MITCHELL JUNE 2000

Basil flavors dishes from soup to pizza, but it really shines in pesto. You can grow enough basil in one Texas summer to keep your freezer stocked with pesto year round (pesto recipes on pages 183–184).

Dean Fearing, longtime chef at the Mansion on Turtle Creek, along with Stephan Pyles and a handful of other Dallas chefs, is credited with inventing modern Southwestern cuisine. When we published his recipe for tortilla soup in 1987, it had already become one of his signature dishes. Since then, Dean has written two cookbooks, The Mansion on Turtle Creek Cookbook *and* Dean Fearing's Southwest Cuisine: Blending Asia and the Americas.

Tortilla Soup

Like most tortilla soups, this version includes chicken. However, this recipe calls for it to be added last—as a garnish. The wise cook prepares the chicken beforehand and reserves the broth for the soup. However, you can also use leftover chicken and canned chicken stock.

3 T. corn oil	1 T. ground cumin
2 corn tortillas, chopped	1 tsp. chili powder
4 cloves garlic, peeled and finely chopped	2 T. canned tomato pureé
1 T. chopped fresh epazote (a pungent Mexican herb, available in Mexican markets) or chopped fresh cilantro	1 bay leaf
	2 qt. chicken stock
1 c. puréed onion	salt
2 c. puréed fresh tomatoes	cayenne

GARNISHES:

1 breast of chicken, cooked and cut into strips

1 avocado, peeled and cubed

3 oz. cheddar cheese, grated

3 corn tortillas, cut into thin strips and fried

In a soup pot, heat corn oil and sauté chopped tortillas with garlic and epazote. Add puréed onion and tomatoes; bring to a boil. Stir in cumin, chili powder, tomato pureé, bay leaf, and chicken stock; return to a boil. Add salt and cayenne to taste and cook 30 minutes.

Strain broth, removing bay leaf and large particles. Ladle soup into warm bowls and add garnishes as desired. **Yield: 6 to 8 servings.**

DEAN FEARING ⁓ OCTOBER 1987

Tortilla Soup Giraud

Lady Bird Johnson shared another version of tortilla soup with our readers in 1990. If you don't have cooked chicken and chicken stock on hand, place 4 lb. chicken pieces, 1 gal. water, 1 tsp. salt, and other seasonings as desired in a large Dutch oven and simmer, covered, until the chicken is tender (about an hour). Let cool; remove and bone chicken, reserving the broth.

1½ medium onions, diced	1 tsp. granulated garlic
1 green pepper, diced	¾ c. cooked garbanzo beans (about half of a 15½-oz. can, drained)
vegetable oil	
2 carrots, sliced in thin rounds	1 lb. cooked and boned chicken, cut into bite-size pieces
¼ bunch celery, diced	2 T. chopped fresh cilantro
2 potatoes, diced	
3½ qt. chicken stock, heated	GARNISHES:
2 T. chili powder	fried corn tortilla strips
1 T. ground cumin	thin slices of lime
1 tsp. white pepper	thin slices of avocado

Sauté onion and green pepper in a small amount of oil 1 minute. Add carrots, celery, and potatoes; sauté 2 minutes. Add hot chicken stock and next 4 ingredients; simmer 5 to 10 minutes or until vegetables are tender.

Stir in garbanzo beans, chicken, and cilantro; heat an additional 5 minutes or until ready to serve. Ladle into warm bowls and garnish with tortilla strips, lime, and avocado. **Yield: About 16 cups.**

LADY BIRD JOHNSON ⁓ JANUARY 1990

Caldo Xochitl

*Many of the regulars at El Mirador Restaurant in San Antonio request Caldo Xochitl,
one of founder Doña María Treviño's legendary soups.*

3 c. cooked El Mirador Rice (recipe follows)	2 c. sliced zucchini
1 (3- to 4-lb.) chicken, cut into pieces	1½ c. diced carrots
2½ qt. water	1½ c. diced celery
2 tsp. salt, or salt to taste	1½ c. diced green pepper
1 tsp. pepper	1 medium onion, peeled and chopped
1 T. ground cumin	1 (16-oz.) can garbanzo beans, drained and rinsed
1 sprig fresh epazote (available in Mexican markets) (optional)	½ c. fresh cilantro, tightly packed
1 sprig fresh basil *or* ½ tsp. dried basil	½ c. chopped green onion without tops
3 bay leaves	1 to 2 jalapeños, seeded, deribbed, and finely chopped
4 whole cloves	1 ripe avocado, cut into small cubes
1 T. dried whole oregano	lemon juice
5 cloves garlic	2 ripe tomatoes, seeded and diced

Prepare El Mirador Rice; set aside.

Combine next 8 ingredients in a large soup pot. Bring mixture to a boil over high heat, skimming off foam that rises to the surface.

In a blender, purée cloves, oregano, and garlic with a little water (about 1 T.) and add to soup mixture. Bring mixture to a second boil, reduce heat, and simmer until chicken is very tender (about 40 minutes).

Remove chicken with a slotted spoon. Shred chicken, discarding skin and bones; set aside.

Add zucchini, carrots, celery, green pepper, onion, and garbanzos to soup mixture and simmer until vegetables are tender but still slightly crisp (about 15 minutes). Stir in shredded chicken.

In a small bowl, combine cilantro, green onion, and jalapeño; set aside.

Sprinkle avocado with lemon juice; set aside.

To serve, place ¼ c. El Mirador Rice in each soup bowl (reserve any remaining rice for another use). Remove bay leaves and epazote from soup and ladle soup over rice. Garnish with cilantro mixture, avocado, and tomatoes. **Yield: 12 servings.**

N O T E : Everything except the vegetable garnishes can be prepared up to 2 days in advance.

*Opposite page: Caldo Xochitl (foreground) and
Calabacita con Carne de Puerco (Mexican Squash with Pork)*

EL MIRADOR RICE

¾ c. long-grain rice	1 large clove garlic, minced
1 tsp. lemon juice	1 tsp. ground cumin
2 T. vegetable oil	¼ tsp. salt
1 medium onion, peeled and chopped	¼ tsp. pepper
2 medium tomatoes, chopped	1 T. chicken bouillon granules
2 medium green peppers, chopped	

Place rice in a medium-size bowl; add hot tap water to cover. Sprinkle lemon juice over rice. Soak rice 5 minutes; rinse in cold water and drain well.

Heat oil in skillet and sauté rice until golden. Stir in onion, tomato, green pepper, garlic, cumin, salt, and pepper; sauté 2 to 3 minutes.

Dissolve chicken bouillon granules in 1 c. very hot water and stir into rice mixture. Bring mixture to a boil; cover, reduce heat, and simmer 15 minutes without removing lid. Fluff rice and serve. **Yield: 6 to 7 cups.**

Doña María Treviño ～ May 1996

Cream of Avocado Soup

Rich and lush, with an underlying zing, this colorful soup suggests guacamole you're allowed to eat with a spoon. San Antonio chef and restaurateur Blanca Aldaco serves it at her Alamo Heights restaurant, Paloma Blanca, where it's especially popular in the summer. Although the soup is best made with chicken base, you can substitute 1 qt. good-quality chicken stock for the first two ingredients.

1½ T. chicken base (a paste form of concentrated chicken stock sold in large supermarkets)

1 qt. cold water

8 oz. heavy cream

¼ c. freshly squeezed lime juice

4 plump, ripe avocados

½ bunch cilantro

2 large jalapeños, stemmed and seeded

salt

GARNISHES:

small dollop or swirl of heavy cream

red, yellow, and blue corn tortilla strips, fried until crisp

avocado cubes

watermelon cubes (in summer)

Combine chicken base and 1 qt. cold water, stirring well; strain. In a blender, combine half of strained liquid with half of the next 5 ingredients and blend until smooth. Pour into a large container and set aside. Repeat with other half of strained liquid and other half of same 5 ingredients and stir into first mixture. Add salt to taste, stirring well, and pour into chilled bowls. Add garnishes as desired. **Yield: 8½ cups (16 to 18 appetizer servings, or 8 to 12 full-size servings).**

BLANCA ALDACO ～ OCTOBER 2002

Paradise Soup

Another great summertime soup, this creamy concoction is served cold. Topped with cucumber, cantaloupe, and chives, it makes an attractive luncheon dish.

3 c. tomato juice

1 c. sour cream or yogurt

¼ c. chopped onion

2 T. lemon juice

¾ c. finely ground or chopped cooked ham

2 T. finely chopped fresh basil

1 to 2 tsp. salt (adjust according to saltiness of ham and tomato juice)

½ c. chopped cucumber

½ c. chopped cantaloupe

finely chopped chives

Mix together first 7 ingredients. Taste; add more salt if necessary. Chill well.

Pour soup into clear parfait glasses or bowls, topping each serving with about 1 T. each of cucumber and cantaloupe and a sprinkling of chives. Serve very cold. Yield: 6 to 8 servings.

JULY 1991

Gazpacho

Gazpacho is a popular Spanish cold soup. It can serve as an appetizer, a liquid "salad," or a meal in itself.

1 clove garlic

1 medium onion, sliced

1 cucumber, sliced

3 tomatoes, peeled

1 green pepper, sliced and seeded

⅛ tsp. salt

⅛ tsp. cayenne

¼ c. white distilled vinegar

¼ c. olive oil

¾ c. tomato juice

GARNISHES:

croutons (1 c. bread cubes tossed with ½ tsp. minced garlic and sautéed in 2 T. olive oil until browned)

1 cucumber, diced

1 medium onion, chopped

1 green pepper, chopped

1 hard-boiled egg, chopped

Purée the first 5 ingredients in a blender or food processor. Stir in salt, cayenne, vinegar, olive oil, and tomato juice, and chill for 2 hours or overnight.

Garnish each bowl of soup with croutons, cucumber, onion, green pepper, and egg just before serving, or serve garnishes in separate bowls and let diners help themselves. **Yield: 8 appetizer servings.**

JANUARY 1996

Governor's Mansion Summer Garden Soup

Former Texas first lady Rita Clements often served this soup at the "Texas White House" during her husband Bill's tenure as governor.

1 large ear fresh yellow or white corn

6 c. chicken stock

1 sprig fresh rosemary (1 to 3 inches), minced

1 sprig fresh thyme (2 to 3 inches), minced

½ tsp. white pepper

1 c. diced sweet red pepper

1½ c. diagonally sliced fresh green beans

⅔ c. sliced green onion

1 c. thinly sliced yellow squash

1 c. thinly sliced zucchini

2 c. chopped cooked chicken breast

salt

Cut corn from cob, scraping cob well to remove all milk; set aside.

Heat chicken stock in a large Dutch oven and add rosemary, thyme, white pepper, and sweet red pepper; simmer 10 minutes. Add corn, beans, and onion; simmer an additional 10 minutes, until beans are just tender. Stir in squashes and chicken. Remove from heat and add salt to taste. Cook 5 more minutes and serve immediately. **Yield: 10 cups.**

RITA CLEMENTS ~ JANUARY 1990

An easy way to cut calories in homemade soup is to make the soup, refrigerate it several hours (or overnight), skim off any fat that has risen to the top, and then heat and serve.

Ham Bone Soup

Adapted from a recipe that appears in The Melting Pot: Ethnic Cuisine in Texas *(Institute of Texan Cultures, 1977), this soup originally depended on fresh vegetables grown in the garden. Other varieties of peas—crowder, cream, or black-eyed—may be substituted for the purple hull peas.*

1 meaty ham bone	1 c. dried butter beans
about 2 qt. water	¼ c. diced turnips
2 large onions, diced	½ c. purple hull peas (fresh or frozen)
3 stalks celery, chopped	1 T. sugar
3 carrots, chopped	¼ tsp. ground cloves
5 medium tomatoes, chopped	2 tsp. salt
3 potatoes, peeled and cubed	½ tsp. pepper
1 c. broken snap beans	1 large ear fresh corn

Combine ham bone and about 2 qt. water (or enough water to cover ham bone) in a large Dutch oven; bring to a boil. Cover, reduce heat, and simmer about 1 hour or until meat is almost tender. Add remaining ingredients except corn; cover and simmer about 2 hours and 15 minutes, stirring occasionally. Cut corn from cob, scraping cob well to remove all milk. Stir in corn and simmer an additional 15 minutes. **Yield: About 13 cups.**

FEBRUARY 1996

Opposite page: Ham Bone Soup (top) and Mary McLeod Bethune's Sweet Potato Pie

Matzo Ball Soup

A favorite Jewish dish, Matzo Ball Soup is traditionally served at Passover.
This recipe is adapted from one in From Generation to Generation *(1993),*
a cookbook compiled by the Sisterhood of Temple Emanu-El in Dallas.

1 (3-lb.) chicken, cut up or whole	1 T. finely minced parsley
1 lb. chicken backs, necks, wings, and giblets (plus any extra on hand to enhance the flavor)	1 carrot, sliced
	3 stalks celery, diced
4½ qt. water, or water to cover	1 T. chicken-flavored bouillon granules
2 cloves garlic	8 black peppercorns
2 onions, chopped	cooked Matzo Balls (recipe follows)
10 whole cloves	additional parsley (optional)
2 bay leaves	additional carrot slices (optional)

Combine all ingredients except Matzo Balls and garnishes in a large Dutch oven. Bring to a boil, reduce heat, and simmer 10 to 15 minutes, skimming off foam that rises to the surface. Cover and continue to simmer 2½ hours. Cool and strain, reserving broth. (Reserve chicken for chicken salad or another use.)

Return broth to Dutch oven and simmer over low heat. Carefully drop in cooked matzo balls and heat about 5 minutes or until hot. Garnish with parsley and/or carrot slices, if desired. **Yield: 4 to 6 servings.**

MATZO BALLS

¾ c. chicken fat (ask your butcher for this ingredient)	¼ tsp. ground ginger
	¼ tsp. white pepper
4 eggs, beaten	1 T. minced parsley
1 c. plus 1 T. matzo meal	2 qt. lightly salted water
¼ tsp. ground nutmeg	

Render chicken fat by frying it in a skillet until it yields ½ c. rendered fat (discard remaining solids). Cool fat and combine with eggs; set aside.

Combine matzo meal and seasonings; add to egg mixture and mix well. Stir in parsley. Cover and refrigerate mixture for several hours.

Dip out dough with teaspoon and roll into small balls about 1½ inches in diameter. Set aside.

Heat 2 qt. lightly salted water in a large Dutch oven; bring to a boil and reduce heat. Drop in matzo balls and simmer 1 hour. Carefully remove matzo balls. **Yield: 24 to 26 matzo balls.**

BARBARA SCHMIDT ～ JANUARY 1997

Opposite page: Company Challah (top) and Matzo Ball Soup

Vegetable Soup with Pumpkin

If you have trouble finding powdered bay leaves, toss in a whole bay leaf instead;
just remember to remove it before serving the soup.

1½ lb. soup meat	1 c. diced carrots
½ lb. soup bone, cracked	1 c. chopped celery
1 onion, chopped	1 c. diced potatoes
½ tsp. powdered bay leaves	1 c. whole kernel corn (cut off the cob, frozen, or canned corn that has been drained)
¼ tsp. freshly ground pepper	
pinch of cloves	4 large fresh tomatoes, chopped, *or* 1 (28-oz.) can diced tomatoes
½ c. chopped celery leaves	
3 qt. cold water	1/4 c. pearl barley
3 c. diced pumpkin	salt and pepper
1 c. thinly sliced red onion	

Trim fat off soup meat; cut meat into ¾-inch cubes. Place meat, soup bone, onion, seasonings, celery leaves, and 3 qt. water in a large soup pot and bring to a boil. Reduce heat and simmer, covered, for 4 hours. Remove soup bone and skim off fat. Add pumpkin, vegetables, and barley; cook 35 to 45 minutes. Season to taste. **Yield: 6 to 8 servings.**

CAROLINE ROSE HUNT　～　JANUARY 1990

Apple-Bacon-Spinach Salad

This recipe is adapted from one that appears in Love Creek Orchards'
Adams Apple Cookbook *(1994 and 2001).*

½ lb. sliced bacon	1 T. lemon juice
2 to 3 cloves garlic, minced	2 T. mayonnaise
1 lb. fresh spinach, washed well and stems removed	1 c. croutons
3 large red apples (unpeeled), cored and diced	½ c. grated Swiss cheese
1 bunch green onions, chopped	

Cook bacon until crisp, reserving ½ c. drippings. Crumble bacon and set aside. Combine drippings with garlic and set aside, preferably for several hours, until just before serving.

Tear spinach into bite-size pieces in salad bowl; add apples and green onions. Combine garlic-bacon drippings mixture with lemon juice and mayonnaise; mix well. Pour over spinach mixture and toss. Add crumbled bacon, croutons, and cheese, and toss again. **Yield: 6 to 8 servings.**

LOVE CREEK ORCHARDS ~ JUNE 1995

Tangy Shrimp and Spinach Salad

Salad fans, rejoice. This colorful salad (pictured on page 106) unites two of your favorite ingredients in an unusual vinaigrette.

1 (6-oz.) jar marinated artichoke hearts	1 bunch green onions (about 8), coarsely chopped
3 to 4 c. (about 5 oz.) loosely packed spinach leaves, washed, stemmed, and torn	12 cherry tomatoes, halved
	1 T. red wine vinegar
¾ lb. fresh medium-size shrimp (about 20), cooked, shelled, and deveined	1 tsp. dry mustard
	1 tsp. dried whole tarragon
8 medium mushrooms, halved lengthwise	

Drain artichoke hearts, reserving ¼ c. liquid. Combine artichoke hearts and next 5 ingredients in a large bowl.

Combine artichoke liquid, vinegar, mustard, and tarragon, stirring until blended. Pour mixture over vegetables and shrimp; toss lightly. **Yield: 4 to 5 salad servings, or 2 main-dish servings.**

NOVEMBER 1997

Opposite page: Apple-Bacon-Spinach Salad

Spinach and Hearts of Palm Salad

This recipe actually uses less than a can of hearts of palm. What to do with the remainder? Toss with tomato slices and a light vinaigrette, and voilà!—another salad.

1 (11-oz.) can mandarin oranges	1 (14-oz.) can hearts of palm, drained
Mandarin Dressing (recipe follows)	8 slices broiled bacon, crumbled
10 c. loosely packed spinach leaves, washed, stemmed, and torn (buy about 1 lb. spinach)	⅓ c. (about 1 oz.) almond slices, toasted
	1 avocado, sliced (optional)

Drain oranges, reserving ¾ c. juice. Prepare Mandarin Dressing; refrigerate.

Slice 4 to 5 stalks of hearts of palm into ½-inch pieces (if not already sliced); reserve remaining hearts of palm for another use. Combine oranges, sliced hearts of palm, and remaining ingredients in a large bowl and toss with ½ c. Mandarin Dressing. Yield: 4 to 6 servings.

MANDARIN DRESSING

¾ c. juice from canned mandarin oranges (above)	1 (0.6-oz.) packet Good Seasons Italian dressing mix
¾ c. olive oil	

Combine ingredients, mixing well. Refrigerate. Yield: About 1½ cups dressing, or enough for 3 large salads.

PEGGI PURCELL ~ NOVEMBER 1997

Opposite page: Confetti Corn Salad

Confetti Corn Salad

Perfect for a special luncheon, this salad features two summertime favorites, corn and tomatoes. If you don't want to stuff the tomatoes, the corn mixture tastes good by itself.

3 ears fresh corn, husked and cleaned	½ tsp. garlic salt
¼ c. vegetable oil	¼ c. chopped red onion
¼ c. cider vinegar	¼ c. chopped green pepper
1½ tsp. lemon juice	¼ c. chopped sweet red pepper
¼ c. minced fresh cilantro	6 large tomatoes
1 tsp. sugar	salt
½ tsp. salt	pepper
⅛ tsp. cayenne	

Cook corn in boiling water to cover for 5 to 7 minutes or until tender. Drain and set aside to cool.

In a large bowl, mix together oil, vinegar, lemon juice, cilantro, sugar, salt, cayenne, and garlic salt; set aside.

Cut kernels off cobs. Add corn, onion, and peppers to oil mixture and mix well. Cover and chill for several hours or overnight.

Cut ½ inch from the stem end of each tomato; scoop out seeds and pulp with a melon baller or spoon and reserve for another use. Sprinkle shells with salt and pepper; drain inverted on a paper towel for 10 minutes. Cut notches in tops of shells to form a zigzag pattern, if desired. Fill each shell with ⅓ c. of chilled corn mixture. **Yield: 6 servings.**

JUNE 1999

More than 100 species of cactus grow in Texas, including prickly pear, the state plant. Its ripe fruits (tunas) can be made into jams and syrups, and its pads can be eaten as a vegetable. But beware—both the tunas and the pads have tiny, painful stickers. It's a good idea to wear heavy gloves or use tongs when gathering or preparing them.

Josie's Cactus Salad

This recipe was judged Best of Show at a 1992 prickly pear cook-off.

3 large tomatoes, diced	1 to 2 serrano peppers, chopped
1 large red or sweet onion, diced	½ bunch fresh cilantro, chopped
4 large nopalitos (young, tender prickly-pear pads) with thorns and "eyes" removed, diced	2 (15-oz.) cans ranch-style beans, drained
2 cloves garlic, chopped	1 (16-oz.) bottle Catalina dressing
	1 (14½-oz.) bag nacho cheese–flavored tortilla chips

Combine all ingredients except chips and chill at least 2 hours. To serve, place salad in a large bowl set on a platter and arrange chips around bowl. Use chips to scoop up salad. Yield: 10 cups.

JOSIE SLONAKER 〜 MARCH 1998

Opposite page (clockwise, from left): Josie's Cactus Salad, Nopalito Pie, and Cactus Fries

Mushroom-Broccoli Salad

*This simple concoction is a refreshing change from the everyday
lettuce-and-tomato combo.*

1 c. sliced fresh mushrooms	½ c. sour cream
1 c. fresh broccoli flowerets	2 T. Italian dressing
½ c. halved cherry tomatoes	1 tsp. prepared mustard
6 to 8 purple onion rings	

Combine mushrooms, broccoli, tomatoes, and onions in a salad bowl.

In a separate bowl, combine remaining ingredients and blend well to make dressing.
Toss salad with just enough dressing to coat vegetables. **Yield: 6 servings.**

JANUARY 1987

Hot German Potato Salad

*If you're watching your cholesterol count, you can substitute 3 T. corn oil
for half the bacon drippings.*

6 new potatoes	2 T. cornstarch
6 slices bacon	¼ c. cider vinegar
½ c. chopped onion	2 T. sugar
⅓ c. finely chopped fresh sweet red pepper	1 tsp. salt
⅓ c. finely chopped green pepper	¼ tsp. white pepper
¼ c. finely chopped celery	1 T. parsley

Boil potatoes; drain well, cut into bite-size pieces, and set aside.

Fry bacon until crisp in a large skillet; remove bacon and drain well, reserving drippings in skillet. Crumble bacon and set aside.

Sauté onion, red pepper, green pepper, and celery in bacon drippings; remove vegetables when tender and set aside.

Blend cornstarch into drippings and add vinegar and 2 c. water; stir until sauce is thickened. Stir in remaining ingredients. Add potatoes, bacon, and sautéed vegetables, then heat briefly until potatoes are hot. **Yield: 4 servings.**

JANUARY 1987

Laura Novosad's Confetti Slaw

Novosad's BBQ and Sausage Market in La Grange serves this slaw (and cold canned peaches) with its famous barbecue. This recipe appears in Legends of Texas Barbecue Cookbook: Recipes and Recollections of the Pit Bosses *(Chronicle Books, 2002) by Robb Walsh.*

1 head green cabbage	4 oz. Wish-Bone Italian Dressing
½ head red cabbage	(or another Italian dressing)
3 large carrots	

Shred cabbage and carrots into a large bowl and stir in Italian dressing. Allow to marinate 1 hour before serving. **Yield: 8 cups.**

LAURA NOVOSAD ~ JUNE 2002

Louise's Cranberry Salad

In 1999, we asked food editors across the state to share some of their favorite holiday recipes with our readers. Cathy Barber, longtime food editor of The Dallas Morning News, *was one of the first to respond. Among the recipes she sent us was her mom's recipe for cranberry salad.*

2 T. unflavored gelatin	2 (16-oz.) cans whole-berry cranberry sauce
½ c. cold water	1 (8-oz.) can crushed pineapple
1½ c. sugar	1 c. chopped pecans

Dissolve gelatin in cold water in a shallow casserole. Add remaining ingredients (including juice from cans) and mix well. Cover and refrigerate overnight. Cut in squares or spoon out to serve. **Yield: 10 to 12 servings.**

CATHY BARBER ~ DECEMBER 1999

Paula Lambert founded the Mozzarella Company in Dallas in 1982 and has gone from producing a few hundred pounds of fresh mozzarella a week to producing more than a quarter of a million pounds of specialty cheeses annually. The company's cheeses have won numerous awards and are sold across the United States.

Tomato-Mozzarella Salad

You can use a mixture of basil varieties—sweet green, purple, lemon, Thai, chocolate, or others—in this salad.

6 to 8 oz. fresh mozzarella, thickly sliced	5 T. balsamic vinegar
3 lb. ripe tomatoes, thickly sliced	salt
1 medium red onion, thinly sliced	freshly ground pepper
1 c. fresh basil leaves, chopped	fresh basil sprigs (optional)
⅓ c. olive oil	

Layer cheese, tomatoes, onion, and basil on four salad plates or in bowls. Drizzle with olive oil and sprinkle with balsamic vinegar. Add salt and pepper to taste, and garnish with basil sprigs, if desired. **Yield: 4 servings.**

JUNE 2000

Opposite page: Tomato-Mozzarella Salad

Tabouli

*Sammy's Lebanese Restaurant in Houston provided this recipe for tabouli,
a Mediterranean salad (pictured on page 15).*

½ c. fresh lemon juice (juice of 4 medium lemons)	1 lb. (4 medium) tomatoes, finely chopped
½ c. cracked wheat (bulgur)	½ bunch (about 6 sprigs) fresh mint, finely chopped, *or* 2 T. dried mint leaves
2 medium yellow onions, finely chopped	
2 T. salt	4 green onions, finely chopped
1 T. cinnamon (optional)	½ c. olive oil
1 lb. (5 bunches) parsley, chopped with a knife	cabbage or romaine lettuce leaves

Combine lemon juice with cracked wheat in a small bowl and set aside while chopping other ingredients. Combine onion with salt and cinnamon and add to cracked-wheat mixture.

Combine parsley, tomatoes, mint, and green onion in a large bowl. Add the cracked-wheat mixture and olive oil; mix well. Chill. Serve on cabbage or romaine lettuce leaves. **Yield: About 14 servings.**

MOHAMED HAMED ✎ AUGUST 1996

Fruited Ham and Blueberry Salad

Fresh blueberries add pizzazz to this attractive salad.

Creamy Orange Dressing (recipe follows)	1 c. sliced celery
leaf lettuce	1 c. sliced almonds
3 c. julienned cooked ham	2 c. fresh blueberries, rinsed and drained
2 c. orange sections	minced fresh parsley

Prepare Creamy Orange Dressing; refrigerate.

Line a large platter with lettuce. Arrange ham in middle of platter. Toss next 4 ingredients and place on platter around ham. Sprinkle with parsley and serve with Creamy Orange Dressing. **Yield: 6 servings.**

CREAMY ORANGE DRESSING

½ c. mayonnaise	2 tsp. grated onion
½ c. sour cream	salt
2 T. frozen concentrated orange juice	cayenne
1 T. chopped parsley	

Combine first 5 ingredients and season to taste with salt and cayenne.

MAY 1992

Grapefruit-Avocado Salad

Okay, it's no fun to peel and section grapefruit, but this salad is worth it.
Don't be surprised if it becomes a favorite.

Poppy Seed Dressing (recipe follows)	3 Ruby Red grapefruits
1 head Bibb lettuce, separated and washed	3 ripe (but not soft) avocados, peeled and seeded

Prepare Poppy Seed Dressing; refrigerate until serving.

Cover a large platter with a single layer of lettuce leaves. Using a paring knife, peel grapefruit in a circular direction, being sure to cut away all white membrane; then separate grapefruit into sections and remove membranes around each section. Drain sections in a colander over a bowl, reserving juice.

Cut avocado lengthwise into 8 sections and dip into grapefruit juice to retain color. Arrange grapefruit and avocado in a circular design on lettuce leaves and serve with Poppy Seed Dressing. **Yield: 6 servings.**

1 white onion, peeled and quartered	⅔ c. white vinegar
1½ c. sugar	2 c. vegetable oil
2 tsp. dry mustard	3 T. poppy seeds
2 tsp. salt	

Purée onion in a blender; strain off 1 T. juice and discard residue. Combine onion juice, sugar, mustard, salt, and vinegar in a blender and process on medium speed. Add oil very slowly, blending until thick. Add poppy seeds and blend again. Refrigerate. **Yield: About 3 cups.**

SHELIA ROGERS ~ MARCH 1987

Mixed Greens–Feta Salad

This recipe was adapted from one provided by Emmett Fox, who at the time was executive chef of the Bitter End in Austin. Emmett and his wife, Lisa, now operate ASTI Trattoria, a restaurant in Austin's Hyde Park neighborhood.

1½ lb. mixed greens	½ c. (4 oz.) crumbled goat's-milk feta
½ red onion, sliced	Mustard Vinaigrette (recipe follows)
½ c. coarsely chopped pecans	

Arrange greens and onion slices on individual salad plates. Sprinkle pecans and feta on top and serve with Mustard Vinaigrette. **Yield: 8 servings.**

MUSTARD VINAIGRETTE

1 shallot (or several green onions), chopped	1 tsp. chopped parsley
1 clove garlic, minced	½ c. balsamic vinegar
1 T. coarse-ground mustard (a spread that includes flecks of mustard seed)	2 T. lemon juice
	salt and pepper to taste
1 tsp. chopped fresh basil	1 c. olive oil (extra-virgin is best)

Whisk together all ingredients except oil. Add oil slowly, whisking until blended. Refrigerate. **Yield: About 1½ cups.**

EMMETT FOX ~ MAY 1998

Holiday Turkey Salad

When you're faced with Thanksgiving or Christmas leftovers, this recipe comes in handy (and makes a nice change from turkey sandwiches). Mandarin oranges add a special touch. Chicken or tuna can be used in place of turkey.

2 c. cubed cooked turkey	¼ tsp. nutmeg
1 c. sliced celery	½ c. toasted slivered almonds
1 c. fresh orange pieces	salt and pepper
½ c. mayonnaise, thinned with orange juice	lettuce leaves
¼ tsp. curry powder	fresh orange sections (optional)

Combine all ingredients; season with salt and pepper. Chill. Serve on lettuce leaves; garnish with orange sections, if desired. **Yield: 4 to 6 servings.**

JANUARY 1983

Sweet Onion and Fried Chicken Salad

Sometimes you just gotta have fried chicken. Here's a different way to serve the Sunday bird.

1 large head leaf lettuce, or a combination of lettuces	½ c. peanut oil
8 cherry tomatoes, halved	2 T. white wine vinegar
½ c. sliced mushrooms	1 tsp. Dijon mustard
1 c. all-purpose flour	1 shallot, minced
½ tsp. salt	1 T. fresh tarragon, *or* 1 tsp. dried tarragon
¼ tsp. coarse-grind black pepper	salt
⅓ c. milk	pepper
2 whole chicken breasts, halved, boned, and cut into ½-inch strips	1 large sweet onion (such as Vidalia or Texas 1015 SuperSweet), thinly sliced

Arrange lettuce leaves, tomatoes, and mushrooms on 4 salad plates; set aside.

In a shallow bowl, mix flour with ½ tsp. salt and coarse-grind pepper. Place milk in a separate bowl. Dip chicken strips into milk and then into flour mixture to coat. Fry chicken in hot oil on both sides for a total of 5 minutes or until golden brown. Drain chicken on paper towels, reserving drippings in pan.

Stir vinegar into drippings, scraping bottom and sides of pan. Pour vinegar mixture into a mixing bowl and stir in mustard. Add shallots and tarragon and season with salt and pepper; set dressing aside.

Arrange chicken strips and onion slices on top of salads. Serve with mustard-tarragon dressing on the side. **Yield: 4 servings.**

APRIL 1990

Melon with Chicken Salad

Chicken salad is great paired with cantaloupe. Remember to allow time for chilling the salad and then arranging everything on lettuce leaves.

2 small ripe cantaloupes	4 c. cooked, cubed chicken
1 T. lemon juice	1½ c. sliced celery
1 T. honey, or to taste	1 c. toasted, chopped pecans, divided
1 c. plain yogurt	salt and pepper
¼ c. mayonnaise or salad dressing	leaf lettuce

Cut rinds from cantaloupe and slice fruit lengthwise; chill.

Mix lemon juice with honey; add yogurt and mayonnaise and stir well. Fold in chicken, celery, and half the pecans. Season with salt and pepper. Chill at least one hour.

Line serving plate with lettuce leaves and arrange melon slices on lettuce. Top with chicken salad and garnish with remaining pecans. **Yield: 8 servings.**

JULY 1991

Melon Mélange

This fruit salad looks terrific served in a glass bowl with tall sides.

1 c. sugar	3⅓ c. cantaloupe balls
½ c. water	3⅓ c. honeydew balls
⅓ c. orange liqueur, *or* ⅓ c. orange juice and ½ tsp. grated orange rind	3⅓ c. watermelon balls

Combine sugar and water and bring just to a boil. Remove from heat immediately, add liqueur (or juice and rind), and chill.

Chill melon balls until ready to serve. Just before serving, arrange balls in a large, clear serving bowl and pour chilled syrup on top. **Yield: 10 servings.**

JULY 1991

Main Dishes

The exuberance of Texas food peaks when it comes to the main event—just scan the recipes in this section for confirmation. Naturally, beef dishes abound, from chicken-fried steak to Irish stew, but the roundup also includes such choices as Pecan-Crusted Teriyaki Chicken, Shrimp with Broccoli and Pine Nuts, and Oven-Roasted Salmon.

And this string of entrées still doesn't take into account what many consider the state's two main food groups: barbecue and Tex-Mex. Both add zing to an already zesty lineup. If you want to wake up a conversation (or start an argument), just ask Texans about their favorite barbecue joint or Mexican restaurant. There are plenty of opinions out there, many of them held sacred.

If you've got a grill (or even better, a full-fledged barbecue pit), you can try your hand barbecuing at home. We'll tell you how to prepare tenderloin, sirloin, spareribs, brisket, chicken, and hot links. We also offer recipes for Smoked Mint Bass Fillets and Grilled Red Snapper. Texans think just about anything can be improved with a little smoke and spice.

And then there's the state's beloved Tex-Mex, where the wealth of delicious dishes tests the fortitude of the most dedicated gourmand. Over the years, we've published an array of recipes for enchiladas, tacos, tamales, chili, and fajitas, some more complicated than others, but all of them tasty and worthy of your time. *¡Buen provecho!*

Vegetarian dishes figure in the mix, too. Don't overlook Fresh Tomato-Mushroom Pizza, Spinach-Mushroom Lasagna, Green Chiles Casserole, and Grilled Portobellos. While there's not a hunk of hamburger or chunk of chicken in the lot, they're still main-dish material.

What's for dinner in Texas? Beef, sure—along with many other enticing entrées. The options are limited only by your imagination.

Jalapeño Beef Stew with Polenta Stars

The Reata (in Alpine and Fort Worth) uses Polenta Stars to dress up one of its specials, Jalapeño Beef Stew. This version is adapted from a recipe that appears in A Cowboy in the Kitchen *by Grady Spears, Robb Walsh, and John Westerdahl (1998). Note that the polenta recipe also works well as a side dish with other entrées.*

6 whole shallots	½ red onion, diced
1 T. olive oil	1 c. port
5 T. unsalted butter	2 c. beef stock (fresh or canned)
1 lb. beef chuck, cut into 1-inch cubes	1 T. rubbed sage
⅓ c. all-purpose flour	1 T. dried whole oregano
3 to 4 jalapeños, seeded and minced	2 tsp. kosher salt, or to taste
2 carrots, cut into 2-inch pieces	1 tsp. freshly ground pepper, or to taste
1 large potato, cut into 2-inch pieces	Polenta Stars (recipe follows)

Toss shallots with olive oil and roast in a 350° oven 35 minutes or until soft and brown. Set aside.

Heat butter in a large, deep saucepan over medium heat. Toss beef with flour to coat and place in hot butter. Increase heat and sauté 5 to 10 minutes. (Don't crowd the meat.) Remove pan from heat and transfer meat to a bowl, reserving drippings in pan; cover meat loosely with aluminum foil and set aside.

Sauté jalapeños, carrots, potato, and red onion in drippings over medium heat, tossing to prevent burning, until onion turns translucent. Stir in wine, beef stock, sage, and oregano. Cook over low heat, with lid slightly ajar, 30 to 40 minutes. Stir in reserved beef-shallots mixture and continue cooking 30 more minutes or until meat and vegetables are done. Season with salt and pepper. Ladle stew into bowls and top with 2 or 3 Polenta Stars. Serve hot. **Yield: 4 servings.**

POLENTA STARS

1 T. olive oil	2 tsp. dried whole thyme
¾ c. minced red onion (about ½ onion)	1 tsp. kosher salt
1 c. minced shallots	1 tsp. freshly ground pepper
8 scallions without tops, thinly sliced	¼ c. unsalted butter
3 c. water	1½ c. quick-cooking polenta
3 c. milk	1 c. grated Asiago or Parmesan cheese

Heat oil in a large, deep saucepan. Add onion, shallots, and scallions; sauté over medium heat about 5 minutes or until wilted. Stir in next 6 ingredients; bring mixture to a boil, then reduce heat to simmer. Pour polenta in with one hand while whisking with the other. After polenta is whisked in, stir with a long-handled wooden spoon 10 to 15 minutes or until mixture thickens and liquid is absorbed. Reduce heat if necessary. Remove saucepan from heat and stir in cheese. Spread polenta evenly in a buttered 9 x 13–inch metal pan, cover with plastic wrap, and refrigerate at least an hour.

At serving time, cut polenta into stars or other shapes (unless serving as a side dish) and bake at 350° for 10 to 15 minutes. (Stars may also be heated by sautéing, grilling, or microwaving.) Serve hot. **Yield: Enough stars for 2 recipes of Jalapeño Beef Stew, or 4 to 6 servings if used as a side dish.**

GRADY SPEARS ～ FEBRUARY 2000

Opposite page: Jalapeño Beef Stew with Polenta Stars

Calabacita con Carne de Puerco

(MEXICAN SQUASH WITH PORK)

This version of calabacita (pictured on page 57) was adapted from a recipe that appears in The Melting Pot: Ethnic Cuisine in Texas *(1977). If you can't find Mexican squash, tatuma squash or zucchini work well as alternatives.*

2 T. vegetable oil	1 tsp. ground cumin
2 lb. pork, cubed	2 ears fresh sweet corn (or 1 c. frozen corn)
2 c. chopped tomatoes	1½ lb. Mexican squash
1 c. diced onion	(or tatuma squash or zucchini), cubed
½ c. diced green pepper	1 tsp. salt, or to taste
2 cloves garlic, minced	

Brown meat in hot oil in a large skillet; drain fat. Stir in tomato, onion, green pepper, garlic, and cumin. Cover, reduce heat, and simmer about 15 minutes. Cut corn from cob. Stir in corn, squash, and salt; cover and simmer about 30 minutes. **Yield: 8 to 10 servings.**

MAY 1996

Aunt Rosie's Campy Goulash

Former managing editor Rosemary Williams developed this dish, which is easily doubled, to take on family campouts. She says, "It's easy, and, best of all, it frees you from worrying about cooking the first (or second) night out."

1 lb. lean ground hamburger or ground turkey	1 T. commercial Italian-seasoning herb blend (a mixture of ground basil, thyme, and oregano), or to taste
1 tsp. Worcestershire sauce, or to taste	
1 clove garlic, minced	salt and pepper to taste
½ medium green pepper, chopped	1 (14½-oz.) can stewed tomatoes
1 small onion, chopped	1 (15-oz.) can pinto beans
1 rib celery, chopped	1 (15-oz.) can tomato sauce with herbs

Combine hamburger, Worcestershire sauce, and garlic in a Dutch oven and brown over low heat; drain well. Add green pepper, onion, celery, and remaining seasonings; cook slowly until onions become translucent. Add tomatoes, beans, and tomato sauce. Simmer slowly at least 1 hour, adding water as necessary. **Yield: 2 to 3 servings.**

ROSEMARY WILLIAMS ~ MAY 1990

Joe Keys' Irish Stew

Joe Keys, an Irishman turned Texan, obtained this recipe for Irish stew from his mother, Cathrine Keys, who thickened it with 4 large potatoes (cooked and mashed) instead of instant potatoes.

2 T. cooking oil	4 carrots, sliced
2 lb. lamb shank, cut into 1-inch chunks	2 leeks, sliced, *or* 8 to 10 green onions, sliced
¼ c. chopped fresh parsley	1 parsnip, sliced
2 T. chopped fresh thyme	4 to 5 ribs of celery, sliced
1 T. salt, or to taste	⅓ c. instant potato flakes (add more for a thicker stew)
1 tsp. pepper, or to taste	

Brown half the meat at a time in hot oil in a large pot. Stir in parsley, thyme, salt, pepper, and 5 c. water. Simmer, covered, about 2 hours or until meat is tender.

Add vegetables, cover, and continue simmering about 20 minutes or until vegetables are done. Add more water if needed.

Whisk instant potatoes into stew; continue simmering about 3 minutes. Taste; season with additional salt and pepper, if desired. Serve in shallow bowls with Irish soda bread or cornbread. **Yield: 10 servings.**

JOE KEYS ～ MARCH 2003

Chili Cook-offs

Texans take seriously making a good bowl of red—hundreds of chili cook-offs take place annually across the state. In the two biggest and best-known contests—the Original Terlingua International Frank X. Tolbert–Wick Fowler Memorial Championship Chili Cookoff and the Terlingua International Chili Championship—cooks have to qualify to compete. Both events take place in the Big Bend town of Terlingua on the same day, the first Saturday in November (related festivities extend over the weekend). The competitions bring together thousands of chili lovers to have a good time as they celebrate the state dish.

Al Hopkins' Chili

Al Hopkins became involved in chili cook-offs in the late 1970s when he worked for Wolf Brand Chili, a cook-off sponsor. For many years, he coordinated the Original Terlingua International Frank X. Tolbert–Wick Fowler Memorial Championship Chili Cookoff.

2 lb. chuck tender, coarsely ground	2 T. ground cumin
1 (8-oz.) can tomato sauce	dash of salt
1 (14½-oz.) can beef broth	dash of ground oregano
1 c. chopped onion	dash of cayenne
¼ c. chili powder	dash of ground coriander

Brown meat in a large pot; drain well. Add remaining ingredients and simmer, covered, 45 minutes or until meat begins to get tender. Taste and adjust seasonings, adding more chili powder or salt if needed. (If chili is too spicy, add a little brown sugar; if too thick, add a little water.) Cook 15 minutes longer or until meat is tender. **Yield: 6 cups.**

AL HOPKINS ∾ AUGUST 1997

Bob Horton's Chili

Bob Horton, a longtime competitor in one or the other of the Terlingua cook-offs, provided this recipe for our August 1997 story on chili. Bob's competition chili is a little spicier than this toned-down version, which he created for eating by the bowlful.

6 T. chili powder	1 tsp. Accent (MSG) (optional)
3 T. onion powder	3 lb. lean, boneless beef roast or round steak, diced or coarsely ground
2 tsp. garlic powder	
½ tsp. black pepper	1 (8-oz.) can tomato sauce
½ tsp. cayenne	1 (14½-oz.) can chicken broth
½ tsp. ground oregano	1 (14½-oz.) can beef broth
1 T. paprika	1 T. ground cumin
¾ tsp. salt, or to taste	1 T. brown sugar

Combine first 9 ingredients in a small bowl; divide into thirds and set aside.

Brown meat in a large pot; drain well. Add tomato sauce, chicken broth, and beef broth, and simmer, covered, 2 hours or until meat is tender, adding ⅓ of the chili powder mixture after each half-hour of cooking. Add cumin and brown sugar with the last portion of the chili powder mixture. (Chili should cook about 30 minutes longer.) **Yield: 6 cups.**

BOB HORTON ∾ AUGUST 1997

Dotty Griffith's Favorite Chili

Longtime Dallas food writer Dotty Griffith shared this recipe from her 1985 book
Wild about Chili.

4 dried ancho chiles, stemmed and seeded	1 (14½-oz.) can unsalted chopped tomatoes, undrained, *or* 1 lb. fresh tomatoes, chopped
4 dried arbol chiles, *or* 1 extra dried ancho chile, stemmed and seeded	2 tsp. salt
2 japones chiles, stemmed and seeded, *or* ½ to 1 tsp. cayenne	¼ lb. chopped beef suet (ask the butcher for this)
1 T. cumin seed	4 lb. lean beef, such as trimmed chuck roast or chuck tender, cut in ¼-inch cubes
7 cloves garlic	1 tsp. sugar
1 tsp. dried chile petins, crushed	1 c. red wine
5 fresh jalapeños, stemmed and seeded	¼ c. masa preparada (a flour-tortilla mix)

Place first 3 ingredients and enough water to barely cover in a small saucepan. Bring chiles to a boil over medium heat and simmer, covered, 15 minutes. Remove chiles, reserving liquid. Place softened chiles, cumin seed, garlic, chile petins, jalapeños, tomatoes, and salt in a food processor and process until smooth; set aside.

In a cast-iron pot or large Dutch oven, render enough suet to make ¼ c. Cook meat in rendered fat over high heat until meat turns gray (cook away most of the liquid, but do not brown); drain excess fat.

Add chiles mixture, sugar, and wine to meat. Add just enough water (2 to 3 c.) to almost cover meat. Bring mixture to a boil, reduce heat, and simmer uncovered about 1½ hours, stirring occasionally. Add water as needed to maintain same level.

Combine masa preparada with just enough water to make a smooth paste; press out all lumps with the back of a spoon. Gradually stir paste into chili to thicken. Taste, adding more salt and chili powder if desired. (For a hotter chili, add some of the reserved liquid from chiles.) Cook about 30 minutes longer over very low heat, stirring frequently. Yield: 10 cups.

DOTTY GRIFFITH ～ AUGUST 1997

Frito Pie

Many Texans consider this simple dish the ultimate comfort food. Aficionados range from those who prefer to slit open a small bag of Fritos lengthwise and use the bag itself as the bowl to those who top the traditional mix with chopped tomatoes, grated carrot, and/or sprouts. As to whether or not the chili should have beans—always a delicate subject—you're on your own.

2 c. small Fritos	shredded cheddar cheese
1 (15-oz.) can Wolf Brand Chili	chopped onions

Place 1 c. Fritos into each of 2 soup or cereal bowls. Heat chili in a small saucepan, pour over Fritos, dividing evenly, and top with shredded cheese and onions. **Yield: 2 servings.**

JANUARY 2004

Threadgill's Chicken-Fried Steak

A Texas institution, Threadgill's in Austin serves up heapin' helpings of Southern specialties and Lone Star atmosphere. According to owner-proprietor Eddie Wilson, the secret to the restaurant's acclaimed CFS is its wet-dry-wet method of preparation. (It seals in the juices.) Eddie uses this same basic recipe, which is adapted from a recipe in The Threadgill's Cookbook *(1996), for frying chicken or center-cut, boneless pork chops.*

2 eggs	2 c. canola oil
2 c. milk (room temperature)	8 (6-oz.) tenderized beef cutlets (room temperature)
3 c. all-purpose flour	Threadgill's Cream Gravy (recipe follows)
2½ tsp. Threadgill's Meat Seasoning (recipe follows)	

Whisk eggs and milk together in a bowl and set aside. Combine flour and Meat Seasoning in another bowl and set aside.

Heat oil in a 14-inch cast-iron skillet over medium heat (or to 375° in an electric skillet). The oil should pop loudly when a drop of egg mixture is dropped in. Dip each cutlet in egg mixture; dredge in flour mixture, shaking off excess; and dip again in egg mixture. Gently place cutlets in hot oil. (As you transfer cutlets from egg mixture to skillet, hold a plate under them to catch drips.) Cook 3 to 5 minutes until breading is set and golden brown. (There will be regular "explosions" of oil as cutlets cook.) Gently turn cutlets with a long-handled meat fork or long metal tongs. Cook another 3 minutes. Carefully remove cutlets from skillet; drain well, reserving cracklings and ⅓ to ½ c. oil in skillet for gravy.

Keep steaks warm while preparing gravy. Place steaks on individual plates and top with hot gravy. **Yield: 8 servings.**

THREADGILL'S MEAT SEASONING

½ c. flaked salt (or substitute regular salt and use 1 T. less)	2 T. white pepper
¼ c. granulated or powdered garlic	2 T. paprika
2 T. granulated or powdered onion	1½ tsp. ground cumin
¼ c. black pepper	1½ tsp. cayenne

Mix ingredients well. Place mixture in a tightly sealed glass or plastic container and store in a dark place for future use. Shake before each use to remix ingredients. **Yield: 1⅓ cups.**

THREADGILL'S CREAM GRAVY

⅓ to ½ c. reserved drippings	½ tsp. black pepper
⅓ to ½ c. all-purpose flour	2 tsp. Worcestershire sauce
1 qt. milk (room temperature)	¼ tsp. Tabasco sauce, or to taste
1 tsp. salt	

Heat reserved drippings over medium heat and sprinkle flour over top. Whisk until mixture becomes a bubbly golden paste. Whisking as you pour, slowly add milk; whisk mixture continuously until it is smooth and thick enough to coat a spoon. Add salt, pepper, Worcestershire sauce, and Tabasco sauce, and whisk until smooth.

EDDIE WILSON ∾ JULY 1996

Opposite page: Threadgill's Chicken-Fried Steak

Broken Spoke's Chicken-Fried Steak

Acclaimed by CFS aficionados for decades, the Broken Spoke's version of the Lone Star classic went public in 1994, when co-owner James White released the recipe in honor of the Austin dance hall's thirtieth anniversary. Co-owner Annetta White, James' wife, says the following adaptation reflects the Spoke's tradition of hand-breading each steak and cooking everything fresh when ordered.

1 large egg	½ c. cracker meal
1 c. buttermilk	1 (3- to 5-oz.) beef cutlet, hand-tenderized
salt to taste	vegetable shortening
pepper to taste	Broken Spoke's Cream Gravy (recipe follows)
½ c. all-purpose flour	

Whip together egg, buttermilk, salt, and pepper in a large bowl; set batter aside.

Blend together flour and cracker meal in another bowl. Place cutlet in cracker mixture and cover both sides well. Submerge cutlet in egg batter, then place it back in cracker mixture, patting both sides again evenly to coat.

Place shortening in a deep fryer or cast-iron skillet and heat to 325°. Place cutlet in fryer and fry until it floats and turns golden. Remove steak from fryer; drain well, reserving ½ c. drippings for gravy. Place steak on plate and keep warm while preparing Cream Gravy. Spoon gravy generously over steak. **Yield: 1 serving.**

BROKEN SPOKE'S CREAM GRAVY

½ c. reserved drippings or shortening	salt to taste
¼ c. all-purpose flour	pepper to taste
1 qt. milk	

Place drippings in a 10- to 12-inch cast-iron skillet and heat until hot. Gradually add flour and cook over low heat until mixture turns brown, stirring constantly to prevent scorching. Add remaining ingredients and cook, stirring constantly, until thick. If gravy gets too thick, thin to desired consistency with water. **Yield: Enough gravy for 6 to 8 steaks.**

JAMES WHITE ∽ JULY 1999

Opposite page: Perini Ranch Steak and some of the accompaniments served at Perini Ranch Steakhouse

Perini Ranch Steaks

This recipe was adapted from one provided by Perini Ranch Steakhouse in Buffalo Gap.

4 large steaks (ribeyes are a good choice)	melted butter or stick margarine (optional)
Perini Ranch Steak Rub (recipe follows)	

Rub steaks with Perini Ranch Steak Rub and refrigerate at least 15 minutes before cooking. Grill over hot mesquite coals and baste with butter, if desired. **Yield: 4 large steaks.**

PERINI RANCH STEAK RUB

2 tsp. cornstarch or all-purpose flour	4 tsp. garlic powder
2 tsp. salt	4 tsp. onion powder
2 T. coarse-grind pepper	1 tsp. paprika
½ tsp. lemon pepper	1 tsp. beef-flavored bouillon granules
½ tsp. ground oregano	

Combine all ingredients, mixing well. If not using right away, store in a tightly sealed glass or plastic container. Shake before each use to remix ingredients. **Yield: About ½ cup seasoning (enough for 4 large steaks).**

TOM PERINI ～ JUNE 1997

Dan's Spoon Venison

Cathy Barber, food editor of The Dallas Morning News, *provided one of her husband's recipes. She calls it "spoon venison" because it's always tender enough to cut with a spoon. Note that Dan prepares the dish in a cast-iron Dutch oven, which he later places in a conventional oven.*

1 T. olive oil	1 c. chicken stock
2 lb. venison shoulder steaks	1 (16-oz.) can tomato sauce
1 T. minced garlic	½ tsp. Cajun seasoning, or to taste
1 medium onion, chopped	1 sprig rosemary
1 lb. mushrooms, sliced, *or* 2 (7-oz.) cans mushrooms, drained	6 fresh basil leaves, minced, *or* ½ tsp. dried basil
1 c. red wine	hot cooked rice

Heat olive oil in a cast-iron Dutch oven (legless) over medium-high heat; sear venison on each side. Remove meat and set aside. Brown garlic, onion, and mushrooms in remaining oil. Stir in wine and next 4 ingredients. Bring to a boil; add seared venison and return to a boil. Cover and bake at 325° about 2 hours. Remove dish from oven and remove rosemary. Stir in basil, replace cover, and let stand in Dutch oven 5 to 10 minutes before serving over rice. **Yield: 4 to 6 servings.**

CATHY BARBER ⁓ DECEMBER 1999

Crisp-Fried Wild Turkey Breast

If you don't have access to a wild turkey breast, a regular turkey breast from the supermarket will do nicely.

2 eggs	1½ c. all-purpose flour
salt and pepper to taste	vegetable oil
1 wild turkey breast	

In a shallow bowl, beat eggs with salt and pepper. Tear strips of turkey off breastbone; dip strips in egg mixture, then flour. Heat 1 inch of oil in a Dutch oven to 375°; drop strips in hot oil. Cover and cook over medium heat until browned. **Yield: 6 to 8 servings.**

SUE SIMS ⁓ NOVEMBER 1987

County Line Smoked Tenderloin

Rick Goss, one of the co-founders of County Line restaurants, which originated in Austin in the mid-1970s, provided this recipe. Rick noted that tenderloin can be prepared on an enclosed smoke pit or on a standard barbecue grill that has a lid. He advised, "The longer and slower you cook the meat, the better the flavor."

1 (5- to 6-lb.) choice whole beef tenderloin, skin removed	juice of 2 limes
lemon-pepper seasoning	2 garlic cloves, pressed
½ c. butter or margarine, melted	salt and pepper to taste

Coat both sides of tenderloin heavily with lemon-pepper seasoning.

Make a "boat" of heavy-duty aluminum foil and place seasoned meat in it. (The boat helps keeps the meat juicy, but if you want a grilled effect, omit the foil and lay the meat directly on the rack.) Cook at a pit temperature of 225°.

Combine remaining ingredients to make a basting sauce; set aside.

After meat has cooked 40 minutes, insert a meat thermometer and check the temperature every 10 to 15 minutes. *Overcooking can occur quickly.* When checking meat, dab basting sauce over exterior.

Remove meat when thermometer reaches 120°–130° (rare) or 140°–150° (medium). Remove at higher or lower temperature depending on degree of doneness desired. (After removal, temperature will continue to rise by about 5°.) Serve immediately, or hold at 120°. **Yield: 10 to 16 servings.**

RICK GOSS ⁓ JANUARY 1987

Fajitas

This recipe calls for a generous amount of cumin, as is typical in Mexican cooking.
Those not accustomed to this flavor should season with caution, tasting frequently.

2 (5-oz.) bottles Lea & Perrins Worcestershire sauce	flour tortillas
½ c. ground cumin	pico de gallo (commercial or homemade; see recipes on page 152 and page 178)
¼ c. garlic powder	grated cheddar cheese
¼ c. freshly ground black pepper	sour cream
juice of 5 limes	guacamole
1 c. vegetable oil	chopped green onions
2½ lb. skirt steak	
2 yellow onions, sliced	

Combine first 6 ingredients in a glass or plastic container. Layer steaks and onions in marinade and marinate overnight in refrigerator.

Remove steaks and onions; discard marinade. Grill over medium-hot mesquite coals 2 to 3 minutes on each side. Turn onions occasionally and remove when soft. Remove meat and slice diagonally across the grain into thin, finger-length strips.

Place strips of meat on flour tortillas along with pico de gallo, cheese, sour cream, guacamole, and green onions, as desired. Roll up tortilla carefully to enclose filling; fold tortilla slightly up at the end so that the delicious contents do not escape as you eat. Yield: 10 servings.

MARTIN LECEA ~ FEBRUARY 1987

Elemental Arracheras

This traditional recipe for fajitas hails from the wood-fire cookouts on northern Mexico ranches.

2 to 2½ lb. skirt steak, trimmed of membrane and fat	1 to 2 medium onions, thickly sliced
juice of 6 to 7 limes	vegetable oil
2 to 3 pickled jalapeños, minced	lime wedges
6 cloves garlic, minced	flour tortillas (preferably thick), warmed
salt to taste	

Place steaks in a shallow glass container. Combine next 3 ingredients and pour mixture over steaks. Refrigerate for at least 6 to 8 hours, turning occasionally.

Remove steaks from refrigerator and drain. Sprinkle salt over steaks and let sit at room temperature for about 45 minutes. Coat onions with oil and place on a piece of foil.

On an outdoor grill, fire up enough charcoal to form a single layer of coals. When coals are covered with gray ash, place steaks directly over the fire; place onions a little to the side, where they'll get less heat. Grill steaks to medium-rare (about 5 to 6 minutes per side); remove from grill. Turn onions occasionally, removing when soft (some edges will be brown and crispy). Allow steaks to sit for 5 minutes before slicing diagonally across the grain into finger-length strips.

Pile meat, onions, and lime wedges on a platter; serve with tortillas. **Yield: 6 generous servings.**

CHERYL ALTERS JAMISON & BILL JAMISON ~ SEPTEMBER 1996

Opposite page: Elemental Arracheras

Mesquite-Grilled Frontier Sirloin

Savory sage and mustard enhance these tasty steaks. You can find mesquite chips at most outdoors stores.

2 T. prepared yellow mustard	2 (18- to 20-oz. and 1-inch-thick) boneless top sirloin strip steaks
2 T. vegetable oil	
6 cloves garlic, dry-roasted until soft	salt
½ tsp. Worcestershire sauce	freshly ground black pepper
½ tsp. crumbled dried whole sage	mesquite chips
8 green onions	4 serrano chiles, halved lengthwise

Combine first 5 ingredients in a food processor or blender. Rub steaks and onions with mixture, season with salt and pepper, and let sit at room temperature for 45 minutes.

On an outdoor grill, fire up enough charcoal to form a single layer of coals. Place a few handfuls of mesquite chips or pods in water to soak. When charcoal is covered with gray ash, scatter mesquite over it and place steaks directly over fire. Place onions and serranos on a small piece of aluminum foil, a little off to the side of the fire, where heat is lower. Grill steaks on one side about 4 to 5 minutes, covering partially with the grill lid (vents open) to trap some of the mesquite smoke. Turn steaks, again cover grill partially, and cook to desired doneness, about 4 more minutes for medium-rare. When you turn steaks, also turn onions and serranos, removing them when soft. Top steaks with onions and serranos; serve immediately. **Yield: 4 servings.**

CHERYL ALTERS JAMISON & BILL JAMISON ∼ SEPTEMBER 1996

Mesquite-Grilled Frontier Sirloin

Bubba Hodges' Egypt Brisket

Bubba Hodges is the pit boss at John's Country Store, a barbecue joint in Egypt, an almost–ghost town just north of Wharton. The store was called G. H. Northington Sr. Mercantile Store when it first opened in 1900. One of Northington's descendants, John Northington, took over the store and changed the name in 1978.

1 (8- to 10-lb.) packer's cut (untrimmed) USDA Select beef brisket	1 c. Tony Chachere's Original Seasoning (or the dry rub of your choice)
	6 c. John Northington's Mop (recipe follows)

Rinse brisket and pat dry. Sprinkle dry rub on both sides, wrap in plastic wrap, and refrigerate overnight.

Set up your smoker for indirect heat with a water pan. Use wood chips, chunks, or logs, and keep up a good level of smoke. Maintain a temperature between 210° and 250°. Place the brisket in the smoker, as far from the heat source as possible. Mop (baste) with mop sauce every 30 minutes, rotating the brisket to cook it evenly, keeping the fat side up at all times. Add charcoal and/or wood every hour or so to keep the fire burning evenly.

After 4 hours, wrap the brisket in heavy-duty aluminum foil with what's left of the mop sauce, including the onions and lemons. Seal and continue cooking over low coals for 4 more hours. (Or place brisket in a roasting pan in a 250° oven.) The meat is done when a thermometer reads 185° at the thick end, or when a probe goes through with little resistance. **Yield: 10 to 12 servings.**

JOHN NORTHINGTON'S MOP

1 c. vegetable oil	3 small onions, sliced
½ c. white vinegar	1 (10-oz.) bottle Lone Star beer
½ c. cider vinegar	3 T. soy sauce
1 c. ranch dressing	2 lemons, cut in half

Combine all ingredients in a large pot, squeezing the lemons as you add them. Simmer for 30 minutes or until the onions are soft. Keep the mop sauce in a pot on top of the smoker so that it stays hot. **Yield: About 6 cups.**

Lorenzo Vences' Sirloin

Cooper's Old Time Pit Bar-B-Q (locations in Llano and Mason) has preserved the "cowboy style" of barbecuing, which is a cross between grilling and smoking. Mesquite wood is burned down to coals in a fireplace and the coals are shoveled into enclosed pits. The meat is cooked by direct heat about 28 to 30 inches above the coals with the lid closed. Lorenzo Vences, who has been pit boss at the Llano location since 1986, estimates that the heat in his pit is between 350° and 400°. When the temperature of the meat reaches 140°, it is moved to a holding pit, where it continues to cook slowly until it is sold. Here's a variation of Lorenzo's sirloin recipe that's designed for a regular-size barbecue pit.

1 (2- to 2½-lb. and 1¾-inch-thick) USDA Choice beef sirloin steak (branded beef such as Black Angus or Certified Hereford preferred)	1 (2- to 2½-lb. and 1 ¾-inch-thick) USDA Choice beef sirloin tip roast
or	salt
	coarse-grind black pepper

Allow meat to come to room temperature and season it with salt and pepper.

Light some mesquite chunks in a charcoal chimney starter (see page 225–226). Pour the hot coals into your firebox. Light another batch of mesquite chunks a few minutes later. Maintain a temperature between 350° and 400° and place the meat at least 18 inches above the coals until it's well browned, or until it reaches an internal temperature of 120°. Add more coals as needed. Douse flare-ups with water from a squirt bottle.

When the meat is well charred, move it to a cooler part of the pit where it can cook indirectly until it reaches the desired temperature. Remove it from the pit when it is firm to the touch, or between 135° and 155°. (Cooper's won't serve any meat that hasn't reached 140°.) At this temperature, the meat will be medium-rare. Remove the meat at 145° for medium and 155° for medium-well. The meat will continue to cook after it is removed, so allow it to rest before carving. **Yield: 4 to 6 servings.**

Drexler's Ribs

James Drexler has been smoking ribs at Drexler's Bar-B-Que in Houston for more than 27 years. Here's his recipe for smoking pork ribs at home. He says, "Sit back, drink a beer, and don't be in a rush. They'll get very tender if you give them enough time."

1 rack pork spareribs (under 3½ lb.)	2 T. salt
2 T. sugar	1 T. garlic powder
¼ c. paprika	1 T. onion powder

Rinse ribs, then dry them. Combine sugar and seasonings and sprinkle on both sides of ribs; rub seasoning mixture in.

Set up your smoker for indirect heat with a water pan. Use wood chips, chunks, or logs, and keep up a good level of smoke. Maintain a temperature between 250° and 300°. Place ribs on smoker, bone side down, as far away from the fire as possible. Cook for 3 to 3½ hours or until a toothpick goes through easily when inserted between the bones. Yield: 2 to 4 servings.

Novosad's Pork Steaks

Novosad's BBQ and Sausage Market in Hallettsville is one of the old Czech barbecue joints where cold canned peaches are a favorite side dish. Third-generation barbecue meister Nathan Novosad owns the market with his wife, Laura. Nathan notes that pork steaks are actually slices of pork shoulder (Boston butt). However, he says, "Don't buy a bone-in Boston butt roast thinking you're going to slice it at home—you'd need a band saw to get through the bone. Ask the butcher to slice it for you."

1 T. salt	½ tsp. ground bay leaf
1 tsp. freshly ground black pepper	2 lb. pork steak
½ tsp. ground sage	

Combine seasonings and sprinkle on steaks, rubbing mixture into meat well.

Set up your smoker for indirect heat with a water pan. Use wood chips, chunks, or logs, and keep up a good level of smoke. Maintain a temperature between 225° and 275°. Place steaks in smoker. Cooking should take 4 to 5 hours. The meat is done when it pulls easily away from the bone. An internal temperature of around 170° is perfect. (This is also the USDA-recommended temperature.) **Yield: 4 servings.**

Ruthie's Pork Shoulder

Louis Charles Henley is the pit boss at Ruthie's Pit Bar-B-Q in Navasota, which specializes in East Texas–style barbecue. (Ruthie is his mom.) Louis says he used to use a "mop" with lots of lemons in it, but now he just depends on his dry rub and good wood— a combination of post oak, pecan, and mesquite—to flavor the meat.

1 (4- to 5-lb.) pork shoulder roast (Boston butt)	your favorite barbecue sauce (optional)
3 T. Louis Charles Henley's All-Purpose Rub (recipe follows)	sliced pickles (optional)
bread or hamburger buns (optional)	sliced onions (optional)

Season the meat with the rub, rubbing it in well.

Set up your smoker for indirect heat with a water pan. Use wood chips, chunks, or logs, and keep up a good level of smoke. Maintain a temperature between 225° and 250°. Smoke the roast 4 to 5 hours, turning it every half-hour or so to ensure even cooking. The meat is done when it pulls easily away from the bone (the USDA recommends an internal temperature of 170°).

Slice meat with an electric knife and serve on bread or buns with your favorite barbecue sauce, sliced pickles, and sliced onions. **Yield: 4 to 6 servings.**

LOUIS CHARLES HENLEY'S ALL-PURPOSE RUB

¼ c. Lawry's Seasoned Salt	2 tsp. garlic powder
1 T. fine-grind black pepper	1 tsp. chili powder

Combine ingredients and store mixture in a tightly sealed container. Shake before each use to remix seasoning. **Yield: ⅜ cup.**

Grilled Portobellos

Looking for something different to cook on the grill? Hearty, saucer-shaped portobellos can serve as a delicious stand-in for hamburgers.

4 medium-size fresh portobello mushrooms, cleaned	¼ tsp. salt
2 T. butter or margarine	⅛ tsp. pepper
2 tsp. minced garlic	1 T. chopped fresh basil or parsley
2 T. balsamic vinegar	

Separate mushroom caps from stems; set caps aside. Coarsely chop enough stems to measure 1 cup; set aside.

In a medium saucepan, melt butter. Add chopped stems and garlic; cook over medium heat, stirring frequently, about 5 minutes or until stems are tender. Stir in remaining ingredients and remove from heat. Transfer mixture to a food processor or blender and process until finely chopped; set aside.

Grill mushroom caps, rounded side up, over hot coals for 2 to 3 minutes or until caps are hot. Turn caps and fill each cavity with ¼ of the mushroom-garlic mixture. Grill 4 to 5 minutes longer or until mushrooms are tender. **Yield: 4 servings.**

N O T E : Mushroom caps may also be cooked on a broiler. Prepare caps as directed; place on broiler pan and broil 4 inches from heat.

N O V E M B E R 1 9 9 8

Roasted Leg of Lamb

For a change of pace, forget the mint jelly and try serving this classic entrée with jalapeño jelly instead. Buy a commercial version or try the recipe on page 186.

1 (5- to 6-lb.) leg of lamb	salt
fresh lemon juice	freshly ground pepper
3 cloves garlic, cut into about 12 slivers	fresh mint (optional)
2 T. unsalted butter, softened	

Trim fat from lamb, leaving only a very thin layer. Drizzle lemon juice over lamb and let sit at room temperature for 30 minutes.

Make about 12 slits randomly throughout the lamb and insert slivers of garlic. Rub butter over lamb to coat; season with salt and pepper.

Place lamb on a rack in a shallow roasting pan. Insert meat thermometer, making sure it doesn't touch fat or bone. Bake at 325° for 2½ to 3 hours or until meat thermometer registers 160°. Let stand 10 minutes before carving. Garnish with fresh mint, if desired. **Yield: 8 servings.**

N O T E : This same cut can be used to prepare butterflied lamb, which is easily cooked outdoors. Remove bone from leg of lamb, then flatten meat to an even thickness. Brush meat with a mixture of melted butter, Dijon mustard, and your favorite herbs. Sprinkle with lemon juice and grill 10 minutes on each side, 5 to 6 inches from hot coals.

S U E S I M S ~ N O V E M B E R 1 9 8 7

Carol McLeod's Fried Chicken

When we were assembling our June 2003 story on Texas fried chicken, the restaurant owners mentioned in the story graciously declined to contribute any recipes (trade secrets, you know). So the author, Gerald McLeod, went to the person he considered the source of the ultimate fried chicken—his mother. Carol McLeod shared her recipe, as well as two of her secrets: Crisco shortening and a large cast-iron skillet with a tight-fitting lid.

1 c. all-purpose flour	1 c. buttermilk
1 T. salt	1 (2½- to 3-lb.) broiler-fryer, cut up
1 T. pepper	⅓ c. Crisco shortening

Mix flour, salt, and pepper in a shallow dish; set aside. Pour buttermilk into a bowl. Dip chicken pieces in buttermilk, shake off excess liquid, and dredge in flour mixture, coating well.

Heat shortening in a 12-inch cast-iron skillet until shortening melts and oil is hot; add chicken and cook over medium heat (reduce heat if chicken is cooking too quickly), turning pieces often until light brown, about 15 to 20 minutes. Reduce heat, add 2 T. water, cover tightly, and simmer, turning two or three times, until thickest pieces are done, about 30 to 40 minutes. **Yield: 8 to 10 pieces fried chicken.**

CAROL McLEOD ∼ JUNE 2003

Carol McLeod's Fried Chicken

King Ranch Casserole

Even meat-and-potatoes types like this casserole (also known as King Ranch Chicken). Despite its name, the origin of this dish is a mystery; the King Ranch doesn't claim it. "We've tried for years to nail down the origin of that recipe," says Martin Clement, who manages the Main House, "but we've never been able to. You can be sure that if we had invented it, it would promote beef or game, not chicken."

1 (3- to 4-lb.) broiler-fryer, cut up	1 large green pepper, chopped
1 tsp. salt	1½ tsp. chili powder
1 (10¾-oz.) can cream of chicken soup	12 corn tortillas
1 (10¾-oz.) can cream of mushroom soup	2 c. shredded Monterey Jack or "Mexican-style" cheese
1 (10-oz.) can Ro-Tel Diced Tomatoes & Green Chilies	garlic powder to taste
1 large onion, chopped	

Place chicken pieces in a large Dutch oven; add water to cover and 1 tsp. salt. Simmer, covered, about 1 hour or until chicken is tender. When cool, remove and bone chicken, reserving broth. Cut or tear meat into small pieces; set aside.

In a large bowl, combine soups with tomatoes, onion, green pepper, and chili powder; mix well and set aside.

Heat reserved chicken broth. Tear tortillas into fourths, dip each piece in warm chicken broth, and place half the tortillas on the bottom of a greased 9 x 13 x 2–inch baking pan or casserole. Continue layering, using half of chicken, half of soup-tomatoes mixture, and half of cheese. Sprinkle with garlic powder. Repeat layers with remaining ingredients. Bake at 350° for 30 to 40 minutes or until cheese has melted and sides of casserole are bubbly. **Yield: 10 to 12 servings.**

JANUARY 2004

Zwiebel Kuchen
(ONION QUICHE)

Fredericksburg Brewing Company provided the original version of this recipe.

1 unbaked 10-inch pastry shell	⅛ tsp. caraway seed
6 oz. sliced bacon	⅛ tsp. ground rosemary
3 medium yellow onions, chopped	pinch of white pepper
3 T. butter or stick margarine	pinch of cayenne
¼ c. bock beer	6 oz. grated Jarlsberg cheese
½ tsp. salt	3 eggs
⅛ tsp. mustard seed	½ c. half-and-half

Bake pastry at 375° until halfway done (about 10 minutes); set aside. Brown bacon; drain, crumble, and set aside.

Sauté onions in butter until translucent. Add beer and seasonings, then reduce mixture over low heat until no liquid remains. Cool.

Combine onion mixture and cheese; place in cooled pastry shell. Mix eggs and half-and-half, pour over onion-cheese mixture, and top with bacon. Bake at 325° for 30 to 35 minutes or until set in the center.

AUGUST 1995

Mexican Macaroni Casserole

Here's a good standby when you're trying to decide what to fix for supper.
Add a green salad and you're set.

1 lb. pork sausage	1 (16-oz.) can whole tomatoes, drained and chopped
1 c. chopped onion	1 T. chili powder
1 c. chopped green pepper	1 tsp. salt
2 c. cooked macaroni	⅓ c. shredded cheddar cheese
½ c. sour cream	green pepper rings (optional)

Sauté sausage, onion, and green pepper in a skillet until sausage is done; drain well. Combine sausage mixture and remaining ingredients except cheese. Spoon into a lightly greased 2-qt. casserole. Sprinkle with cheese and bake at 350° for 20 to 25 minutes or until bubbly. Garnish with green pepper rings, if desired. **Yield: 6 to 8 servings.**

ALICE SEDBERRY ～ 2004

Opposite page: Breast of Pheasant Grand-mère (left) and Bread Pudding with Lemon Sauce

Breast of Pheasant Grand-mère

Adapted from a recipe that appears in Houston Is Cooking 2000, *by retired* Houston Chronicle *food editor Ann Criswell, this elegant entrée goes well with wild rice. Preparation involves flambéing, so be sure to use a skillet without a nonstick finish. For a lower-fat dish, remove skin from breasts, reduce butter to ¼ c., and use only 4 slices of bacon.*

2 (3-lb.) pheasants	8 slices lean bacon, coarsely cut
1 tsp. salt	12 large white button mushrooms, quartered
dash of freshly ground pepper	¼ c. brandy
1 tsp. chopped fresh rosemary	1 c. dry white wine
½ c. all-purpose flour	2 medium potatoes, peeled, boiled, and diced
½ c. unsalted butter	½ c. pearl onions, boiled and stemmed

Remove pheasant breasts by cutting with a sharp knife along breastbone to wing bone; reserve remainder for another use. Sprinkle breasts with salt, pepper, and rosemary, and dust lightly with flour. Melt butter in a heavy skillet (one without a nonstick finish) and sauté breasts over low heat for 10 minutes or until golden brown. Remove breasts, reserving drippings, and place in a shallow baking dish; set aside.

Sauté bacon and mushrooms in same skillet until bacon is cooked but not crisp. Add brandy and flambé, lighting carefully with a taper match from a safe distance. Stir in wine, potatoes, and onions, and spoon over pheasant breasts. Bake at 350° for 10 to 15 minutes or until done. **Yield: 4 servings.**

ANN CRISWELL ～ FEBRUARY 2000

Spinach-Mushroom Lasagna (top) and Tangy Shrimp and Spinach Salad

Spinach-Mushroom Lasagna

One 10-oz. pkg. frozen chopped spinach, thawed and drained, may be substituted for the fresh spinach.

1 (15-oz.) carton ricotta cheese	8 oz. lasagna noodles (uncooked), divided
1 egg, beaten	2 bunches fresh spinach (about 1½ lb.), washed and stemmed
2 c. shredded mozzarella cheese, divided	
1 (28-oz.) jar spaghetti sauce, divided	2 c. sliced fresh mushrooms

Combine ricotta cheese, egg, and 1 c. shredded mozzarella in a medium-size bowl; set aside.

Pour half the spaghetti sauce in the bottom of a lightly greased 9 x 13–inch baking dish. Cover sauce with half the noodles. Spread the cheese-egg mixture over the noodles, followed by the spinach, mushrooms, remaining mozzarella cheese, remaining noodles, and remaining sauce. Pour 2 T. water into each corner of the dish. Cover dish securely with aluminum foil and bake at 350° for 1 hour and 15 minutes. Do not unseal until cooking time is complete. Remove from the oven, uncover carefully, and let stand for 10 to 15 minutes before serving. **Yield: 6 to 8 servings.**

NOVEMBER 1997

Fresh Tomato-Mushroom Pizza

Use your favorite boxed or fresh pizza dough (enough for a 12-inch pie) for this delectable pizza.

1 medium yellow onion, diced	¼ tsp. freshly ground black pepper
3 cloves garlic, minced	1 (12-inch) unbaked pizza crust
1 green pepper, diced	8 oz. ricotta cheese
¼ lb. white mushrooms, thinly sliced	½ to ¾ lb. Provolone cheese, grated
3 T. olive oil	2 ripe tomatoes, sliced ¼-inch thick
3 T. finely chopped fresh basil	1 (6-oz.) jar marinated artichoke hearts, drained
½ tsp. salt	¼ c. grated Asiago or Parmesan cheese

In a skillet over medium heat, sauté onion, garlic, green pepper, and mushrooms in olive oil until vegetables are soft. Stir in basil, salt, and pepper. Drain excess liquid from mixture and set aside.

On unbaked crust, spread ricotta cheese, then add grated Provolone, tomato slices (salted and peppered to taste), sautéed vegetable mixture, and artichoke hearts. Sprinkle with Asiago or Parmesan cheese. Bake at 500° about 15 minutes or until pizza crust is light brown and cheese is bubbly. **Yield: 2 to 4 servings.**

JUNE 2000

Zelné Závitky
(STUFFED CABBAGE LEAVES)

Czechs as well as many other ethnic groups make a version of stuffed cabbage. This recipe is adapted from one that appears in the Czech Heritage Cookbook *(1994).*

1 medium onion, chopped and divided	5 oz. chicken broth or water
2 T. vegetable oil, divided	1 egg, slightly beaten
1 lb. ground pork	1 small head cabbage
1 tsp. salt	1 c. tomato juice
½ tsp. pepper	1 c. half-and-half
2 T. uncooked rice	1 T. all-purpose flour

Sauté half the onion in 1 T. oil. Stir in ground pork, salt, and pepper; cover and cook over low heat for 10 minutes. Drain well. Add rice and broth; cover and cook over low heat about 10 minutes or until meat is tender. Remove from heat; add egg and mix well. Set aside to cool.

Remove 8 cabbage leaves and drop into boiling water. Cook a few minutes; drain well. Place about ⅛ of the pork-rice mixture on each cabbage leaf, dividing mixture evenly. Roll up cabbage leaves, tucking in ends; fasten with toothpicks.

Finely shred remaining cabbage. Sauté cabbage and remaining onion in remaining oil for about 5 minutes or until cabbage is soft. Spread half the sautéed mixture in a lightly greased 4-qt. casserole or large baking pan. Place cabbage rolls on top and cover with remaining sautéed cabbage mixture. Pour tomato juice over top of cabbage; cover and bake at 350° for 20 minutes.

Mix half-and-half and flour. Remove dish from oven; pour cream mixture over top of cabbage. Cover and bake 10 minutes more or until cabbage is tender. **Yield: 4 to 6 servings.**

NOVEMBER 1996

Pan-Fried Pork with Peaches

This recipe is adapted from one that appears in Texas Morning Glory: Memorable Breakfast Recipes from Lone Star Bed and Breakfast Inns *(Great Texas Line, 2002) by Barry Shlachter. It's often on the menu at Cook's Cottage and Suites in Fredericksburg, where there's an abundance of fresh peaches in the summertime.*

4 (¼-inch-thick) pork loin cutlets (ask your butcher to cut these)	2 green onions (tops and bottoms), minced
2 T. all-purpose flour	1 T. green peppercorns
salt and pepper	½ c. chicken stock
3 T. vegetable oil	3 large ripe peaches, peeled and sliced
2 T. dry sherry	juice of ½ lemon

Dust cutlets with flour and season with salt and pepper. Heat oil in saucepan and quickly sauté pork until just cooked through, or about 4 to 6 minutes. Remove cutlets and set aside.

Deglaze pan drippings with sherry, stirring up any bits that cling to the bottom of the pan. Stir in green onions and peppercorns and heat through. Add chicken stock and heat rapidly to reduce and slightly thicken the mixture. Just before serving, return cutlets to the pan, gently stir in peach slices, and heat thoroughly. Drizzle with lemon juice and serve immediately. **Yield: 4 servings.**

BARRY SHLACHTER ～ JULY 2003

Grilled Country Sausage on Warm Red Cabbage

This savory dish makes a wonderful entrée for a winter evening.

¼ c. dried currants	2 bay leaves
1 tsp. toasted caraway seeds	1 T. chopped fresh sage leaves
½ c. apple cider vinegar	1 lb. German, Polish, or hot Italian sausage
1 medium red onion, sliced	½ c. Dijon or stone-ground mustard
1 T. olive oil	1½ tsp. cayenne
2 lb. red cabbage, thinly sliced	1 T. lemon juice
2 Granny Smith apples, peeled, cored, and sliced	additional sage leaves
¼ c. honey	

Soak currants and caraway seeds in vinegar for 15 minutes; drain.

In a large saucepan, brown onions in olive oil over high heat. Add cabbage and apples; cook for 5 minutes. Reduce heat and add currants–caraway seeds mixture, honey, bay leaves, and sage; cook for 30 minutes.

Grill or roast sausage until done. Combine mustard, cayenne, and lemon juice while sausage is cooking; set aside.

Remove bay leaves, place cabbage mixture on warm plates, top with sausage, and garnish with additional sage leaves and mustard sauce. **Yield: 4 servings.**

STEPHEN McINERNEY ～ AUGUST 1995

Sauerbraten with Gingersnap Gravy

Try this adaptation of a classic German dish when you know you'll have a span of time at home; the roast needs to marinate for 4 days before cooking.

1 (4-lb.) beef rump roast	½ c. vegetable oil
2 onions, thinly sliced	½ tsp. salt
8 peppercorns	2 c. boiling water
4 whole cloves	10 gingersnaps, crushed
1 bay leaf	½ c. sour cream
½ c. cider vinegar	1 T. all-purpose flour
½ c. red wine	

Place roast in a deep ceramic or glass bowl. Add onions, peppercorns, cloves, and bay leaf. Combine vinegar, wine, and 1 c. water; pour over meat. Chill, covered, for 4 days, turning meat twice each day.

Remove meat from marinade, reserving marinade. Dry well with paper towels. Strain marinade; reserve onions and 1 c. liquid.

In a Dutch oven, brown roast on all sides in hot oil. Turn roast and sprinkle with salt. Pour 2 c. boiling water around meat. Add gingersnaps; simmer, covered, 1½ hours, turning roast often. Add onions and 1 c. strained marinade; cook 2 additional hours or until meat is tender. Remove roast; keep warm.

Strain cooking liquid into a large saucepan. Mix sour cream with flour in a small bowl. Add a small amount of cooking liquid to sour cream mixture; stir until smooth, then stir mixture into the remaining cooking liquid. Cook over low heat, stirring, until gravy is thickened and smooth. Slice meat in ¼-inch-thick slices and serve with gravy. Yield: 8 to 10 servings.

MARCH 1996

Steamed Pork Dumplings

For these dumplings, look for round "shao-mai" wrappers. They should be about 3 to 3½ inches in diameter, paper-thin, and nearly white. Can't find shao-mai wrappers? Use square wonton skins and trim the corners. Unsteamed dumplings—and dumpling wrappers—freeze well.

¾ lb. ground pork	1 T. chopped green onions
2 c. (½ lb.) Chinese cabbage, chopped and squeezed dry	1 T. freshly minced ginger
3 T. soy sauce	2 (30-count) pkg. dumpling wrappers
1 tsp. salt	cabbage leaves
1 T. sesame oil	Garlic-Soy Dipping Sauce (recipe follows)

Mix first 7 ingredients. Place 2 tsp. of mixture in each wrapper. Fold in half and pinch edges with tucks to form a standing half-moon shape. Seal edges with a bit of cold water. Place dumplings on a cookie sheet lined with parchment or waxed paper and refrigerate.

Line the bottom of a steamer with cabbage leaves so the dumplings won't stick. Place dumplings in steamer and steam at medium heat 20 minutes. Drizzle with Garlic-Soy Dipping Sauce. **Yield: About 46 dumplings.**

GARLIC-SOY DIPPING SAUCE

3 T. soy sauce	2 tsp. minced fresh garlic
2 T. white vinegar	pinch sugar
2 tsp. sesame oil	

Combine ingredients and let stand 5 to 10 minutes before using (to give garlic time to permeate soy sauce).

APRIL 1996

Steamed Pork Dumplings

Pecan-Crusted Teriyaki Chicken

This flavorful dish requires marinating the chicken at least 8 hours before baking.

¾ c. teriyaki sauce	1 large egg, beaten
1 tsp. ground ginger	1½ c. finely chopped pecans
1 tsp. garlic powder	½ c. all-purpose flour
4 lb. frying chicken pieces (breasts, legs, and thighs)	

Combine teriyaki sauce, ginger, and garlic powder in a large plastic bag; add chicken pieces. Press air out, secure top, and turn bag over several times to coat chicken pieces. Refrigerate 8 hours or overnight.

Remove chicken, reserving marinade, and set aside. Combine egg and 2 T. reserved marinade; set aside.

Combine pecans and flour on a large plate. Dip chicken pieces into egg mixture, then roll in pecan mixture, coating all sides. Place chicken pieces, skin side up, on a rack placed in a large baking pan. Bake at 350° for 50 minutes or until chicken is tender. Cool slightly, then serve. **Yield: 8 servings.**

DECEMBER 1993

Vietnamese Skewered Beef

This recipe is adapted from one that appears in Paula Tran's Living and Cooking Vietnamese *(1990). Nước mắm (fish sauce) and Asian chili sauce are available at Asian import stores and at many grocery stores.*

1 lb. tender, lean beef	2 T. *nước mắm* (fish sauce)
4 stalks lemongrass, root and leaves removed, chopped fine, *or* 1 tsp. minced lemon peel	1 tsp. salt
	1 tsp. black pepper
1 T. minced ginger root	Asian chili sauce (optional)

Cut beef into very thin, 4-inch-long slices. Combine lemongrass, ginger, *nước mắm*, salt, and pepper. Spread ½ to 1 tsp. of mixture on each strip of beef and roll into a ball. Place five balls on each of four skewers and grill over hot coals or under broiler for 6 to 7 minutes. Serve with Asian chili sauce, if desired. **Yield: 4 servings.**

JUNE 1996

Vietnamese Skewered Beef

Long-Life Noodles with Chicken, Pork, & Shrimp

For Chinese-food aficionados, this dish is destined to become a favorite.

½ tsp. salt	½ lb. cooked chicken, sliced or shredded
½ lb. dried Chinese rice noodles	2 T. minced fresh garlic
2 T. plus 2 tsp. vegetable oil, divided	2 T. minced fresh ginger
2 T. soy sauce	¼ c. sliced green onions
1 T. sherry or cooking wine	½ c. carrots, thinly sliced
½ tsp. red pepper flakes (or more, to taste)	½ c. snow peas
2 T. cornstarch, divided	½ c. sweet red pepper strips
¼ lb. raw shrimp, peeled and diced	½ c. mushrooms, sliced
¼ lb. cooked pork, sliced or shredded	1 c. chicken broth

Combine 2 to 3 qt. water and ½ tsp. salt in a 4-qt. saucepan and bring water to a boil; add noodles. When noodles are tender, drain and rinse in cold water. Drain again, place in a bowl, and stir in 2 tsp. vegetable oil. Set aside.

In a large bowl, combine soy sauce, sherry, red pepper flakes, and 1 T. cornstarch. Stir in shrimp, pork, and chicken; set aside.

Heat remaining 2 T. oil over medium-high heat in a wok or large, heavy skillet. Stir-fry garlic and ginger lightly. Add, in order, meat mixture, green onions, carrots, snow peas, sweet red pepper, and mushrooms, taking care to keep ingredients moving. Stir-fry until shrimp is opaque.

Mix chicken broth with remaining 1 T. cornstarch and pour over all ingredients, continuing to stir. Heat a few more minutes until sauce boils and thickens. Stir in noodles. **Yield: 4 main-dish servings or 8 appetizer servings.**

APRIL 1996

Peanut-Chicken Dijon

This recipe includes a sour cream sauce that is spooned over the chicken just before serving. For a lighter sauce, you can use nonfat or low-fat sour cream or plain yogurt.

¼ c. butter or margarine, divided	1 c. sour cream
5 T. Dijon mustard, divided	2 to 3 T. chopped parsley
6 boneless, skinless chicken breasts, pounded thin	¼ tsp. salt
1½ c. finely chopped roasted peanuts, divided	¼ tsp. white pepper
¼ c. peanut oil	

In a saucepan over medium heat, melt 2 T. butter. Add 3 T. mustard and whisk until smooth. Remove from heat. Brush chicken with mustard mixture, then coat using 1 c. chopped peanuts. Set aside.

Melt remaining butter in a large skillet (large enough to cook all chicken breasts at the same time) over medium heat and stir in oil. Add chicken and sauté 3 minutes on each side or until done. Remove chicken, set aside, and keep warm.

Discard butter, oil, and any dark peanuts from skillet. Add sour cream, remaining mustard, parsley, salt, and pepper to skillet; stir until smooth and heated through. If desired, spoon a portion of sauce over each chicken breast and garnish with remaining peanuts. **Yield: 6 servings.**

AUGUST 1994

Opposite page: Long-Life Noodles with Chicken, Pork, & Shrimp

Paella Valenciana

Abel Justo, owner of the Mediterranean Restaurant and Bar in Houston, provided this recipe. If you don't have a paella pan, use any deep-sided, 5-qt., ovenproof pan, preferably with two handles. Abel suggested serving the traditional Spanish dish with radishes, sliced green pepper, Spanish olives, and a bottle of good red wine.

¼ c. plus 2 T. vegetable oil	12 peeled shrimp
1 lb. boneless lean pork, cubed	1 c. uncooked risotto or long-grain rice
1 lb. boneless chicken, cut into small pieces	¼ lb. green peas (fresh or frozen)
4 small squid, cleaned and sliced into rings (optional)	⅓ lb. green beans (fresh or frozen)
1 medium onion	1 (4-oz.) jar pimientos, drained and sliced
1 T. Hungarian (sweet) paprika	2 c. chicken broth
3 medium tomatoes, peeled and chopped	several drops yellow food coloring (optional)
8 mussels in shells, scrubbed thoroughly (discard any that are open or cracked)	¼ lb. fresh snow peas
	2 cloves garlic
8 soft-shelled or steamer clams in shells, scrubbed thoroughly (discard any that are open or cracked)	1 T. chopped fresh parsley
	¼ tsp. ground saffron
4 unpeeled shrimp, rinsed well	1 tsp. salt, or to taste
1 tsp. salt	

Brown pork and chicken in hot oil in a paella pan or a large ovenproof pan. Add squid, if desired. Add onion and paprika; cook until onion is transparent. Strain mixture with a colander, reserving liquid.

Return meat-onion mixture to pan. Add tomatoes. Cook 4 minutes over medium-high heat. Remove pan from heat; set aside.

Heat reserved liquid in another pan; add mussels, clams, and *unpeeled* shrimp. Cook 2 minutes over medium-high heat; add 1 tsp. salt. Remove from heat and set aside.

Return paella pan with meat-onion mixture to heat. Stir in *peeled* shrimp. Add rice, green peas, green beans, and pimientos. Cook 1 minute, stirring constantly. Add chicken broth and food coloring. Bring mixture to a boil and continue boiling 10 minutes. Place mussels, clams, and unpeeled shrimp mixture along with raw snow peas on top of meat-onion mixture. Reduce heat and simmer for 20 minutes.

Place garlic, parsley, and a small amount of water in mortar and mash thoroughly (or process in a blender until liquefied). Distribute evenly over paella mixture. Sprinkle saffron and salt over top of mixture. Bake at 400° for about 12 minutes or until broth is absorbed. **Yield: 6 to 8 servings.**

ABEL JUSTO ∼ JANUARY 1996

Paella Valenciana

Shrimp in Olive Oil and Garlic

The Mediterranean Restaurant and Bar also serves this savory seafood dish. Fast and easy, it features a delightful blend of flavors. Try it with saffron-flavored rice and a simple green salad.

2 T. olive oil	2 to 3 cloves garlic, chopped
1 lb. large shrimp, peeled, cleaned, and deveined	¼ c. chopped parsley
2 to 3 cayenne (or Thai) peppers, seeded	½ tsp. salt

Sauté shrimp and peppers in hot olive oil in a large pan. As soon as shrimp turn white, stir in garlic, parsley, and salt. Sauté about 3 minutes. Serve hot. **Yield: 3 servings.**

ABEL JUSTO ~ JANUARY 1996

Shrimp in Olive Oil and Garlic

Cactus Shrimp with Cactus-Lime-Butter Sauce

This spectacular dish from Texas chef Jay McCarthy features a brilliant fuchsia sauce with a sweet-tart, creamy taste. Note that tunas (prickly pear fruits) aren't available all the time; look for them in stores from midsummer to late fall.

5 prickly pear tunas, dethorned and peeled	½ lb. large or medium shrimp, peeled and deveined
1 (8-oz.) box tempura mix	¼ c. cornstarch
1 T. achiote paste	peanut oil
Cactus-Lime-Butter Sauce (recipe follows)	

Pulse tunas briefly in a food processor or blender; strain. Set aside 1 c. puréed tunas and reserve remaining ¼ c. for Cactus-Lime-Butter Sauce.

Combine 1 c. tempura mix and the achiote paste in a blender or food processor; pulse until smooth. Place mixture in a medium-size bowl, add 1 c. puréed tunas, and mix well. Chill.

While tempura-tuna mixture is chilling, prepare Cactus-Lime-Butter Sauce.

Dust shrimp with cornstarch. Dip each shrimp individually into tempura-tuna batter and fry in hot oil (375°) until golden brown, frying only 3 to 4 at a time. Drain well. Serve with Cactus-Lime-Butter Sauce. **Yield: 3 to 4 appetizer servings or 2 main-dish servings.**

CACTUS-LIME-BUTTER SAUCE

¼ c. white wine	¼ c. heavy cream
½ bunch cilantro, minced and stems removed	¼ lb. unsalted butter (room temperature)
1 shallot, minced	¼ c. prickly pear tuna purée (reserved earlier)
1 lime	

Combine wine, cilantro, and shallots in a heavy 2-qt. saucepan. Cook over medium heat until wine is almost gone.

While the wine is reducing, zest the lime; set aside. Juice the lime; set juice aside.

When the wine has reduced to almost nothing, add lime zest, lime juice, and cream, stirring constantly with a whisk. Reduce heat and simmer for 3 to 5 minutes. Remove from heat for about 5 minutes.

While the pot is still hot, slowly begin whisking in butter, 1 T. at a time, until smooth. Strain through a fine sieve. Fold in the cactus purée. *Keep sauce warm—if it becomes too cold or too hot, the sauce will separate and you'll have to begin the process again.* **Yield: Enough sauce for Cactus Shrimp.**

JAY McCARTHY ～ MARCH 1998

Shrimp and Broccoli with Pine Nuts

Kitty Crider, food editor of the Austin American-Statesman, *says this elegant entrée can serve as a colorful one-dish meal. She sometimes makes it with pasta instead of rice.*

1½ bunches broccoli, cut into 2-inch florets	1½ lb. large shrimp, peeled and deveined
1 T. fresh lemon juice	¼ lb. pine nuts
8 T. butter at room temperature, divided	salt and pepper
2 c. hot cooked brown rice	parsley (optional)
1 sweet red pepper, seeded and chopped	sweet red and yellow pepper strips (optional)
4 garlic cloves, finely chopped	

Steam broccoli in a large covered pot until crisp-tender, about 6 minutes. Combine broccoli, lemon juice, and 3 T. butter in a large bowl. Add rice and 2 T. additional butter. Toss lightly and set aside.

Melt remaining 3 T. butter in a large skillet over medium heat and sauté red pepper and garlic, covered, until pepper is soft. Add shrimp and pine nuts to garlic mixture; sauté until shrimp are pink and cooked through. Add rice mixture to shrimp and toss lightly until heated through. Season with salt and pepper. Garnish with parsley sprigs and strips of red and yellow pepper, if desired. **Yield: 6 servings.**

KITTY CRIDER ∿ DECEMBER 1999

Shrimp and Broccoli with Pine Nuts

Gerling Family Cajun Gumbo

When Cajun cooks exchange recipes, you often hear, "First, you make a roux." A cooked mixture of oil and flour that provides a perfect avenue for blending flavors, a roux is indispensable in Cajun cooking. Austin food stylist Fran DeCoux Gerling, a native of Bridge City, shared this recipe for gumbo, and yes, it starts with a roux. If you don't want to make the roux from scratch, use 1 c. commercial roux and omit the first two ingredients and the first paragraph of the procedure.

1 c. vegetable oil	½ tsp. white pepper, or more to taste
1 c. all-purpose flour	1 tsp. paprika
2 cloves garlic, pressed	½ to 1 tsp. cayenne
2 c. onion, coarsely chopped	2 lb. fresh shrimp, peeled and deveined
3 c. celery, coarsely chopped	3 chicken thighs, cooked, deboned, and cut into large pieces
3 c. chicken broth, *or* 1½ c. chicken broth and 1½ c. shrimp broth	1 lb. frozen precooked crawfish tails (optional)
1 c. beef broth	1 c. (¼ lb.) mild link sausage, sliced thin and then halved
1 green pepper, seeded and coarsely chopped	gumbo filé (a seasoning used in Creole and Cajun cooking)
1 c. puréed cooked shrimp, *or* 1 (6-oz.) container fresh oysters, undrained, puréed	2 tsp. thinly sliced green onions (optional)
2 tsp. salt	hot cooked rice

Heat oil in a large, heavy skillet over high heat until it is very hot, almost smoking. Add flour and stir quickly with a long-handled whisk or wooden spoon so that the roux browns evenly. *Use caution, and avoid splashing mixture on your skin.* Reduce heat to medium and stir continuously for about 15 minutes or until roux turns a dark caramel color. (Immediately remove any bits of blackened flour; they give the roux a bitter flavor.)

Stir garlic, onion, and celery into roux and cook until vegetables are clear. (If roux is very thick, add a small amount of chicken broth until it stirs easily.) Remove pan from heat.

In a 6-qt. soup pot, combine broths and roux-vegetable mixture and stir until roux is dissolved. Stir in green pepper, puréed shrimp or oysters, salt, white pepper, and paprika. Add cayenne gradually, tasting as you go. Bring mixture to a boil, then simmer for about 1 hour. Add 2 lb. fresh shrimp, chicken, crawfish tails, and sausage. Simmer another 20 minutes. Sprinkle on gumbo filé and garnish with green onions, if desired. Serve over rice. **Yield: About 5 quarts.**

NOTE: If gumbo is too spicy, stir in 1 to 2 tsp. honey; it helps even out the flavors. For a darker color, add Kitchen Bouquet, 1 tsp. at a time. (Gumbo looks richer if it is a dark caramel color.) This dish keeps well in the refrigerator for 3 to 4 days and also freezes well.

FRAN DeCOUX GERLING ⌁ 2003

Crawfish (or Shrimp) Étouffée

Fran also shared this recipe for Crawfish (or Shrimp) Étouffée. If you like, use ¾ c. commercial roux and omit the first two ingredients and the first paragraph of the procedure.

¾ c. vegetable oil	1 tsp. white pepper
¾ c. all-purpose flour	½ tsp. black pepper
½ c. chopped white onion or shallots	1 tsp. salt
⅔ c. chopped celery	2 tsp. paprika
⅓ c. chopped green pepper	2 lb. peeled crawfish tails or peeled, deveined shrimp
2 T. finely chopped fresh parsley	1 c. finely chopped green onion
3 c. Seafood Stock (recipe follows) or chicken broth or water	½ c. unsalted butter
	3 to 4 c. hot cooked rice
1 tsp. cayenne	cayenne pepper sauce (optional)

Heat oil in a heavy skillet over high heat until it is very hot, almost smoking. Add flour and stir quickly with a long-handled whisk or wooden spoon so that the roux browns evenly. (*Use caution, and avoid splashing mixture on your skin.*) Reduce heat to medium and stir continuously for about 15 minutes or until roux turns a dark caramel color. (Immediately remove any bits of blackened flour; they give the roux a bitter flavor.)

Remove skillet from heat and stir in onion, celery, green pepper, and parsley. Set aside.

Heat stock in a 6- to 8-qt. saucepan and stir in roux mixture with a whisk until well blended. Add cayenne, white pepper, black pepper, salt, and paprika. Simmer mixture for about 10 minutes.

In another skillet, sauté crawfish and green onion in butter for 4 to 5 minutes; stir into stock mixture. Simmer for about 10 minutes, then taste and adjust seasonings. Serve over rice. Pass cayenne pepper sauce for those who like it extra hot. **Yield: 7 cups.**

NOTE: You can buy frozen, peeled crawfish tails year round or live crawfish in season, which varies from one locale to another.

SEAFOOD STOCK

1 medium onion, unpeeled and halved	1½ lb. rinsed crawfish shells with heads or shrimp shells or fish carcasses
1 clove garlic, unpeeled and halved	
2 celery ribs with leaves, cut in half	

Place ingredients in a 3- to 4-qt. saucepan and add water to cover. Bring to a boil; reduce heat and simmer, uncovered, for about 1½ hours. Add more water as necessary to maintain 2 qt. stock. Strain; store stock in freezer if not used immediately. **Yield: 2 quarts.**

FRAN DeCOUX GERLING ～ DECEMBER 1996

Crawfish (or Shrimp) Étouffée

Oysters on the Half Shell with Caper Sauce

If you like oysters, you'll want to try this recipe, which features a savory breadcrumb topping. Served with Caper Sauce, it's a great company meal.

Caper Sauce (recipe follows)

6 slices cooked bacon, drained and divided

¼ c. plus 3 T. finely chopped black olives, divided

¼ c. plus 2 T. chopped pimiento, divided

¼ c. butter or stick margarine, melted

1 T. lemon juice

rock salt

3 dozen oysters on the half shell, drained

⅓ c. dry breadcrumbs

Prepare Caper Sauce; refrigerate at least an hour before serving.

Crumble 2 slices bacon and reserve for garnish. Crumble remaining bacon slices and combine with ¼ c. finely chopped black olives, 3 T. chopped pimiento, butter, and lemon juice; set aside.

Sprinkle a thin layer of rock salt in a large shallow pan. Arrange oysters (in shells) over salt. Place 1 tsp. bacon-olive-pimiento mixture on each oyster and top with breadcrumbs. Garnish with remaining bacon bits, olives, and pimiento. Bake at 450° for 5 to 7 minutes. Serve with Caper Sauce. **Yield: 3 dozen oysters.**

CAPER SAUCE

1 c. coarsely chopped parsley

¼ c. coarsely chopped green onions

2 T. capers

1 clove garlic

¼ c. mayonnaise

1 T. lemon juice

½ T. prepared mustard

Combine parsley, green onions, capers, and garlic in a blender and purée. Add remaining ingredients and blend well; store in refrigerator.

FULTON OYSTERFEST ⌒ OCTOBER 1984

Seasoned Fried Fish

While fried fish is certainly nothing new, the use of specially seasoned tostadas and fresh rosemary in the breading gives this fish a delightful texture, appearance, and taste. Look for Julio's Tostadas at H-E-B grocery stores.

1 (10-oz.) bag Julio's Tostadas (other brands will work but not as well)	2 large eggs
¼ c. all-purpose flour	1 to 2 lb. fresh fish fillets (catfish works well)
3 T. minced fresh rosemary	2 T. olive oil
½ tsp. garlic powder	juice of 1 lime
½ tsp. Tony Chachere's Creole Seasoning	Tomatillo and Green Chile Sauce (see recipe on page 129) (optional)
salt and pepper to taste	

Crush enough tostadas (3 to 4 oz.) to equal 1½ c. coarse crumbs. Combine crumbs, flour, and seasonings in a shallow bowl; mix well and set aside.

Beat eggs in another shallow bowl. Dip fillets, one at a time, in beaten eggs and then coat with crumb mixture. Fry in hot oil over medium heat in a large skillet, turning once to brown both sides. Cook until almost done, then squeeze lime juice over fillets while still in the pan. Turn heat off and let fillets remain in pan a few minutes longer. Drain well and serve immediately (with Tomatillo and Green Chile Sauce, if desired). **Yield: 4 to 6 servings.**

MICHAEL A. MURPHY ∼ 2004

Baked Lemon Catfish

You can't go wrong with catfish baked with lemon juice and fresh vegetables.

4 catfish fillets	½ c. melted butter or stick margarine
¼ c. minced celery	⅓ c. lemon juice
½ c. diced carrots	salt and pepper to taste
¼ c. chopped green onions	

Place fillets on a length of aluminum foil 4 inches longer than fish; set aside.

Sauté vegetables in butter and spread mixture over fillets. Sprinkle with lemon juice, salt, and pepper. Seal foil well, place on cookie sheet, and bake at 350° for 20 to 25 minutes, depending on thickness of fillets. **Yield: 4 servings.**

JANUARY 1992

Fried Catfish

This recipe is adapted from one provided by the owners of Pipe Creek Junction Cafe.

2 c. all-purpose flour	2 c. cracker-meal mix or finely ground cornmeal
1½ tsp. baking powder	2 lb. catfish fillets, cut in 4-inch-long strips (about ½ oz. each)
4 T. fajita seasoning, divided	
1 egg	vegetable oil

Combine flour, baking powder, and 1½ tsp. fajita seasoning in a medium-size bowl or pie plate; set aside. Combine egg, 1 qt. cold water, and 1½ tsp. fajita seasoning in a large bowl or plastic container; set aside. Combine cracker meal and 1 T. fajita seasoning in another container suitable for dredging; set aside.

Dredge fillets in flour mixture, then gently drop them into egg batter; remove fillets, holding them against inside of container for about 5 seconds to allow batter to drip off. Dredge fillets thoroughly in cracker-meal mixture (should look dry on the outside). Fry in deep hot oil (375°) for 7 to 10 minutes or until golden brown; drain on paper towels. **Yield: 4 servings.**

DON AND GINGER LEE ∼ JULY 1997

Fried Catfish

Grilled Blackened Catfish

This recipe is adapted from one provided by the owners of Catfish Corner in Abilene. They warn that it produces a lot of smoke, so be sure your kitchen is well ventilated.

½ tsp. salt	2 tsp. lemon pepper
1½ tsp. paprika	1 tsp. Lawry's Seasoned Salt
1 tsp. onion powder	1 c. unsalted butter, melted
1½ tsp. garlic powder	6 (6- to 8-oz.) catfish fillets
1½ tsp. cayenne	

Combine first 7 ingredients; set aside.

Heat a large cast-iron skillet or griddle over high heat until a drop of water placed on it sizzles. Dip each fillet in melted butter; sprinkle seasoning mixture on both sides (about ½ T. per fillet), patting into fish by hand. Place fillets in hot skillet and drizzle each with about 1 T. melted butter. Cook quickly, about 2 minutes per side. **Yield: 6 servings.**

DAN JACOBY AND MARVIN MORRIS ⌒ JULY 1997

Catfish Parmesan

Catfish fillets baked in a crumb coating flavored with Parmesan cheese— what could be simpler?

¼ c. milk	2 T. toasted sesame seeds
1 egg	2 T. olive oil
⅓ c. breadcrumbs	1 garlic clove, cut in half
¼ c. grated Parmesan cheese	4 catfish fillets
1 T. finely chopped parsley	salt and pepper

Blend milk and egg in a shallow bowl; set aside. Combine breadcrumbs, cheese, parsley, and sesame seeds on waxed paper or in a shallow dish. Lightly oil a baking dish large enough to hold the fillets in a single layer and rub the interior with cut side of garlic clove. Dip fillets in milk mixture and roll in crumb mixture. Place fillets in baking dish, drizzle with remaining olive oil, and sprinkle with salt and pepper. Bake at 400° for 20 minutes or until fish is flaky.

JANUARY 1992

Oven-Roasted Salmon

WITH TWIN SAUCES AND PAPAYA-AVOCADO RELISH

Depending on the size of your dinner plates and the amount of sauce you like, you may have some Tomatillo and Green Chile Sauce left over. No problem—just use it to make enchiladas the next day.

½ tsp. chili powder	2 oz. white wine
¼ tsp. ground cumin	Ancho Chile Sauce (prepare ahead; recipe follows)
¼ tsp. ground coriander	Tomatillo and Green Chile Sauce (prepare ahead; recipe follows)
¼ tsp. garlic powder	
¼ tsp. onion powder	Papaya-Avocado Relish (prepare ahead; recipe follows)
6 (6-oz.) salmon fillets, skin removed	

Combine chili powder, cumin, coriander, garlic powder, and onion powder; blend well. Sprinkle on both sides of fillets.

Spray a heavy nonstick skillet with no-stick cooking spray and heat until just below the smoking point. Place each fillet in skillet, top side down. Sear fish on both sides until browned (about 3 to 4 minutes per side), but do not blacken. Add white wine and place pan in a 350° oven to finish cooking (about 8 to 10 minutes). Remove from oven and keep warm.

To serve, cover half of each dinner plate with Ancho Chile Sauce and the other half with Tomatillo and Green Chile Sauce. Carefully place a fillet in the middle of each plate. Spoon 2 T. Papaya Avocado Relish over one corner of each fillet (serve remainder with the meal). **Yield: 6 servings.**

ANCHO CHILE SAUCE

1 tsp. olive oil	1½ c. chicken stock
1 medium onion, diced	⅓ c. diced raw sweet potato
2 cloves garlic, peeled and cut in half	1 T. honey
1 medium tomato, diced	½ tsp. ground cumin
2 dried ancho chiles, soaked in warm water and seeded	1 T. minced fresh cilantro

Heat olive oil in a medium saucepan until just below the smoking point. Add onion and garlic, reduce heat, and sauté about 6 minutes or until mixture has browned. Add tomato and sauté another minute. Add chiles, chicken stock, and sweet potato; simmer 15 to 20 minutes or until sweet potatoes are tender.

Place mixture in a blender and purée until smooth. Return blended mixture to saucepan; add honey, cumin, and cilantro. Heat thoroughly. Add more chicken stock if sauce is too thick. Sauce may be strained through a fine sieve for a smoother appearance.

TOMATILLO AND GREEN CHILE SAUCE

½ tsp. olive oil	2 c. husked and halved tomatillos
½ medium onion, diced	1½ c. chicken stock
2 cloves garlic, peeled and cut in half	½ bunch parsley, chopped
¼ c. canned diced green chiles, or 1 fresh Anaheim pepper, diced	½ bunch cilantro, chopped

In a saucepan, heat olive oil until just below smoking point. Add onion, garlic, chiles, and tomatillos. Sauté approximately 5 minutes or until mixture has browned. Add chicken stock and simmer 20 minutes. Remove from heat; cool.

Pour cooled mixture into a blender, add parsley and cilantro, and purée until smooth.

PAPAYA-AVOCADO RELISH

1 papaya, peeled, seeded, and diced (if you can't find papayas, use a mango instead)	1 tomato, seeded and diced
	1 fresh jalapeño, seeded and minced
½ avocado, peeled, seeded, and diced	2 T. minced cilantro
½ red onion, peeled and diced	1 T. honey

In a medium bowl, combine all ingredients and toss gently. Refrigerate 1 hour before serving.

THOMAS PALMER ～ MARCH 1993

Opposite page: Oven-Roasted Salmon with Twin Sauces and Papaya-Avocado Relish

Smoked Mint Bass Fillets

This recipe involves applying both a paste and a "mop," but most of the work is done the night before. Because the mop is applied before and after cooking, this recipe can be prepared in any type of smoker.

¾ c. fresh mint	1 T. vegetable oil
¼ c. coarse salt (preferably), *or* 3 T. table salt	1½ lb. bass fillets
¼ c. sugar	1 c. mint tea, brewed from 2 mint tea bags
2 T. coarse-grind or cracked black pepper	additional fresh mint (optional)
2 T. fresh lemon juice	

Combine first 6 ingredients in a food processor and purée (mixture will be paste-like). Cover fillets with a thick coating of mint mixture, wrap in plastic, and refrigerate overnight.

Remove fillets from refrigerator and let sit at room temperature for about 15 minutes. Heat smoker to a temperature of 180° to 200°. Transfer paste-covered fillets to a small rack. Drizzle each fillet with enough tea to moisten coating well. Place rack in smoker and cook fillets until opaque and easily flaked, about 30 to 45 minutes. Drizzle with additional mint tea and garnish with fresh mint, if desired. Serve immediately. **Yield: 4 servings.**

CHERYL ALTERS JAMISON AND BILL JAMISON ～ SEPTEMBER 1996

Grilled Snapper

Smoking enhances the flavor of red snapper in this entrée.

½ tsp. lemon-pepper seasoning	2 T. lemon juice
¼ tsp. ground basil	¼ lb. clarified butter
½ T. chopped fresh parsley	½ tsp. smoke flavor
½ tsp. paprika	lemon slices
garlic salt	additional fresh parsley
1 whole red snapper, cleaned	

Combine lemon-pepper seasoning, basil, parsley, paprika, and garlic salt. Sprinkle mixture on fish.

In a bowl, combine lemon juice, butter, and smoke flavor; baste snapper, reserving remaining sauce. Place snapper in well-oiled fish-grilling basket and grill over medium heat (coals burned down to gray). Close lid and smoke for 15 minutes. Turn fish basket and cook another 10 minutes or until fish flakes. Baste with more lemon-butter sauce and serve with lemon slices and fresh parsley. **Yield: 2 to 3 servings.**

MIKE COUNIHAN ～ JANUARY 1987

Smoked Mint Bass Fillets

Tamale Tips

Tamale recipes may call for freshly prepared ("wet") *masa* or *masa harina*, a dry ingredient. In many parts of Texas, freshly prepared masa for tamales can be bought by the pound at tortilla factories. Masa harina can be found in the baking section of most grocery stores. If you can't find freshly prepared masa in your area, use the tamale dough recipe within the Bean Tamales recipe on the next page.

If you put a coin in the bottom of the steamer, it will rattle gently while the tamales steam, as long as the steamer has enough water in it. If it stops rattling, then you know to add more boiling water. Be careful not to get water on the tamales; it will dilute the flavor.

Tamales can be refrigerated for a week. They also freeze well. To reheat, steam them for best results; you can also grill them or pop them into a microwave oven for a few minutes.

Tamales are ideal for entertaining since they can be prepared ahead, frozen, and then steamed just before guests arrive.

Bean Tamales

Rod Santana, author of The Mexican Kitchen with Rod Santana *(1992), provided this recipe, which has homemade refried beans in the filling. Note that Rod just tucks under one end of the tamales and leaves the other end open.*

1 lb. pinto beans	Bean Tamale Dough (recipe follows)
1 T. salt	1 (8-oz.) pkg. corn husks, washed, soaked in warm water for several hours or until very pliable, drained, and patted dry
2 cloves garlic	

Sort and wash beans; place in a large Dutch oven. Add water almost to top of pot (about 1 qt.); bring to a boil. Add salt and garlic. Cover and simmer for 2 to 3 hours, adding more boiling water as needed to maintain water level. Remove beans from heat once they are soft and have lost their "pinto" spots. Remove garlic cloves. Scoop cooked beans into a skillet with a slotted spoon. Add about 1½ c. liquid from Dutch oven. Mash with a potato masher over low heat until mixture is well blended.

To assemble tamales, spread about 1 T. dough on the bottom half of each corn husk, spreading thinly to make about a 4-inch-wide strip. Place 1 T. bean mixture in center of strip and roll lengthwise toward center. Fold down the top half of the husk, which has no dough on it, to make a cylinder. Fold pointed end of husk up toward center. Continue procedure until all dough is used.

To steam tamales, use a steamer or large pot with a rack or metal colander placed inside. Add enough water to fill pot below rack level and keep tamales above water. Place tamales upright, open end up, on rack and cover with a clean, folded dishtowel. Bring water to a boil. Cover and steam for 1 hour or until tamale dough pulls away from husk; add more boiling water as necessary. **Yield: 2 dozen tamales.**

BEAN TAMALE DOUGH

1 c. shortening (or lard, for more authentic tamales)	1 tsp. salt
2½ c. masa harina	2 c. water
1 T. ground red chile (not chili powder)	

Beat shortening until fluffy. Add remaining ingredients and beat until mixture is light and fluffy or until a spoonful floats in a glass of cold water.

ROD SANTANA ~ DECEMBER 1995

Red Chile Tamales

This recipe requires preparing a filling, a sauce, and a dough; assembling the tamales; and, finally, steaming them. Why would anyone go to all this trouble? Judge for yourself after you unwrap the first corn shuck.

1 (5-lb.) pork roast, Boston butt, or shoulder, *or* 3 (3-lb.) chickens	about 1 c. pork (or chicken) broth
4 cloves garlic, pressed, *or* 3 to 4 tsp. garlic powder	Tamale Dough (prepare ahead; recipe follows)
1 T. salt	1 (8-oz.) pkg. corn husks, washed, soaked in warm water for several hours or until very pliable, drained, and patted dry
1 T. ground cumin	
4½ c. Red Chile Sauce (prepare ahead; recipe follows)	

Combine meat and next 3 ingredients in a large pot. Add water to cover; bring to boil. Cover, reduce heat, and simmer 2½ hours or until meat is tender. Drain meat, reserving broth; set broth aside.

Bone meat and shred with a fork. Add chile sauce to meat and enough broth to make mixture soupy but not watery. Set aside. (Refrigerate meat–chile sauce mixture properly while preparing tamales.)

To assemble tamales, evenly spread about 1 to 2 T. dough on each corn husk. (Use 2 T. for a fat tamale.) Place about the same amount of the meat–chile sauce mixture in the center. Fold sides of husk inward to center, lengthwise, so that they overlap. Fold pointed end toward center, then fold wider end down over pointed end, completely enclosing filling. Continue procedure until all dough is used.

To steam tamales, use a steamer or large pot with a rack or metal colander placed inside on top of a layer of clean corn shucks. Add enough water to fill pot below rack level and keep tamales above water. Place tamales upright on rack (see photograph on page 135) and cover with another layer of shucks. Bring water to a boil. Cover and steam for 1 hour or until tamale dough pulls away from husk; add more boiling water as necessary. Yield: 7½ to 10 dozen tamales.

RED CHILE SAUCE

2 c. ground red chile (not chili powder)	2 tsp. ground oregano
2 cloves garlic, pressed, *or* 2 tsp. garlic powder	1 tsp. salt
2 tsp. ground cumin	2 (8-oz.) cans tomato sauce

Combine ingredients with 2 qt. water in a large pot and simmer until slightly thickened. Yield: Enough sauce for 7½ to 10 dozen tamales, plus some left over. (Leftover sauce can be used to make enchiladas or chilaquiles.)

RED CHILE TAMALE DOUGH

7½ lb. freshly prepared masa	1 T. salt, or to taste
1 lb. lard	about 1⅔ c. Red Chile Sauce
3 c. pork (or chicken) broth	

Combine first 4 ingredients. Add enough Red Chile Sauce to give the dough a tint. Beat until mixture is light and fluffy or until a spoonful floats in a glass of cold water. **Yield: Enough dough for 7½ to 10 dozen tamales.**

ROSA GUERRERO　～　DECEMBER 1995

Fresh Corn Tamales

For the best flavor, make these tamales in June, right after the corn has been harvested.

18 ears fresh sweet corn (with husks on)	½ tsp. pepper
6 T. butter or stick margarine	

Remove husks and silks from corn just before cooking, reserving 2 dozen of the most pliable green husks. Steam ears of corn for 20 to 30 minutes or until tender. Rinse reserved husks; drain and pat dry. Set aside. Cut corn from cob. Place corn in food processor or blender and chop until finely ground. Add remaining ingredients, mixing well.

To assemble tamales, spoon 2 T. corn mixture onto the center of each green husk. Fold sides of husk inward to center, lengthwise, so that they overlap. Fold pointed end toward center and fold wider end down over pointed end, completely enclosing filling. If husks are difficult to fold, tie a string around the middle of each tamale. Continue procedure until all corn mixture is used.

To steam tamales, use a steamer or large pot with a rack or metal colander placed inside. Add enough water to fill pot below rack level and keep tamales above water. Place tamales upright on rack (see photograph on page 135). Bring water to a boil. Cover and steam 15 to 20 minutes to heat throughout. **Yield: 2 dozen tamales.**

MARGARET VICTOR ⌁ DECEMBER 1995

WHILE FRESH CORN TAMALES (ABOVE) GO TOGETHER QUICKLY, TRADITIONAL TAMALES—THOSE WITH MASA—TAKE A LOT OF TIME TO MAKE. THE SOLUTION IS TO ROUND UP FAMILY MEMBERS AND FRIENDS TO HELP, WHICH MAKES THE WORK MORE PLEASANT. THIS ACTIVITY IS CALLED A TAMALADA, AND IN MANY MEXICAN-AMERICAN HOMES IN TEXAS, IT'S A JOYFUL OCCASION THAT TAKES PLACE ANNUALLY A FEW WEEKS BEFORE CHRISTMAS. THE RITUAL PROVIDES AN OPPORTUNITY TO GATHER IN THE KITCHEN, LAUGH, AND EXCHANGE STORIES WHILE PREPARING DOZENS OF TAMALES TO USHER IN THE HOLIDAY SEASON.

Opposite page: Red Chile Tamales

Enchilada Tips

San Antonio Mexican-food restaurant consultant and cooking instructor Jim Peyton wrote our January 2002 story on enchiladas. Jim has also written three cookbooks: *La Cocina de la Frontera* (1994), *El Norte: The Cuisine of Northern Mexico* (1995), and *Jim Peyton's New Cooking from Old Mexico* (1999). He offers these tips for novice enchilada makers.

- When making enchiladas, you'll need to soften the tortillas with oil, which makes them pliable enough to roll without cracking and prevents them from becoming soggy during baking. The traditional way to do this is to heat about ½ inch of cooking oil in a small skillet over medium heat until a drop of water instantly vaporizes. Using tongs, you then place a tortilla in the oil and cook it for 15 to 20 seconds, but don't allow it to become crisp. Then you remove it from the oil and place it on absorbent towels to drain.

    A much easier, less messy, and healthier way to do this is to spray or brush lightly both sides of the tortillas with regular cooking oil (commercial cooking sprays work fine). Then place them (6 to 12 at a time) in a plastic tortilla warmer, or wrap them in a tea towel, and microwave on HIGH for 30 to 60 seconds or until they are very hot and pliable.

- Specifying an accurate number of dried chiles in recipes is difficult because they vary greatly in size and moisture content. For example, a bag of ancho chiles often contains chiles of vastly different sizes. Specifying weight is equally difficult, as a very dry chile can weigh half that of one that is less dry. Try to use chiles that are not so dry that they crack when bent. A little experience will guide you to the right amount of chiles for your own taste.

- Remember, it's always a good idea to wear gloves when working with chiles, and be sure to avoid touching your eyes and face.

- To peel fresh chiles, use kitchen tongs to hold individual chiles over a gas flame until skin is charred on all sides. (If you don't have a gas range, you can roast several chiles at a time under a broiler or in a toaster oven or on a grill.) Place roasted chiles in a paper bag or a heat-proof plastic freezer bag and allow to "sweat" for 15 to 20 minutes. Upon rinsing, the skins will come off easily.

- Adding a teaspoon or two of white vinegar and a couple of bay leaves greatly enhances red chile sauces, especially those made with dried New Mexico chiles.

Tex-Mex Enchiladas

Learn to make this quintessential Texas dish and you'll never be lonely.

12 corn tortillas, softened (see Enchilada Tips, page 138)	½ c. minced onions (optional)
12 oz. grated mild cheddar cheese	Ancho Chile Sauce (prepare ahead; recipe follows)

Using about three-fourths of the cheese, place a small amount just off center in each tortilla, sprinkle on some of the onion (if desired), and roll up. Place enchiladas in a shallow baking pan, or place 3 of them on each of 4 ovenproof serving plates. Ladle sauce generously over enchiladas, sprinkle with remaining cheese (and remaining onion, if desired), and bake at 350° for 10 to 15 minutes or until cheese melts and sauce bubbles. **Yield: 1 dozen enchiladas (4 servings).**

ANCHO CHILE SAUCE

4 ancho chiles (anchos are dried poblanos)	¾ c. tomato sauce
2 T. oil	4 cloves garlic, chopped
2 oz. (about ¼ c.) ground beef	1 tsp. dried whole oregano
2 T. all-purpose flour	about 1¼ tsp. salt
1½ tsp. ground cumin	

Using kitchen tongs to turn them, toast chiles on a griddle or skillet over medium heat until just fragrant (20 to 30 seconds on each side), but do not scorch. Rinse chiles under cold running water, remove stems and most of the seeds and veins, chop coarsely, and place in blender. Fill blender with very hot water and soak chiles 20 minutes.

Discard soaking water. Add 1 c. fresh water to chiles and blend mixture 2 to 3 minutes or until smooth. Add 3 c. water and blend again for 1 minute. Pour mixture through a strainer, pressing lightly but not forcing skins through, into a bowl (a food mill works well for this step); set aside.

Heat oil in a saucepan over medium heat, add ground beef, and cook until browned, stirring constantly. Add flour and continue cooking and stirring for about 2 minutes. Add cumin and continue cooking for 20 seconds. Stir in about ½ c. puréed chiles, allow sauce to thicken, and then gradually stir in remaining purée. Add tomato sauce, bring mixture to a boil, reduce heat, and simmer for a few minutes.

While sauce is simmering, grind garlic and oregano to a paste in a *molcajete* (a round stone bowl used for grinding), or use a mortar and pestle or a spice grinder; add to sauce. Stir in ¾ tsp. salt and continue simmering, uncovered, 20 to 25 minutes or until mixture coats a spoon. Add more salt to taste and continue cooking 1 minute; remove sauce from heat. **Yield: About 3 cups (enough for 1 dozen enchiladas).**

JIN PEYTON ∽ JANUARY 2002

West Texas/New Mexico–Style Enchiladas

Preparing the Red Chile Sauce takes some time, but the results are worth it!

12 oz. grated, mild cheddar cheese (or combination of cheddar and mozzarella)	12 corn tortillas, softened (see Enchilada Tips, page 138)
	Red Chile Sauce (prepare ahead; recipe follows)

Using about three-fourths of the cheese, place a small amount just off center in each tortilla and roll up. Place enchiladas in a shallow baking pan, or place 3 of them on each of 4 ovenproof serving plates. Ladle sauce generously over enchiladas, sprinkle with remaining cheese, and bake at 350° for 10 to 15 minutes or until cheese melts and sauce bubbles. **Yield: 1 dozen enchiladas (4 servings).**

RED CHILE SAUCE

8 dried New Mexico red chiles	2 bay leaves
3 cloves garlic, chopped	1 tsp. white vinegar
1 tsp. dried whole oregano	¾ tsp. salt
3 T. oil, divided	2 T. all-purpose flour

Using kitchen tongs, toast chiles on a griddle or skillet over medium heat until just fragrant (15 to 20 seconds on each side), but do not scorch. Rinse chiles under cold running water, remove stems and most of the seeds and veins, chop coarsely, and place in a blender. Fill blender with very hot water and soak chiles 20 minutes.

Discard soaking water. Add garlic, oregano, and 1 c. fresh water to chiles and blend mixture 2 to 3 minutes. Pour mixture through a strainer, pressing lightly but not forcing skins through, into a large measuring cup. (A food mill works well for this step.) Stir in enough additional water to bring mixture to a total of 3½ c.; set aside.

Heat 2 T. oil in a large saucepan over medium heat and stir in strained chile mixture, bay leaves, vinegar, and salt. Bring mixture to a boil, decrease heat, and simmer, stirring frequently, for 20 minutes (mixture will become slightly thicker).

While the sauce simmers, make a roux by heating remaining oil in a small saucepan over medium heat, adding flour, and stirring until mixture *just* begins to brown (about 1 minute). Remove from heat and set aside.

When the chile mixture has thickened, stir in about 1 tsp. roux and continue simmering about 2 minutes. If necessary, continue adding roux until the sauce just coats a spoon, then remove from heat. Remove bay leaves and set aside. **Yield: 2½ cups (enough for 1 dozen enchiladas).**

JIM PEYTON ∽ JANUARY 2002

Opposite page (from left): Enchiladas con Crema, Tex-Mex Enchiladas, and West Texas/New Mexico-Style Enchiladas

Enchiladas del Jardín

(GARDEN ENCHILADAS)

These enchiladas work particularly well served on individual plates and cooked in a microwave. Cook each plate of 3 enchiladas on medium for about 2 minutes or until thoroughly heated.

12 corn tortillas, softened (see Enchilada Tips, page 138)

Garden Filling (prepare ahead; recipe follows)

Tomatillo Sauce (prepare ahead; recipe follows)

¾ c. grated mozzarella cheese

Place about 2 T. filling just off center in each tortilla and roll up. Place enchiladas in a shallow baking pan, or place 3 of them on each of 4 ovenproof serving plates. Ladle sauce over enchiladas, sprinkle with ¾ c. mozzarella cheese, and bake at 350° for 10 minutes or until heated through and cheese has melted. **Yield: 1 dozen enchiladas (4 servings).**

Preparing Enchiladas del Jardín (Garden Enchiladas)

GARDEN FILLING

1 (10-oz.) pkg. frozen spinach, thawed	⅓ to ½ c. roasted, peeled, and chopped poblano chiles or canned green chiles
1 medium to medium-large zucchini, cut into 1-inch pieces	½ tsp. dried whole oregano
1 T. olive oil	¼ tsp. salt, or to taste
¼ c. minced white onion	½ c. grated cotija cheese or feta cheese
1 clove garlic, minced	¾ c. grated mozzarella cheese
¼ c. minced black olives	1½ tsp. lime juice

Wrap spinach in a towel and squeeze well to remove as much moisture as possible. Place spinach and zucchini in the bowl of a food processor and process briefly until zucchini is minced; set aside.

Heat oil in a large saucepan over medium heat, add onions, and cook until soft but not browned. Add garlic and cook about a minute longer, but do not allow garlic to brown. Add zucchini-spinach mixture, olives, chiles, and oregano; continue to cook, stirring often, for 5 minutes (filling should be cooked through but still a little crunchy). Add salt; cool mixture. Stir in cheeses and lime juice and set aside (refrigerate if not using immediately). Yield: About 4 cups (enough for 1 dozen enchiladas, plus about 2 cups extra, which can be used in another dish, such as quesadillas).

TOMATILLO SAUCE

2 to 4 serrano chiles	2 T. oil
1 lb. tomatillos, husks removed	1 clove garlic, minced
¼ c. coarsely chopped cilantro	1 T. smooth peanut butter (optional)
¼ c. coarsely chopped white onion	½ tsp. salt, or to taste

Combine serranos and 3 c. water in a saucepan; bring to a boil, cover, and simmer for 10 minutes. Add tomatillos, replace lid, and continue simmering for 8 minutes more. (The tomatillos should be cooked through, but not falling apart.) Remove tomatillos and serranos from pot, reserving the liquid; cool.

Remove stems and seeds from serranos and place in the bowl of a food processor or blender. Add tomatillos, cilantro, and onions. Blend mixture for about 30 seconds (sauce should be well blended, but still retain some texture); set aside.

Heat oil in a saucepan over medium heat, add garlic, and cook for about 20 seconds (do not allow garlic to brown). Add chiles-tomatillo mixture, ½ c. reserved cooking liquid, and peanut butter, and simmer 10 to 15 minutes or until the sauce firmly coats a spoon. Add salt and cook another minute; remove from heat and set aside. Yield: About 2 cups (enough for 1 dozen enchiladas).

JIM PEYTON ～ 2002

Enchiladas con Crema

Adapted from a dish served at El Café de Tacuba in Mexico City, these enchiladas have a French influence and are similar to Enchiladas Suizas (page 145).

2 boneless, skinless chicken-breast halves	Spinach-Poblano-Cream Sauce (prepare ahead; recipe follows)
salt	
12 corn tortillas, softened (see Enchilada Tips, page 138)	3 oz. grated manchego cheese (or Swiss cheese)

Place chicken in a saucepan with enough water to cover. Bring to a boil; cover, reduce heat, and simmer gently for about 10 minutes or until cooked. Remove chicken and cool. Shred chicken, add salt to taste, and set aside.

Place about 1 T. shredded chicken just off center in each tortilla and roll up. Place enchiladas in a shallow baking pan, or place 3 of them on each of 4 ovenproof serving plates. Ladle sauce over enchiladas, sprinkle with cheese, and bake at 350° for 5 minutes or until heated through and cheese has melted. Place enchiladas under broiler for about 2 minutes or until cheese just begins to turn golden. **Yield: 1 dozen enchiladas (4 servings).**

SPINACH-POBLANO-CREAM SAUCE

1 (10-oz.) pkg. frozen spinach, thawed	2 c. whipping cream, divided
2 T. peeled, seeded, and minced fresh poblano chiles or canned green chiles	3 T. butter
	¼ tsp. salt, or to taste

Wrap spinach in a towel and squeeze well to remove as much moisture as possible. Measure 2 T. spinach and set aside (reserve remainder for another use).

Place 2 T. spinach, chiles, and 1 c. cream in a blender; blend for 15 seconds or until vegetables are just puréed. Melt butter in a saucepan over medium heat and stir in chile mixture and remaining cream. Simmer until slightly thickened (about 5 minutes), stir in salt, and remove from heat. **Yield: About 2 cups (enough for 1 dozen enchiladas).**

JIM PEYTON ~ JANUARY 2002

Enchiladas Suizas
(SWISS ENCHILADAS)

These enchiladas are easy to make and less spicy than most.

12 tomatillos , husked

about 5 c. chicken stock

2 medium garlic cloves

1 small onion

½ c. chopped cilantro

salt and pepper

8 corn tortillas

vegetable oil

8 oz. Swiss cheese, grated

In a saucepan, place tomatillos and enough chicken stock to cover. Add garlic, onion, and cilantro. Simmer until tomatillos are soft; purée in blender. Add salt and pepper to taste and set aside.

Soften tortillas in hot oil. Spoon about 1 T. cheese into each tortilla and roll up, reserving some cheese for the top. Place tortillas in a baking dish and cover with tomatillo sauce. Sprinkle with remaining Swiss cheese. Bake at 325° for 15 minutes or until enchiladas are thoroughly heated and cheese is melted. **Yield: 8 enchiladas.**

MARTIN LECEA ~ FEBRUARY 1987

Easy Enchilada Casserole

For enchilada flavor without all the fuss, try this simple dish.

¾ lb. lean ground beef

2 to 3 tsp. vegetable oil

1½ T. Williams Chili Seasoning

4½ T. all-purpose flour

garlic salt and pepper to taste

½ (8-oz.) can tomato sauce

3 c. water

1 dozen corn tortillas, torn into thirds

1½ c. chopped onion

2 c. grated Monterey Jack or cheddar cheese, divided

Brown ground beef in hot oil; drain. Stir in chili seasoning, flour, garlic salt, and pepper; cook over low heat several minutes, stirring constantly. Stir in tomato sauce and 3 c. water and continue cooking for about 5 minutes. Layer chili sauce, tortillas, onion, and 1½ c. cheese (ending with sauce) in a greased 2-qt. baking dish. Sprinkle remaining cheese over top. Bake at 375° for 20 to 30 minutes or until bubbly. **Yield: 4 servings.**

NOLA McKEY ~ 2004

Pueblo Tacos

Adapted from a recipe provided by the former Wyngs restaurant on the Tigua Indian Reservation in El Paso, this colorful entrée takes time to prepare; you may want to make the sauce the day before.

10 to 12 Pueblo Taco Shells (prepare ahead; recipe follows)	1 head lettuce, shredded
3 (16-oz.) cans refried beans, *or* 6 c. homemade refried beans	24 oz. shredded cheddar cheese
	5 medium tomatoes, diced
4¾ c. Taco Meat Filling (prepare ahead; recipe follows}	20 oz. sour cream
1 qt. Chile Colorado Sauce (prepare ahead; recipe follows)	20 oz. pico de gallo (commercial or homemade; see recipes on pages 152 and 178)

Place Pueblo Taco Shells on large plates. Spread each shell with about ½ c. refried beans. Sprinkle about ⅓ c. Taco Meat Filling evenly over refried beans and top with about ⅓ c. Chile Colorado Sauce. Layer each shell with lettuce, cheese, and tomatoes; top with generous dollops of sour cream and pico de gallo. **Yield: 10 to 12 Pueblo Tacos.**

PUEBLO TACO SHELLS

The base for a Pueblo Taco consists of a large round of fried bread. It's similar to Indian fry-bread, a sweet bread served with honey.

7 c. all-purpose flour	1⅛ c. vegetable oil, divided
1 T. baking powder	about 1 c. warm water
1 T. salt	

Combine flour, baking powder, and salt in a large bowl. Into a separate bowl, pour 5 T. oil. Sprinkle flour mixture over oil and mix about 2 minutes. Add enough warm water to make a soft dough. Mix dough for a few minutes and turn out onto a lightly floured board.

Knead dough for about 5 minutes until shiny and elastic. Divide dough into 10 to 12 balls, each about 2½ inches in diameter. Roll out each ball into a 6-inch round.

Heat remaining vegetable oil in a heavy skillet over medium heat. Gently place each bread round in hot oil and fry for 30 seconds, then flip and fry for another 30 seconds. Remove bread from oil and drain well. Repeat procedure with remaining bread rounds. **Yield: 10 to 12 Pueblo Taco Shells.**

TACO MEAT FILLING

2 lb. lean hamburger	2 (1-oz.) pkg. Lawry's Taco Seasoning
1 large (baking size) potato, peeled and diced	

Sauté hamburger and potato together until meat is almost done. Add seasoning mix and cook a little longer until potatoes are tender. Yield: About 4¾ cups, or enough for 10 to 12 Pueblo Tacos.

CHILE COLORADO SAUCE

Faint-hearted souls, beware—this sauce registers hot, *even by Texas standards. Be sure to wear rubber gloves and to protect your eyes while working with the chiles.*

¾ lb. dried red chiles	2 tsp. ground cumin
¼ oz. (about 1 T.) dried chile petins	1 bay leaf
1 tsp. salt	¾ tsp. ground oregano
1½ tsp. granulated garlic	

Rinse red chiles with cold water; drain. Remove stems and allow the loose seeds to fall off. Place red chiles and chile petins in a large pot and add 2 qt. water. Bring water to a boil, remove from heat, and strain chiles, reserving cooking liquid.

Place cooked chiles in blender and add some cooking liquid (enough to make a thick sauce). Blend for at least 2 minutes. Pour sauce through a strainer placed over a large saucepan; stir sauce with a spatula to force sauce through strainer. Discard leftover skin and seeds.

Add salt and spices to sauce, stir, and bring mixture to a boil. Reduce heat and simmer for about an hour, stirring every 15 to 20 minutes. Yield: About 1 quart, or enough for 10 to 12 Pueblo Tacos.

THE FORMER WYNGS RESTAURANT　～　OCTOBER 1996

Tex-Mex Tacos (foreground) and Tacos de Carne Guisada

Tex-Mex Tacos

For maximum taste per bite, layer the ground beef, guacamole, beans, and cheese sideways rather than vertically. Note also that the shells should be just crisp enough to hold their shape, but still pliable. If they are too crisp, they will be difficult to fill and will break with the first bite.

1 T. plus 1 tsp. vegetable oil	8 Taco Shells (prepare ahead; recipe follows)
½ c. minced onion	1 c. refried beans (homemade or canned), heated
2 cloves garlic, minced	1 c. grated mild cheddar cheese
1 lb. lean ground beef	1 c. guacamole
1 tsp. chili powder, or to taste	1½ c. shredded lettuce
1 tsp. dried whole oregano	1 c. finely chopped tomato
½ tsp. ground cumin	salsa
½ tsp. salt, or to taste	

Heat oil in a skillet over medium heat, add onion, and cook until it begins to soften. Add garlic and cook another minute. Add ground beef, increase heat slightly, and cook until done, stirring to break meat into small pieces. Stir in chili powder, oregano, cumin, and salt; cook 1 minute more. Add ¾ cup water, bring to a simmer, and cover. Continue simmering over low heat 15 to 20 minutes or until most of the liquid evaporates, stirring about every 3 minutes; reduce heat and keep warm until serving time.

To assemble tacos, spread about 2 T. beans on one side of each shell, then sprinkle about 2 T. cheese onto the beans. Spread about 2 T. guacamole onto the other side of each shell, then spoon some of the filling into the shell between the two sides. Top with lettuce, tomato, and any remaining cheese; serve with salsa. **Yield: 8 tacos.**

TACO SHELLS

vegetable oil	8 corn tortillas

Heat about ¾-inch of oil in a medium-size skillet until a drop of water instantly vaporizes when dropped into the oil. Using kitchen tongs, place one tortilla in the hot oil and allow it to cook for a few seconds. Flip tortilla over and cook another few seconds. Grab one edge of tortilla with tongs and fold it into a wide V-shape (half of it will be out of the oil) and allow it to cook until it begins to crisp, about 15 to 20 seconds. Then grasp the cooked portion with tongs, immerse the uncooked portion, and continue cooking until it's also semi-crisp. If necessary, place tongs between the two sides of the tortilla to keep them apart. Remove tortilla, drain on paper towels, and place it on an ovenproof platter in a 225° oven. Repeat procedure with remaining tortillas. **Yield: 8 taco shells.**

Puffy Tacos

You'll need a tortilla press to make the shells for these unusual tacos. A large metal spatula is also helpful. Be sure the oil is at the proper temperature. Note: It takes practice to form the V-shaped shells without breaking them; puffy tostadas are an alternative.

1 T. plus 1 tsp. vegetable oil	½ tsp. salt, or to taste
½ c. minced onion	8 Puffy-Taco Shells (recipe follows)
2 cloves garlic, minced	1 c. guacamole
1 lb. lean ground beef	1 c. shredded lettuce
1 tsp. chili powder, or to taste	1 c. finely chopped tomato
1 tsp. dried whole oregano	salsa
½ tsp. ground cumin	

Heat oil in a skillet over medium heat, add onion, and cook until it begins to soften. Add garlic and cook another minute. Add ground beef, increase heat slightly, and cook until done, stirring to break meat into small pieces. Stir in chili powder, oregano, cumin, and salt; cook 1 minute more. Add ¾ c. water, bring to a simmer, and cover. Continue simmering over low heat for 15 to 20 minutes or until liquid evaporates, stirring about every 3 minutes; keep warm until serving time.

Prepare Puffy-Taco Shells. Spoon some of the beef mixture into each shell (or on top of each shell, if making puffy tostadas). Top each taco with guacamole, lettuce, tomato, and salsa. **Yield: 8 tacos.**

PUFFY-TACO SHELLS

2 c. masa harina	vegetable oil
1⅛ c. to 1⅓ c. warm water	

Combine masa harina and water; prepare dough according to package directions and divide it into 12 balls (enough for 12 shells, which allows for some mistakes).

To make each shell, place a piece of waxed paper (or plastic wrap) a little larger than the tortilla press on the base of the press. Place a ball of dough onto the waxed paper just off center toward the hinges, then cover it with another piece of waxed paper. Close the press firmly to make a thin circle 4 to 5 inches in diameter.

Heat 1 inch of oil in a small skillet over medium heat until a drop of water instantly vaporizes when dropped into the oil. Remove dough round from press and peel off the top piece of waxed paper. Invert dough round and remove remaining waxed paper. Place dough on a metal spatula and submerge into hot oil. Using spatula, move some of the oil over top of dough. The dough should begin to puff immediately and begin to turn golden; if it doesn't, increase the heat. Using side of spatula, press down on center of shell to form an indentation to hold the filling (or leave shell flat if you want puffy tostadas); continue cooking a few more seconds until shell is golden brown and crispy. Drain well on paper towels. Repeat procedure with remaining tortillas. **Yield: 1 dozen taco shells.**

Opposite page: Puffy Tacos

Baja-Style Fish Tacos

Fresh fish can be used in this recipe, but commercially available frozen fish is so appropriate that using fresh is hardly worth the effort. (Gorton's Tenders in Original Batter is a good choice.)

1 lb. frozen, battered fish fillets	1 c. finely shredded green or purple cabbage
Pico de Gallo (recipe follows)	salsa
Spicy Tartar Sauce (recipe follows)	lime halves
8 large corn tortillas	

Bake fish according to package directions. While fish is baking, prepare Pico de Gallo and Spicy Tartar Sauce.

A few minutes before fish is done, heat a heavy, ungreased skillet over medium heat. Just after fish comes out of the oven, heat tortillas one by one in the skillet until very hot and just beginning to harden. Remove tortillas to a large platter or individual plates. For each taco, place a small bed of shredded cabbage over a little less than half of each tortilla, then spoon a little Pico de Gallo over it. Top mixture with 1 to 2 pieces of fish, depending on size; spoon some of the cabbage and Spicy Tartar Sauce on top and fold tortillas into tacos. Serve with salsa and lime halves. **Yield: 8 tacos.**

PICO DE GALLO

1 medium tomato, finely chopped

3 serrano chiles, seeded and finely chopped

¼ c. finely chopped white onion

¼ c. finely chopped cilantro

Combine ingredients and chill.

SPICY TARTAR SAUCE

½ c. tartar sauce

½ tsp. prepared mustard

1 T. minced pickled jalapeños

Blend ingredients and chill.

Chico's-Style Tacos

Chico's Tacos didn't provide this recipe, but it's close enough to the original that a transplanted El Pasoan declared it a cure for the withdrawal symptoms she experienced after moving to Colorado.

¾ lb. lean ground beef	½ tsp. salt
¾ tsp. salt, or to taste	12 small corn tortillas
3 large (or 4 small) jalapeños, stems removed	vegetable oil
¼ c. canned crushed tomatoes	about 8 oz. mild cheddar cheese, finely grated

Combine raw ground beef and 1 c. water in a medium-size pot. Heat nearly to simmering, stirring to break up the meat, and add 3½ c. water. Bring mixture to a simmer, skimming off any film that rises to the surface. Reduce heat, add salt and jalapeños, and simmer, covered, for 20 minutes or until jalapeños are soft. Strain mixture, reserving broth in a large pot. Set aside meat-chile mixture to cool.

Bring strained broth to a simmer, add tomatoes, and continue simmering for 2 to 3 minutes. Reduce heat, keeping broth warm.

When meat-chile mixture has cooled, remove meat and set aside. Remove seeds and veins from jalapeños if desired. Combine chiles, ½ tsp. salt, and ¾ c. water in a blender; purée and set aside.

Unless the tortillas are very fresh (they can be rolled up tightly without cracking or unrolling), you'll need to soften them by frying one at a time in hot oil for 5 to 10 seconds or just until softened; drain on paper towels. Place a heaping tablespoon of cooked meat just off center of each tortilla, roll into a tight cylinder, and secure in the middle with a toothpick. Using kitchen tongs, place tacos in ½-inch-deep hot oil; fry a few minutes or until crisp and golden brown, turning once. Drain well.

Place 3 tacos in each of 4 large, shallow soup bowls; ladle some reserved broth over them. Top each bowl with about ½ c. cheese and serve with reserved jalapeño sauce. **Yield: 4 servings.**

Tacos al Carbón

In both Mexico and the United States, tacos al carbón are made with different cuts of meat, poultry, and fish, but in Texas, they're usually made with fajitas (skirt steak), along with some or all of the accompaniments listed. You can buy flour tortillas for this recipe, but it's more gratifying to make your own (see Flour Tortillas recipe on page 32).

1½ lb. char-broiled fajitas, boneless steak, or chicken	guacamole
Pico de Gallo (see page 152)	salsa
12 flour tortillas, warmed	

Slice fajitas diagonally across the grain. Divide fajitas and Pico de Gallo among tortillas and add guacamole as desired. Garnish with your favorite salsa and fold tortillas into tacos. **Yield: 1 dozen tacos.**

Carne Guisada (shown here in soft tacos)

Tacos de Carne Guisada

The filling for these tacos is carne guisada, a thick, chili-flavored beef stew.

3 T. plus 1 tsp. vegetable oil, divided	1 T. chili powder
2 lb. very lean stew meat, cut into ¾-inch chunks	½ tsp. ground cumin
1 medium onion, chopped	2 T. canned tomato purée
2 cloves garlic, minced	salt and pepper to taste
½ green pepper, chopped	2 T. all-purpose flour
1 medium tomato, chopped	8 to 10 flour tortillas, warmed

Brown meat in 2 T. hot oil in a large skillet over medium-high heat. Add onion, garlic, and green pepper; reduce heat and cook until vegetables begin to soften, about 2 to 3 minutes. Add tomato, chili powder, and cumin; cook another minute. Stir in tomato purée, salt, pepper, and enough water to cover the contents. Simmer, covered, until meat is tender, about 1 hour and 45 minutes, adding water as necessary to keep liquid level about half that of the meat.

Just before stew is done, make a roux: Heat 1 T. plus 1 tsp. oil in a small saucepan over medium heat; add flour, whisking constantly, and cook until mixture begins to turn golden and has a nutty odor. Remove from heat and set aside.

When meat is done, whisk 1 tsp. roux into stew; continue simmering for about 30 seconds. If necessary, add more roux in small increments until liquid is thick enough to bind ingredients together. Divide mixture among flour tortillas. **Yield: 8 to 10 tacos.**

Carne Guisada

Carne guisada can be used as a filling for tacos or served by itself as a main dish.
This recipe is from The Melting Pot: Ethnic Cuisine in Texas.

2 T. vegetable oil	2 cloves garlic, pressed
3 lb. round steak, cubed	½ tsp. ground cumin
1 T. all-purpose flour	½ tsp. salt
2 T. chopped onion	⅛ tsp. pepper
2 T. chopped green pepper	½ (8-oz.) can tomato sauce
2 T. chopped tomatoes	½ (10-oz.) can Ro-Tel Diced Tomatoes & Green Chilies

Brown meat in hot oil in a large skillet; drain. Stir in flour to coat meat while cooking over low heat. Stir in ¼ c. water and remaining ingredients. Continue simmering about 30 to 45 minutes or until meat is tender and sauce is thickened. Serve with tortillas; garnish with avocado slices and grated cheese, if desired. **Yield: 6 to 8 servings.**

MAY 1996

Breakfast Tacos

Like tacos al carbón, breakfast tacos are made with a variety of ingredients,
but they almost always start with scrambled eggs.

1 T. vegetable oil	salt and pepper to taste
1 onion, peeled and chopped	12 flour tortillas, warmed
12 slices bacon, chopped, *or* 1 c. chorizo	1 c. refried beans and/or 1 c. hash brown potatoes, warmed
6 eggs	salsa
3 T. milk	
1 c. grated cheddar cheese	

Heat oil in a large skillet over medium heat, add onion, and sauté until golden. Add bacon and/or chorizo and cook until done. Drain well and set aside.

Combine eggs, milk, cheese, salt, and pepper in a bowl, stir with a fork until well blended, and pour into skillet on top of bacon mixture. Cook without stirring until egg mixture begins to set on the bottom, then begin stirring to break up the curds. Continue cooking and stirring until eggs are thickened, but still moist.

Divide scrambled eggs among tortillas and add refried beans and/or potatoes as desired. Garnish with your favorite salsa and fold tortillas into tacos. **Yield: 1 dozen tacos.**

JIM PEYTON ～ 2003

Nopalitos con Huevos

Note that this recipe was designed for fresh cactus. Most canned or other commercially
prepared cactus is pickled in brine or vinegar.

½ lb. bacon, cut into large pieces	1 large tomato, chopped
1 medium onion, chopped	6 eggs, beaten
2 cloves garlic	salt to taste
1 (4-oz.) can chopped green chiles	1 c. grated cheddar cheese
1 lb. nopalitos (tender young prickly pear pads), coarsely chopped	flour or corn tortillas (optional)
1 tsp. chili powder	home-fried potatoes (optional)
	refried beans (optional)

Fry bacon; drain, reserving enough bacon drippings in pan to sauté onions and garlic. When onions are transparent, add chiles, nopalitos, chili powder, and tomato. Cook 5 minutes and stir in eggs and salt. When eggs are scrambled, top with grated cheese and bacon and serve with tortillas, home-fried potatoes, and refried beans, if desired. **Yield: 4 servings.**

TONI TURNER ～ AUGUST 1991

Green Chiles Casserole

This recipe is adapted from one that appears in Texas Morning Glory: Memorable Breakfast Recipes from Lone Star Bed and Breakfast Inns *(Great Texas Line, 2002) by Barry Shlachter. It's served at the Governor's Inn in Austin.*

10 eggs	1 tsp. baking powder
2 c. cottage cheese	½ tsp. salt
2 c. Monterey Jack or cheddar cheese	salsa
2 (4.5-oz.) cans chopped green chiles	sour cream
½ c. all-purpose flour	

Break eggs into a large bowl and beat until light. Add remaining ingredients except salsa and sour cream, blending thoroughly. Pour into a well-greased 2-qt. baking dish and bake at 350° for about 1 hour or until top of casserole is browned and center is firm. Cool for 5 minutes before slicing. Serve with salsa and sour cream. **Yield: 8 to 10** servings.

BARRY SHLACHTER ∽ JULY 2003

Pan-Fried Pork with Peaches (left) and Green Chiles Casserole

Mushroom, Ham, and Swiss Cheese Omelet Roll

This recipe was provided by Hoopes' House, a bed and breakfast in Rockport.

12 large eggs	2 T. butter
1 lb. sliced fresh mushrooms	Dijon-style mustard
1 tsp. garlic powder	¾ lb. thinly sliced honey-cured ham
1 tsp. salt	1 lb. thinly sliced baby Swiss cheese
½ tsp. black pepper	

Lightly grease a 10 x 15–inch jelly roll pan, line pan with waxed paper, and then grease paper; set aside.

Combine eggs and ¾ c. water and beat well. Pour mixture into prepared pan and bake at 350° for 10 to 15 minutes or until omelet is set.

Sauté mushrooms, garlic powder, salt, and pepper in butter in a small skillet until mushrooms are soft; set aside.

When omelet is done, invert onto a greased piece of aluminum foil and gently peel off waxed paper. Spread a thin layer of mustard on top of omelet; layer with ham, cheese, and sautéed mushrooms. Roll up jelly-roll fashion lengthwise, then wrap tightly in foil. Place on a cookie sheet and bake an additional 10 to 15 minutes or until cheese is melted. Remove foil, slice, and serve immediately. **Yield: 6 to 8 servings.**

PAULA SARGENT ∽ 2003

Rosemary–Cream Cheese Eggs

This recipe (pictured on page 43) is adapted from one that appears in Texas Morning Glory: Memorable Breakfast Recipes from Lone Star Bed and Breakfast Inns *(Great Texas Line, 2002) by Barry Shlachter. It's a popular dish at the Star of Texas Bed and Breakfast in Brownwood. For more than two people, simply double or triple the recipe.*

4 eggs	3 sprigs rosemary, snipped into small pieces
¼ c. cream	3 T. cream cheese
1 tsp. salt	

Whip eggs, cream, and salt together in a small bowl. Pour mixture into a hot, lightly greased skillet, sprinkle rosemary on top, and scramble until slightly runny. Gently fold in dollops of cream cheese. **Yield: 2 servings.**

BARRY SHLACHTER ∽ JULY 2003

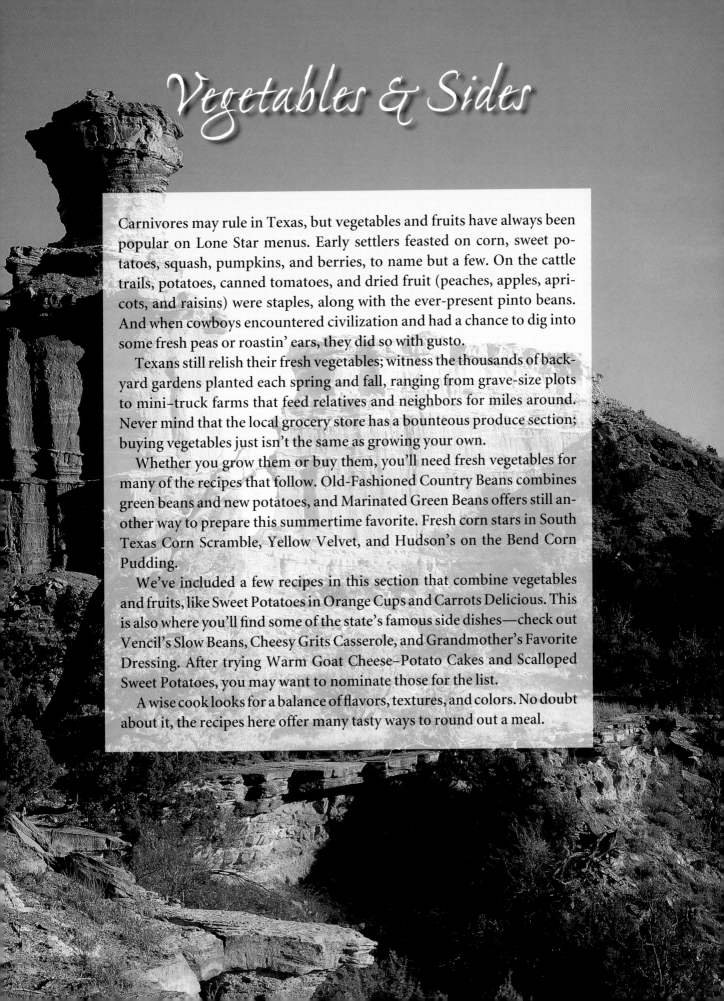

Vegetables & Sides

Carnivores may rule in Texas, but vegetables and fruits have always been popular on Lone Star menus. Early settlers feasted on corn, sweet potatoes, squash, pumpkins, and berries, to name but a few. On the cattle trails, potatoes, canned tomatoes, and dried fruit (peaches, apples, apricots, and raisins) were staples, along with the ever-present pinto beans. And when cowboys encountered civilization and had a chance to dig into some fresh peas or roastin' ears, they did so with gusto.

Texans still relish their fresh vegetables; witness the thousands of backyard gardens planted each spring and fall, ranging from grave-size plots to mini–truck farms that feed relatives and neighbors for miles around. Never mind that the local grocery store has a bounteous produce section; buying vegetables just isn't the same as growing your own.

Whether you grow them or buy them, you'll need fresh vegetables for many of the recipes that follow. Old-Fashioned Country Beans combines green beans and new potatoes, and Marinated Green Beans offers still another way to prepare this summertime favorite. Fresh corn stars in South Texas Corn Scramble, Yellow Velvet, and Hudson's on the Bend Corn Pudding.

We've included a few recipes in this section that combine vegetables and fruits, like Sweet Potatoes in Orange Cups and Carrots Delicious. This is also where you'll find some of the state's famous side dishes—check out Vencil's Slow Beans, Cheesy Grits Casserole, and Grandmother's Favorite Dressing. After trying Warm Goat Cheese–Potato Cakes and Scalloped Sweet Potatoes, you may want to nominate those for the list.

A wise cook looks for a balance of flavors, textures, and colors. No doubt about it, the recipes here offer many tasty ways to round out a meal.

Marinated Green Beans

*Looking for the perfect picnic vegetable? These green beans need no reheating,
and they're great paired with fried chicken.*

1 lb. fresh green beans	1 tsp. freshly grated lemon rind (yellow part only)
½ c. finely chopped shallots	1 T. minced fresh dill
1 T. champagne vinegar	salt and pepper to taste
1 T. fresh lemon juice	1 T. extra virgin olive oil

Wash beans, remove strings, and cut into julienne strips. Cook beans in boiling salted water, covered, about 7 minutes or until crisp-tender. Rinse in cold water and drain well; set aside.

Combine shallots, vinegar, lemon juice, lemon zest, dill, salt, and pepper in a glass or plastic container. Add olive oil and whisk until marinade is smooth. Add green beans and toss. Marinate in the refrigerator several hours. Serve cold or at room temperature. Yield: 6 servings.

SUE SIMS 〜 NOVEMBER 1987

Green Beans Oregano

Former Houston Chronicle *food editor Ann Criswell shared this favorite holiday recipe
with our readers in December 1999. Note that frozen green beans work fine in this recipe.
Just prepare them without salt according to package directions and drain well.*

6 c. (about 2 lb.) fresh green beans	2 (4-oz.) cans sliced mushrooms, drained
6 to 8 slices crisply cooked low-sodium bacon	¼ to ½ tsp. crushed dried whole oregano
2 (10¾-oz.) cans condensed cream of mushroom soup	1 (1-oz.) pkg. onion soup mix, divided

Wash beans and remove strings. Cut beans into pieces, if desired. Cook beans in boiling unsalted water, covered, about 7 minutes or until crisp-tender; drain.

Place beans in a large bowl. Chop or crumble 4 or 5 slices of bacon (reserve remainder for garnish) and add to beans, along with soup, mushrooms, oregano, and ½ pkg. onion soup mix (reserve remainder for another use). Stir well, cover, and refrigerate overnight to allow flavors to blend (very important). Bake in a 3-qt. casserole, uncovered, at 350° for 30 to 40 minutes. Garnish with remaining bacon just before serving. Yield: 10 to 12 servings.

ANN CRISWELL 〜 DECEMBER 1999

Old-Fashioned Country Beans

This recipe is adapted from A Date with a Dish, a Cookbook of American Negro Recipes *by Freda DeKnight (1948). If you don't have new potatoes on hand, substitute small red potatoes.*

¼ lb. to ½ lb. lean bacon	2 tsp. salt
2 lb. fresh green beans	¼ tsp. cayenne
2 small onions, chopped	1 lb. new potatoes, unpeeled
1 tsp. sugar	

Cut bacon into chunks, cover with water, and boil 20 minutes in a large Dutch oven.

Wash beans. Remove strings, snap beans in half, and add to Dutch oven. Add onion, sugar, salt, cayenne, and water to cover. Bring to a boil, cover, reduce heat, and simmer 15 minutes. Add new potatoes, replace cover, and simmer 45 minutes to 1 hour or until potatoes are tender. **Yield: 6 servings.**

JUNE 1988

Carrots Delicious

Apples and carrots team up in this slightly sweet vegetable dish.

10 medium carrots, peeled and sliced crosswise	⅓ c. firmly packed brown sugar
4 to 6 large red apples, peeled, cored, and sliced into eighths	salt and pepper
3 T. butter or margarine	minced parsley

Combine carrots and apples in a greased 9 x 13–inch baking dish; set aside.

Melt butter in a small saucepan over low heat; add brown sugar, stirring until sugar has dissolved. Pour sauce over carrot-apple mixture and toss gently. Sprinkle with salt and pepper. Cover and bake at 350° for 35 minutes. Sprinkle with minced parsley before serving. **Yield: 8 to 10 servings.**

CAROL ADAMS ~ JULY 1989

Copper Penny Carrots

This dish will keep in the refrigerator for several days.

2 lb. carrots, sliced into rounds	1 c. sugar
1 small green pepper, thinly sliced	¾ c. vinegar
1 medium onion, thinly sliced	1 tsp. prepared mustard
1 (10¾-oz.) can condensed tomato soup	1 tsp. Worcestershire sauce
½ c. vegetable oil	salt and pepper

Cook carrots in boiling salted water, covered, about 7 minutes or until crisp-tender. Rinse in ice water and drain well. Layer carrots, green pepper, and onion in a glass or plastic container; set aside.

Combine remaining ingredients in a small saucepan and cook over low heat until thoroughly blended. Pour over vegetables and marinate in refrigerator several hours or overnight. Serve cold. **Yield: 12 servings.**

BETTY KEMP ~ MARCH 1987

Savory Red Cabbage

Currant jelly and red wine add a bit of elegance to this cabbage recipe.

1 large head of red cabbage	¼ c. sugar
2 T. bacon fat or vegetable oil	1 tsp. salt
¾ c. red wine	dash of white pepper
3 T. red currant jelly	¼ tsp. ground cloves

Wash, drain, and shred cabbage. Heat bacon fat in a large pot. Stir in cabbage and cook 5 minutes. Add remaining ingredients and continue cooking a few minutes, mixing well. Cover and simmer 25 minutes. Serve hot. **Yield: 8 to 10 servings.**

MARCH 1996

Okra and Tomatoes

This recipe is adapted from A Date with a Dish, a Cookbook of American Negro Recipes *by Freda DeKnight (1948).*

1 onion, diced	1 (28-oz.) can peeled whole tomatoes, undrained and chopped
1 green pepper, seeded and chopped	
3 T. butter or margarine	pinch of sugar
½ lb. fresh okra, washed and cut into ½-inch slices	salt and pepper to taste

Sauté onion and green pepper in butter in a large skillet until tender. Add okra and continue cooking 5 minutes. Add tomatoes, sugar, salt, and pepper; cover and cook over medium heat 15 minutes. Remove cover and let simmer 5 minutes longer. Yield: 6 servings.

JUNE 1988

Fried Squash

This recipe came to us from John White, who once cooked for the J. A. Matthews Ranch, near Albany. Like many chuck-wagon cooks, he used shortening for frying, but vegetable oil works fine, too.

1 c. cornmeal	6 medium-size yellow summer squash, sliced ¼-inch thick
¼ c. all-purpose flour	
¼ c. shortening	salt and pepper

Combine cornmeal and flour in a shallow container. Dredge squash in cornmeal-flour mixture and fry in hot shortening until brown. Season to taste. Yield: 6 servings.

JOHN WHITE ⌇ OCTOBER 1982

Fried Green Tomatoes

This recipe calls for shortening, but you can use bacon drippings or vegetable oil as an alternative.

4 large, semi-green tomatoes, peeled and sliced ¼-inch thick	⅔ c. cornmeal
salt and pepper	shortening

Season tomatoes with salt and pepper. Dredge each tomato slice in cornmeal and fry in 1 inch of hot shortening until brown. **Yield: 4 to 6 servings.**

JULY 1996

Fried Green Tomatoes

Onion Rings

When we ran our story on catfish restaurants in July 1997, the owners of Catfish Corner in Abilene declined to give us their secret recipe for fried catfish, but they did fork over this tasty recipe for onion rings.

2 large onions	2 T. Lawry's Seasoned Salt
5 c. all-purpose flour	1 qt. buttermilk (room temperature)
2 T. pepper	vegetable oil
2 T. granulated garlic or garlic powder	

Peel onions; cut into ¼-inch slices and separate into rings. Combine flour and seasonings. Dip onion rings into buttermilk, then into flour mixture; repeat. Fry rings in deep hot oil (350°-375°) until golden brown. Drain on paper towels. **Yield: 3 to 4 servings.**

DAN JACOBY AND MARVIN MORRIS ～ JULY 1997

Ranch-Style Black-Eyed Peas

Leave it to Texans to find another way to cook black-eyed peas.

4 peeled tomatoes, chopped	picante sauce
1 medium onion, chopped	2 c. cooked black-eyed peas
salt and pepper	

Combine tomatoes, onion, and 2 T. water in a saucepan; stir in salt, pepper, and picante sauce to taste. Cook over medium heat until onion is tender and mixture has reduced considerably. Adjust seasonings if necessary.

In a separate saucepan, combine ⅔ c. tomato mixture (reserve any remainder for another use) and black-eyed peas; cook over low heat until thoroughly blended. **Yield: 4 to 5 servings.**

ANN WILLIAMS ～ MARCH 1987

Vencil's Slow Beans

Vencil Mares, who opened the Taylor Café in 1948, knows a thing or two about cooking pinto beans. "Don't be in a rush to cook beans," he advises. "They taste best when they are cooked very slowly." He added that a Crock-Pot (or another brand of slow-cooker) is the perfect cooking vessel for home-cooked pintos. This recipe is adapted from a recipe that appears in Legends of Texas Barbecue Cookbook: Recipes and Recollections from the Pit Bosses *by Robb Walsh (Chronicle Books, 2002).*

2 c. dried pinto beans	1 tsp. black pepper
½ onion, finely chopped	1 c. finely chopped bacon
1 T. chili powder	1 tsp. salt, or more to taste

Sort beans to remove any stones or grit. Rinse in a colander and place beans in a slow-cooker with 6 c. water. Stir in remaining ingredients and cook on high for 2 hours. Reduce heat and simmer for 8 hours or overnight. Add more water as needed. **Yield: About 6 cups.**

NOTE: A variation of this recipe is Vencil's Beans and Sausage, which consists of a bowl of these beans topped with sliced Czech sausage and a little chopped onion. Vencil serves this dish with saltines and offers hot sauce for those who want to add more spice.

ROBB WALSH ~ JUNE 2002

Ranch-Style Pinto Beans

If you like your beans spicy, add this simple recipe to your repertoire.

1 lb. dried pinto beans	1 onion, chopped
¼ lb. salt pork	1 (14½-oz.) can diced tomatoes
1 tsp. salt	3 T. chili powder

Sort beans to remove any stones or grit. Rinse well and place in a large Dutch oven. Cover with water and soak overnight.

Add enough water to cover beans by 1 inch. Add salt pork and salt; simmer 30 minutes. Add remaining ingredients and simmer 2 to 3 hours longer, adding enough water to prevent sticking. **Yield: About 6 cups.**

JOHN WHITE ~ OCTOBER 1982

Opposite page: Mescal Black Beans

Mescal Black Beans

These savory beans can be cooked on a conventional stovetop or in a camp-style Dutch oven over coals on the ground.

1 link (about 4 oz.) chorizo or other spicy sausage	juice of 1 lime
1 to 2 cloves garlic, minced	3 T. chopped fresh cilantro
3½ c. fresh-cooked black beans, drained, *or* 2 (15- to 16-oz.) cans black beans, rinsed and drained	½ c. to ¾ c. crumbled goat cheese, crumbled queso fresco, or grated Monterey Jack, at room temperature
3 T. mescal or tequila	lime slices (optional)

Place chorizo in a Dutch oven and fry over medium heat until just cooked through. Remove chorizo with a slotted spoon and set aside. Drain fat, leaving a thin film on the bottom of the pot. Sauté garlic in remaining fat 1 minute or until just lightly colored.

Return chorizo to Dutch oven. Add beans, mescal, and lime juice; stir well. Place Dutch oven over medium heat and simmer briefly (until beans are heated through). Stir in cilantro, top with cheese, and garnish with lime slices, if desired. **Yield: 6 servings.**

CHERYL ALTERS JAMISON & BILL JAMISON ∼ SEPTEMBER 1996

Cowboy Beans and Rice

Don't mistake this concoction for New Orleans–style beans and rice.
The flavor is completely different, but still spicy.

1 c. chopped onion

1 T. bacon drippings or vegetable oil

3 c. cooked pinto beans, drained,
or 1 (27-oz.) can pinto beans, drained

1 (6-oz.) can tomato paste

1 (4-oz.) can diced green chiles

1 tsp. sugar

1 tsp. chili powder

1 smoked ham hock

3 c. hot cooked rice

In a large Dutch oven over medium heat, sauté onion in bacon drippings until translucent. Stir in beans, tomato paste, chiles, sugar, chili powder, and 2 c. water; add ham hock. Bring to a boil; reduce heat and simmer, uncovered, 45 minutes.

Remove ham hock; cut meat off bone and dice. Stir meat into beans and serve over rice. **Yield: 4 cups.**

OCTOBER 1990

Rice Olé

This is an easy recipe for Spanish rice.

1 c. chopped onion

1 c. chopped green pepper

½ c. finely chopped celery

1 T. butter or margarine

1 tsp. chili powder

1 tsp. garlic salt

1 (14½-oz.) can peeled whole tomatoes,
drained and chopped

3 c. cooked rice

Sauté onion, green pepper, and celery in butter in a large saucepan until tender. Add remaining ingredients and mix well. Cook over low heat until thoroughly heated, stirring constantly. **Yield: 6 servings.**

OCTOBER 1990

Scalloped Sweet Potatoes

This version of baked sweet potatoes works for everyday meals, not just holidays.

4 lb. raw sweet potatoes, peeled and sliced thin	¼ tsp. white pepper
3 c. light cream or half-and-half	1 c. firmly packed brown sugar
¼ tsp. salt	

In a heavy saucepan, combine sweet potatoes, cream, salt, and pepper; cook over low heat until mixture comes to a boil. Remove from heat and transfer mixture to a greased 2½- to 3-qt. baking dish or a 9 x 13–inch pan. Bake, covered, at 375° for 30 minutes. Sprinkle top of sweet potatoes with brown sugar, then continue to bake, uncovered, at 350° for 20 to 30 minutes. **Yield: 8 to 10 servings.**

SUE SIMS 〜 NOVEMBER 1987

Sweet Potatoes in Orange Cups

Scooped-out oranges make pretty containers for fluffy mashed sweet potatoes.

10 sweet potatoes	1 T. grated orange peel
½ c. unsalted butter	½ tsp. cinnamon
2 T. firmly packed brown sugar	¼ tsp. ground nutmeg
½ tsp. salt	6 oranges
¼ c. bourbon	chopped pecans
½ c. chopped pecans	marshmallows

Cook sweet potatoes in boiling water about 1 hour or until tender. Let cool to touch; peel and mash. Add butter while potatoes are hot, then add remaining ingredients except oranges, pecans, and marshmallows. Taste and adjust seasonings if necessary.

Cut oranges in half and scallop edges with a sharp paring knife. Remove pulp from oranges and squeeze to make ¼ c. juice (reserve remainder for another use). Stir juice into sweet potato mixture.

Place orange shells in a baking dish, fill shells with sweet potato mixture, and cover with aluminum foil. Bake at 325° about 30 minutes. Remove foil and top with chopped pecans and/or marshmallows. Return to oven for a few minutes to melt marshmallows, then serve hot. **Yield: 12 servings.**

MARY FAULK KOOCK 〜 DECEMBER 1983

Yellow Velvet

Kitty Crider, food editor of the Austin American-Statesman, *notes that this rich vegetable dish is especially popular during the Christmas holidays. She adds, "You can substitute frozen corn on the cob for the fresh corn, but the flavor won't be quite as good."*

4 to 6 ears fresh corn, husked and cleaned	1 lb. yellow squash, trimmed and sliced
½ c. chopped sweet red pepper	Tabasco sauce to taste
½ c. heavy cream	6 T. butter, cut into pats, or less to taste
2 tsp. sugar	green onion (optional)
salt and pepper to taste	additional sweet red pepper (optional)

Cut enough kernels off cobs to measure 2 c. In a medium saucepan, combine corn, red pepper, cream, sugar, salt, and pepper; simmer, covered, for 20 minutes.

In another saucepan, cook squash, covered, in a small amount of salted water 15 to 20 minutes or until soft. Drain squash and purée in a blender or food processor. Add squash to corn mixture; cover and simmer 15 minutes more. (Recipe can be prepared ahead to this point.) Season with Tabasco sauce and additional salt and pepper, if desired. Stir in butter about 10 minutes before serving. Garnish with green onion and sweet red pepper, if desired. **Yield: 6 servings.**

KITTY CRIDER ～ DECEMBER 1999

South Texas Corn Scramble

This hearty dish works well for breakfast or brunch. Try it with tortilla chips and picante sauce on the side.

3 ears fresh corn, husked and cleaned	1 (2¼-oz.) can sliced black olives, drained
3 T. butter or margarine	8 eggs, slightly beaten
1 small onion, chopped	1 c. cubed cooked ham
2 T. chopped jalapeños	1 c. shredded cheddar cheese

Cook corn in boiling water to cover 5 to 7 minutes or until tender. Drain and set aside to cool.

In a medium skillet, sauté onion and jalapeños in butter until tender. Cut kernels off cooled cobs. Add corn and olives to onion mixture. Add eggs; cook over medium heat, stirring constantly, until eggs just begin to set. Stir in ham and cheese. Cover and cook over low heat until eggs are done and cheese is melted. **Yield: 6 servings.**

JUNE 1999

Hudson's on the Bend Corn Pudding

Hudson's on the Bend restaurant, near Austin, has served this unusual pudding for more than ten years. We adapted the original recipe to serve fewer people.

4 ears fresh corn, husked and cleaned	½ sweet red pepper, diced
¾ c. all-purpose flour	½ Anaheim pepper, diced
¼ c. sugar	5 eggs
2 T. plus 1½ tsp. baking powder	½ c. heavy whipping cream
1 tsp. salt	6 T. butter, melted
¾ tsp. cayenne	1 (8½-oz.) can cream-style corn
½ green pepper, diced	sweet red pepper rings (optional)

Cook corn in boiling water to cover 5 to 7 minutes or until tender. Drain and set aside to cool.

In a large bowl, combine flour, sugar, baking powder, salt, and cayenne; set aside.

Cut cooled kernels off cobs. Add diced peppers and set aside.

Place eggs in another large bowl and whisk lightly. Whisk in cream, melted butter, and cream-style corn. Slowly pour egg mixture into flour mixture, stirring constantly. Stir in diced peppers and corn. Pour pudding into a greased and floured 10-inch quiche pan or pie plate; bake at 375° for 40 to 45 minutes or until pudding is golden brown and firm. Allow to cool slightly before slicing. Top with sweet red pepper rings, if desired, and serve warm. **Yield: 8 to 10 servings.**

JEFF BLANK ～ JUNE 1999

Cheesy Grits Casserole

While it's not exactly low-calorie, this versatile side dish is popular at holiday gatherings. It's especially good with ham or sausage.

1½ c. grits	1 tsp. salt
½ c. butter or stick margarine	½ tsp. garlic salt
1 lb. Velveeta or other pasteurized, processed cheese loaf, cut into cubes	1 T. Lawry's Seasoned Salt
	⅔ tsp. Tabasco sauce
3 eggs, beaten	paprika

Cook grits in 6 c. unsalted boiling water for 5 minutes or until thick. Remove from heat and add butter and cheese; stir until both are melted. Add eggs and remaining seasonings except paprika. Pour mixture into a lightly greased 2½-qt. baking dish and bake at 350° for 1 hour or until grits are set. Sprinkle with paprika. **Yield: 12 servings.**

BEVERLY WILLIAMS ～ MARCH 1987

Grandmother's Favorite Dressing

Grandmother's Favorite Dressing

If you don't have a recipe for your grandmother's dressing, try this one instead.
Plan ahead by saving leftover bread, biscuits, and cornbread in your freezer.

4 c. day-old breadcrumbs	1½ tsp. rubbed sage
4 c. crumbled cornbread	1 tsp. salt
4 c. crumbled biscuits	¼ tsp. pepper
¼ c. chopped green onions (with tops)	½ c. butter or stick margarine, melted
¾ c. chopped onion	2 eggs, slightly beaten
1 c. chopped celery	2 to 4 c. defatted turkey broth or chicken broth
¼ c. minced fresh parsley	parsley (optional)

In a large bowl, combine first 10 ingredients; toss well. Add butter, eggs, and broth (mixture should be extra moist, just this side of soupy). Mix well, but toss lightly.

Place dressing in a well-greased 2½-qt. baking dish. Bake uncovered at 325° about 30 minutes or until browned. Garnish with parsley, if desired. **Yield: About 12 cups.**

NOTE: To cook dressing with turkey, loosely stuff body cavity with dressing before roasting turkey according to directions. Place remaining dressing in a well-greased baking dish, refrigerate, and then bake during last 30 minutes of turkey-roasting time. Before serving, blend dressing from turkey with that baked separately.

ANN CRISWELL ~ DECEMBER 1999

Warm Goat Cheese–Potato Cakes

We made the potato cakes in 12 three-inch ramekins, but a muffin pan would work just as well.

2 russet potatoes, peeled and sliced thinly	½ tsp. salt
18 oz. chèvre (goat cheese)	⅛ tsp. white pepper
3 eggs	¼ c. olive oil, divided
½ c. heavy cream	¾ c. sliced black olives

Boil potatoes until tender; drain and set aside.

Blend cheese, eggs, cream, salt, and pepper. Grease each of 12 ramekins with 1 tsp. oil and layer with 1½ T. cheese mixture, 3 or 4 potato slices, then another 1½ T. cheese mixture.

Place ramekins on a cookie sheet and bake at 350° about 25 minutes. Cool 10 minutes, then invert each ramekin onto a plate. Top each cake with black olives. **Yield: 1 dozen potato cakes.**

JEAN-LUC SALLES ~ MAY 1998

Cold Peanut-Sesame Noodles

Peanut butter with noodles? It's a winning combination in this unusual side dish.

8 oz. egg noodles	2 T. sugar
¼ c. sesame oil	1 c. chicken broth
⅓ c. plus 1 T. creamy peanut butter	½ tsp. white pepper
1½ T. distilled white vinegar	2 cucumbers, peeled, seeded, and julienned
2 tsp. Hunan pepper sauce	2 scallions, minced
1½ tsp. minced fresh red chile *or* red pepper flakes to taste	5 T. minced cilantro

Boil noodles in a large pot of well-salted water until tender. Drain, cool in cold water, and drain again. Toss noodles with sesame oil. Cover and refrigerate 1 hour.

In a large bowl, combine peanut butter and next 6 ingredients. Add cold noodles and toss well. Add remaining ingredients, toss well, and serve. **Yield: 4 to 6 servings.**

AUGUST 1994

Sauces, Spreads, & More

If this were a cookbook from a less imaginative state, this section might accurately be called Miscellaneous. However, nothing in Texas fits this bland description, so we chose a phrase we feel better characterizes the assortment of foodstuffs that often accompany Lone Star fare. Some of them, like pico de gallo and Cafe Annie's Pickled Jalapeño Salsa, can show up on the table at every meal—even at breakfast. (Both add real kick to egg dishes.)

Speaking of jalapeños, we offer a tasty recipe for jelly made from the fiery fruit, as well as jelly recipes using the fruits of two native species—mustang grapes and prickly pear. The fruits of the latter are called *tunas* in Spanish.

You'll find some salsa recipes here that didn't quite fit in the first section of the cookbook; they're meant to be eaten as part of a meal rather than as a snack. Of course, you never know—Fresh Mango-Jícama Salsa or Peach-Onion Salsa might be great with tortilla chips. Hmm . . . .

Many of our sauce recipes go with specific main dishes, so you'll find some of them in that section (and cross-referenced in the index). However, while you're here, be sure to check out The Day After the Night Before Barbecue Sauce, which came from one of the all-time-great chuck-wagon cooks, the late Richard Bolt. Before his death in 1977, Richard compiled some of his recipes and a fraction of his stories in a little cookbook called *Forty Years behind the Lid.* You'll find more of Richard's recipes in the Dutch-Oven Dishes section.

Some of our more recent recipes are winners, too. Be sure to try our trio of pestos—Mediterranean Pesto, Mexican Pesto, and Thai Pesto—which were developed by Austin herb gardener and cookbook author Lucinda Hutson. You'll be amazed at the versatility of these simple concoctions. Not only do they work served on the side, they can serve as the basis for an appetizer, salad, or side dish.

"Miscellaneous"? To describe menu extras ranging from pico de gallo to pesto? We think you'll agree the term just doesn't suffice.

Barbecue Sauce

You can use this mixture as a basting sauce or just offer it on the side when you serve the meat. Many barbecue cooks use no sauce at all while the meat is cooking, preferring instead to let the smoke from the pit provide the flavor.

1 pt. white distilled vinegar	1½ c. ketchup
1 heaping tsp. medium-grind black pepper	¾ c. to 1 c. sugar
1 heaping tsp. cayenne	¼ c. Worcestershire sauce
1 whole red chile, ground, *or* 1 T. chili powder	1 T. salt or to taste

Combine first 4 ingredients and 3 pt. water in a large soup pot and bring to a boil. Set aside half of mixture to use as a basting sauce for meat.

Combine remaining half of mixture with ketchup, sugar, Worcestershire sauce, and salt; blend well. Serve with barbecued meat. **Yield: 1 quart.**

JOANNE SMITH ～ DECEMBER 1982

The Day After the Night Before Barbecue Sauce

The following recipe is adapted from one that appears in Forty Years behind the Lid *(1974) by Richard Bolt, a longtime Texas chuck-wagon cook. Evidently, the sauce was good for hangovers as well as for barbecue. The author wrote, "Of course we all know black coffee helps an early morning headache and for some reason cowboys are prone to have Sunday Morning Headaches. Never figured this out unless it is because their Saturday night tea is a little strong for them at times."*

1 c. strong—very strong—black coffee	½ c. butter or stick margarine
1½ c. Worcestershire sauce	2 T. sugar
1 c. ketchup	1 T. salt
¼ c. lemon juice	

Combine all ingredients in a small saucepan. Simmer mixture 30 minutes over low heat, stirring occasionally. Cowboys drink it straight; the rest of you will enjoy this over beef. **Yield: About 3 cups.**

SEPTEMBER 1994

Maggi's Pico de Gallo

*This recipe is similar to the pico de gallo recipe on page 152;
however, this one has less cilantro.*

2 medium tomatoes, finely chopped	1 T. finely chopped fresh cilantro
2 or more serrano chiles, finely chopped	salt and pepper to taste
1 onion, finely chopped	pinch of sugar

Combine ingredients and chill before serving. **Yield: About 2½ cups.**

MAGGI STEWART ～ DECEMBER 1981

Cafe Annie's Pickled Jalapeño Salsa

*Chef Robert Del Grande, the owner of Cafe Annie's in Houston, provided this recipe.
The piquant flavor of the fiery salsa makes a nice combination with grilled steaks, fish,
chicken, pork chops, and, of course, tortilla chips.*

6 to 12 fresh jalapeños, stems removed	⅓ c. white wine vinegar
12 tomatillos, husks removed and cut into chunks	2 T. sugar
½ white onion, chopped	1½ tsp. salt
2 cloves garlic, chopped	1 c. chopped fresh cilantro (about 1 bunch)

Combine all ingredients except cilantro in a pot, add ⅔ c. water, and bring to a boil.
Cover, reduce heat, and simmer about 10 minutes or until tomatillos are soft. Remove
from heat and allow mixture to cool.

Transfer cooled mixture (including liquid) to a blender. Add cilantro and purée until
smooth and uniformly green. Refrigerate. Serve cold or at room temperature. **Yield:
About 3½ cups.**

ROBERT DEL GRANDE ～ NOVEMBER 1992

THE NEXT TIME YOU GRILL FISH, TRY IT WITH ONE OF THE FOLLOWING THREE SALSAS. ADAPTED FROM RECIPES IN *GULF COAST COOKING* BY VIRGINIA ELVERSON (SHEARER PUBLISHING, 1991), THEY APPEARED IN OUR JANUARY 1993 ISSUE.

Avocado Salsa

(FOR GRILLED FISH)

2 Roma tomatoes	juice of 1 lime
1 small jalapeño	½ c. diced onion
2 to 3 avocados	¼ tsp. salt

In a very hot iron skillet, roast tomatoes. Cool and dice, including the charred skin; set aside.

Wearing gloves, cut jalapeño in half and remove seeds and membrane. Dice and add to tomatoes.

Peel and seed avocados, dice, and toss with lime juice. Add avocados, onion, and salt to tomato mixture and mix well. Serve at room temperature. **Yield: 2 cups.**

Poblano-Mango Salsa

(FOR GRILLED FISH)

2 poblano chiles	zest of ½ lime
1 large firm mango	1 tsp. maple syrup
juice of 1 lime	½ tsp. salt

Roast poblanos in a very hot iron skillet over a gas flame or on a grill until charred on all sides. Transfer to a plastic bag, seal loosely, and let steam 10 minutes or more.

Peel and seed mango and cut it into thin strips. Combine mango with lime juice, lime zest, maple syrup, and salt, mixing well.

Remove seeds and membranes of roasted poblanos, rub charred skin off, and cut into thin strips. Toss with mangos and adjust seasonings to taste. Allow to stand 30 minutes. Serve at room temperature. **Yield: 1 to 1½ cups.**

Fresh Mango-Jícama Salsa

(FOR GRILLED FISH)

1 c. chopped mango	1 poblano chile
1 c. chopped jícama	2 T. chopped fresh cilantro
¼ c. lime juice	⅜ tsp. salt

Mix mango and jícama with lime juice; set aside.

Roast poblano in a very hot iron skillet over a gas flame or on a grill until charred on all sides. Transfer to a plastic bag, seal loosely, and let steam 10 minutes or more.

Remove seeds and membrane of poblano, rub charred skin off, and chop. Combine with mango-jícama mixture, cilantro, and salt; mix well. Allow to stand for about 3 hours. Serve at room temperature. **Yield: About 2½ cups.**

Peach-Onion Salsa

This recipe works well as an accompaniment to seafood or poultry.

2 firm, ripe, unpeeled peaches, diced	1 T. olive oil
½ c. chopped sweet onion	½ tsp. cumin
2 T. minced sweet red pepper	½ tsp. salt
2 T. minced green pepper	⅛ tsp. pepper
1 T. fresh lime juice	minced jalapeño to taste
1 T. finely chopped fresh cilantro	

Combine ingredients in a large bowl; cover and refrigerate for 30 minutes. Recipe can be prepared 2 hours ahead and refrigerated. **Yield: 1½ cups.**

JULY 1994

Corn Relish

Try varying the proportions of oil and vinegar as well as the vegetables.

3 (12-oz.) cans of shoepeg or white corn, drained	⅓ c. vinegar
2 medium tomatoes, chopped	⅓ c. vegetable oil
¼ c. chopped green onions	salt and pepper to taste
¼ c. chopped green pepper	pinch of sugar, or to taste

Combine all ingredients and refrigerate 1 day before serving.

SARAH LIVELY ～ NOVEMBER 1988

Citrus Relish

This interesting relish works well with a surprising number of dishes.

2 Ruby Red grapefruits	¼ tsp. cinnamon
2 oranges	¼ tsp. allspice
2 c. sugar	1 c. chopped pecans

Wash fruit, cut into quarters, and remove seeds. *Do not peel.* Grind fruit in meat grinder (using medium blade) or in food processor. Add remaining ingredients and blend. Chill several hours before serving. Store in tightly covered container in refrigerator. Will keep several weeks. **Yield: 2 pints.**

JANUARY 1983

Mediterranean Pesto

GARDENER, CHEF, AND COOKBOOK AUTHOR LUCINDA HUTSON
WROTE OUR JUNE 2001 STORY ON CULINARY HERBS, MANY OF
WHICH THRIVE IN TEXAS. TO ILLUSTRATE THE VERSATILITY OF
SOME OF HER FAVORITES, LUCINDA ALSO DEVELOPED THREE VERY
DIFFERENT PESTO RECIPES. IF YOU KNOW ABOUT ONLY ONE TYPE
OF PESTO, YOU'RE IN FOR A DELIGHTFUL SURPRISE.

Mediterranean Pesto

This more-or-less traditional pesto tastes great tossed with pasta and chopped Roma tomatoes. Or try it spread on toasted baguette slices and topped with crumbled goat cheese, chopped sweet red pepper, and leaves of fresh basil or rosemary.

3 to 4 cloves garlic, peeled	¾ c. olive oil
2 c. basil leaves (use purple basil, if you can find it)	2 tsp. minced rosemary
¼ c. chopped sun-dried tomatoes	¼ tsp. crushed dried red chile, or more to taste
¼ c. pine nuts or walnuts	additional olive oil (optional)
½ c. freshly grated Parmesan cheese	

In a blender or food processor, grind first 5 ingredients. Slowly add ¾ c. olive oil; add rosemary and dried red chile; blend lightly. Use immediately, or spoon into a jar, cover with a thin layer of olive oil, and refrigerate until needed. **Yield: About 1 cup.**

Use your imagination when it comes to making (and serving) pestos. Fresh herbs, oil, and nuts are the primary ingredients.

Mexican Pesto

Toss this pesto with steamed squash, or try it stirred into rice or pasta salad. Of course, it's also good spread on toasted baguette slices, perhaps topped with chopped Roma tomatoes, grilled shrimp, and a few pumpkin seeds. Or try it on warm corn tortillas.

2 to 3 cloves garlic, peeled	2 tsp. fresh lime juice
½ c. Italian parsley or basil	1 to 2 serrano chiles, seeded and minced, or more to taste
½ c. oregano leaves (including 2 T. Mexican oregano leaves, if possible)	¾ c. olive oil
¼ c. pumpkin seeds	additional olive oil (optional)
¼ c. freshly grated Parmesan cheese	

In a blender or food processor, blend all ingredients except olive oil. Slowly add ¾ c. olive oil and blend until smooth. If not using immediately, spoon into a jar, cover with a thin layer of olive oil, and refrigerate until needed. **Yield: About 1 cup.**

Thai Pesto

Try this pesto stirred into a salad of rice vermicelli, grated carrots, chopped green onions, bean sprouts, sliced cucumbers, grilled shrimp, and crushed peanuts. It's also good spread on toasted baguette slices and topped with thinly sliced cucumber, crushed honey-roasted peanuts, grated carrots, and sprigs of mint or basil.

4 cloves garlic, peeled	½ c. cilantro leaves
½-inch piece fresh ginger, peeled	½ tsp. lime zest
2 or more Thai peppers, stemmed	2 T. fresh lime juice
3-inch piece lemon grass, lightly mashed	¾ c. dry honey-roasted peanuts
1½ c. Thai basil leaves or leaves from a combination of basils	about ¾ c. peanut oil
½ c. mint leaves	salt
	crushed red pepper

In a blender or food processor, chop first 4 ingredients. Slowly add basil leaves and next 5 ingredients; grind to a thick paste. Add enough oil to achieve the desired consistency. Add salt and crushed red pepper to taste. If not using immediately, spoon into a jar and refrigerate until needed. **Yield: About 1 cup.**

> *Author Lucinda Hutson says one of her favorite herbs is Mexican mint marigold. "I call it 'Texas tarragon,'" she says, "because it can be used to season many of the same dishes as tarragon—poultry, fish, and even apple pie."*

Cactus Jelly

(PRICKLY PEAR JELLY)

Making this jelly requires more than culinary skill—gathering and preparing prickly pear fruit (tunas) is not for the faint-hearted. Look for fully ripe (dark purple) tunas in the fall. Always use tongs to pick the fruit and wear rubber gloves while preparing it.

1 gal. cactus tunas (prickly pear fruit)	1½ (1.75-oz.) pkg. (about 2.5 oz. total) powdered fruit pectin
½ c. lemon juice	6 c. sugar

Wearing thick rubber gloves, and using an ice pick or fondue fork to hold the tunas, burn stickers from each tuna over a candle or gas flame. Scrape away the burned-sticker residue from tunas with the edge of a sharp knife; wash well. Continue wearing rubber gloves (to keep the juice from dyeing your hands purple) and peel tunas.

Cut peeled tunas into quarters and place them in a large saucepan, seeds and all, with just enough water to show through the fruit. Bring to a gentle boil, cover, and allow fruit to cook about an hour.

Strain juice from pulp and seeds; place 3¾ c. juice in a large, heavy pot, reserving any remaining juice for another use. Stir in lemon juice and fruit pectin. Bring mixture to a boil and add sugar. Allow mixture to cook 3 minutes, stirring frequently.

Remove jelly from heat and allow it to cool 45 minutes. Skim off foam and pour jelly into hot, sterilized jars, leaving ¼-inch headspace; wipe jar rims. Cover at once with metal lids and screw on bands. Process in boiling-water bath 5 minutes. **Yield: 6 half-pint jars.**

HAZEL BEESLEY ∼ MAY 1982

Jalapeño Jelly

You can vary the proportions of jalapeño and green pepper to control the hotness of this jelly. For a milder jelly, you can also remove the seeds from the jalapeños; for a hotter jelly, leave in the seeds. Remember to wear gloves and to avoid touching your eyes or skin when working with jalapeños.

1 c. chopped fresh jalapeño	6 c. sugar
½ c. chopped green pepper	2 (3-oz.) pkg. liquid pectin
1½ c. cider vinegar, divided	

Combine jalapeño, green pepper, and ½ c. vinegar in blender and process lightly. Refrigerate mixture overnight.

Combine pepper mixture, sugar, and remaining 1 c. vinegar in a large, heavy pot; cook over medium heat, stirring constantly, until mixture reaches a full rolling boil. Remove from heat and let stand exactly 5 minutes. Skim off foam. Stir in liquid pectin quickly and thoroughly. Pour hot jelly into hot, sterilized jars, leaving ¼-inch headspace; wipe jar rims. Cover at once with metal lids and screw on bands. Process in boiling-water bath 5 minutes. **Yield: 6 half-pint jars.**

NOTE: For a simple party dish, place an 8-oz. block of cream cheese on a serving platter, top it with 1 c. jalapeño jelly (let the jelly drip over the sides), and surround cheese with party crackers.

DECEMBER 1982

Mustang Grape Jelly

Mustang grapes grow wild in many parts of South Texas. Although the grapes are a bit sour, you can use them to make delicious jelly. Be sure to wear rubber gloves when gathering or handling wild grapes, which can irritate the skin. If you extract more juice than you need, you can dilute it with water, sweeten it, and serve it as a beverage, or you can simply freeze the juice and make more jelly later.

about 5 lb. ripe (dark purple) mustang grapes

7 c. sugar

1 (1.75-oz.) pkg. powdered fruit pectin

Sort and wash grapes thoroughly; remove stems and place grapes in a large, heavy pot. Crush grapes slightly and add enough water to cover them. Bring mixture to a boil, cover, reduce heat, and simmer, stirring frequently, about 15 minutes or until grape skins begin to pop. *When grapes slip out of their skins easily, they are ready to press.*

Press mixture through a colander lined with a jelly bag or medium-textured cloth. Press all the juice from the grapes, but do not force the pulp through the colander. Cover juice and let sit 8 hours in refrigerator.

Pour clear juice off the top and discard sediment on the bottom. (For the clearest jelly, strain juice again through a double thickness of damp cheesecloth.) Combine 5 c. juice (reserve remainder for another use) with pectin in a large Dutch oven and stir well. Cook over high heat, stirring occasionally, until mixture comes to a full rolling boil. Add sugar, stirring constantly, and return to a full rolling boil; continue boiling and stirring 1 minute. Remove from heat and skim off foam with a metal spoon.

Quickly pour hot jelly into hot sterilized jars, leaving ¼-inch headspace; wipe jar rims. Cover at once with metal lids and screw on bands. Process in boiling-water bath 5 minutes. **Yield: 8 half-pint jars.**

JULY 1981

Desserts

Over the years, we've published scores of dessert recipes in *Texas Highways*, including such tasty standards as rum cake and buttermilk pie. However, many of the recipes reflect the land's abundance, highlighting peaches, pears, apples, oranges, blueberries, sweet potatoes, pumpkins, pecans, and other bounty.

Beulah's Pecan Pie, Fresh Sweet Potato Bundt Cake, and Apple Dumplings serve as prime examples; each is chock-full of grown-in-Texas goodness.

Other finales included here relate directly to the cultural traditions of the different ethnic groups that settled the state. Desserts, perhaps because they're often associated with certain holidays, tend to be passed down through the generations more than any other type of food. For example, Swedish Texans celebrate Christmas with pepparkakor (ginger cookies) and spritsar (spritz cookies). Mexican-Americans associate the same holiday with two cookie-like treats of their own, bizcochitos and buñuelos. Some ethnic desserts, like Nopalito Pie, Streusel-Filled Coffee Cakes, and the Cajun-inspired Gateau du Sirop (Syrup Cake) find their way onto menus year round.

Many of these treats have become so popular that cooks in other ethnic groups make them, too. Texas is a melting pot, especially when it comes to food.

But not all the desserts found here are traditional. If you're looking for something unusual, consider Mexican Kahlua Pie, Raspberry Salsa over Ice Cream, or Rose Petal Pound Cake. Plain or fancy, Texas sweets will make you glad you saved room for dessert.

Beulah's Pecan Pie

Eddie Wilson of Threadgill's restaurant in Austin provided his mother's recipe for pecan pie, which also appears in The Threadgill's Cookbook *(1996). He said, "If at least one person in ten doesn't think the pie is scorched, it's not done enough to set the crispy sweetness of the pecans and brown sugar."*

1½ c. firmly packed brown sugar	1½ tsp. vanilla
2½ T. all-purpose flour	2½ c. pecan pieces (not halves)
¼ c. butter or stick margarine, melted	1 unbaked (10-in.) pastry shell
5 large eggs	vanilla ice cream (optional)
1⅓ c. light corn syrup	chopped pecans (optional)
¼ c. molasses	fresh mint (optional)

Combine sugar, flour, butter, and eggs in a bowl and whisk together. Add corn syrup, molasses, and vanilla; whisk until smooth. Arrange pecan pieces in unbaked pastry shell and pour liquid mixture over pecans. (The nuts will rise to the top during baking.) Bake at 350° for 50 to 60 minutes or until filling is completely set in the center. Cool on a rack about an hour before serving. Serve with vanilla ice cream and garnish with chopped pecans and mint, if desired. **Yield: One 10-inch pie.**

EDDIE WILSON ⁓ JULY 1996

Beulah's Pecan Pie

Chocolate-Pecan Pie

For the prettiest pie, place the pecan halves as directed below. However, if you want to arrange them on top of the pie filling before baking (for simplicity's sake), just omit the corn syrup and the second baking step.

2 T. butter or stick margarine	4 eggs, beaten
2 (1-oz.) squares unsweetened chocolate	1 tsp. vanilla
1¼ c. light corn syrup	⅔ c. chopped pecans
¼ c. firmly packed brown sugar	1 unbaked (9-in.) pastry shell
½ c. granulated sugar	30 to 40 pecan halves
⅓ c. all-purpose flour	light corn syrup (optional)
⅛ tsp. salt	

Heat butter and chocolate together in the top of a double boiler (or in a small bowl in a microwave oven) just until melted. In a large mixing bowl, combine chocolate mixture, syrup, sugars, flour, and salt; mix well. Stir in eggs, vanilla, and pecans; mix well and pour into pastry shell. Bake at 350° for 1 hour or until pie is set. Arrange pecan halves on top of pie immediately; brush them with corn syrup, if desired. Return pie to oven for about 5 minutes. Cool pie thoroughly before slicing. **Yield: One 9-inch pie.**

MARCH 1987

Mexican Kahlua Pie

Coffee flavor oozes from this rich dessert, which requires about 20 Double-Stuf Oreos. Use a food processor or blender to make the crumbs.

1½ c. finely crushed Double-Stuf Oreo cookie crumbs, divided	1 tsp. vanilla
6 T. butter or stick margarine, melted	⅓ c. Kahlua liqueur
½ c. finely chopped pecans or walnuts	4 Heath bars, crushed
1 pt. whipping cream	1 qt. coffee-flavored ice cream, softened
	chocolate shavings (optional)

Combine 1¼ c. cookie crumbs, butter, and nuts in a greased 10-inch pie plate, pressing mixture firmly onto bottom and sides. Bake at 350° for 10 minutes. Set aside to cool.

Whip cream with vanilla and Kahlua. Measure 2 T. whipped cream mixture; reserve in refrigerator for garnish. Gently fold crushed candy bars into remaining whipped cream mixture. Gently combine mixture with ice cream, pour into cooled cookie crust, and freeze.

Remove from freezer 15 minutes before serving. Top with remaining ¼ c. cookie crumbs; garnish with reserved whipped cream and chocolate shavings. **Yield: 8 servings.**

JEAN GRAHAM ~ SEPTEMBER 1990

Nannie's Pear-Mincemeat Pie

Note that the filling recipe makes enough filling for 12 pies, but it freezes well so you don't have to use it all at once. You might want to cut the recipe by half the first time you make it.

2 c. Mincemeat Filling (recipe follows)	2 unbaked (8- or 9-in.) pastry shells
	½ c. chopped pecans

Spread filling in an 8- or 9-inch unbaked pastry shell. Sprinkle top of filling with pecans.

Roll out second pastry; place on top of filling and flute edges. Make 4 slits in top crust, each about 1 inch long. Bake at 375° about 40 minutes or until filling bubbles up in slits. Serve warm or at room temperature. **Yield: One 8-inch or 9-inch pie.**

MINCEMEAT FILLING

about 10 lb. firm cooking pears	1 T. cinnamon
3 lemons, quartered and seeded (leave peel on)	5 lb. brown sugar
1½ lb. ground beef	1 T. cider vinegar
2 lb. raisins	1 tsp. ground cloves
2 T. salt, or less to taste	1 tsp. allspice

Peel and core enough pears to measure 4 qt.; place in container of food processor. Add lemons and process lightly (do not purée); set aside.

Cook ground beef in a Dutch oven until well done. Add pear-lemon mixture and remaining ingredients, mix well, and refrigerate 4 hours. Boil 20 minutes, stirring constantly. Cover tightly and refrigerate overnight. Boil 20 minutes again; pack into pint containers, allowing room for expansion. Freeze if not using right away. **Yield: 12 pints, or enough filling for 12 pies.**

N O T E : This recipe may also be used to make empanadas. To make 16 empanadas, you'll need 1 c. filling, to which ¼ c. chopped pecans has been added, and 4 unbaked pastry shells. Roll out pastry shells; cut 4-inch circles and spread 1 heaping tsp. filling on half of each circle. Fold half of circle over the other half and press edges together with a fork. Sprinkle empanadas with sugar and bake on a cookie sheet at 375° about 15 minutes or until golden.

KITTY CRIDER ～ DECEMBER 1999

Opposite page: The filling for Nannie's Pear-Mincemeat Pie makes tasty empanadas.

Yam Pie

Our senior editor, Ann Gallaway, tasted this dessert at the East Texas Yamboree booth of the 1996 Texas Folklife Festival and proclaimed it "one of the best pies I've ever eaten."

2 to 3 sweet potatoes, unpeeled	½ tsp. allspice
¼ c. butter or stick margarine, melted	2 eggs, beaten
1 c. sugar	¾ c. milk
¼ tsp. salt	1 tsp. vanilla
1 tsp. cinnamon	1 unbaked (9-in.) pastry shell

Scrub sweet potatoes and cook in boiling water 20 minutes or until soft; drain and peel. Mash enough sweet potatoes to measure 2 c. (reserve remainder for another use). Set aside to cool completely.

Combine next 5 ingredients in a large mixing bowl and mix well. Add mashed sweet potatoes and eggs; beat until smooth. Gradually add milk and vanilla, beating well. Pour filling into pastry shell. Bake at 350° for 1 hour or until set. Serve pie warm or cold. **Yield: One 9-inch pie.**

EAST TEXAS YAMBOREE ~ OCTOBER 1997

Mary McLeod Bethune's Sweet Potato Pie

This recipe (pictured on page 61) was adapted from one that appears in Celebrating Our Mothers' Kitchens *by the National Council of Negro Women, Inc. (1994).*

1 c. butter or stick margarine, softened	9 medium sweet potatoes or yams, baked, peeled, and mashed
½ c. sugar	3 eggs, beaten
½c. firmly packed brown sugar	2 c. milk
½ tsp. salt	1 T. vanilla
¼ tsp. ground nutmeg	2 unbaked (9-in.) pastry shells

Combine butter, sugars, salt, and nutmeg in a large mixing bowl; beat with an electric mixer at medium speed until creamy. Add sweet potatoes and beat until smooth. Add eggs and beat until blended. Combine milk and vanilla; gradually add to sweet potato mixture, beating well. Pour filling into pastry shells, dividing evenly. Bake at 350° about 1 hour or until set. Cool completely on wire racks. **Yield: Two 9-inch pies.**

FEBRUARY 1996

Nopalito Pie

Some folks in Benavides, where this recipe originated, think this pie tastes like apple pie, especially if served warm and topped with ice cream. For the uninitiated, nopalitos are tender young prickly pear pads.

20 to 24 nopalitos with thorns and "eyes" removed, diced

pastry for double-crust 9-inch pie

1 c. sugar

3 T. all-purpose flour

¾ tsp. cinnamon

1 T. butter or stick margarine

slice of prickly pear tuna (fruit)

Cook nopalitos, covered, for 3 minutes in enough boiling, lightly salted water to cover; drain. Rinse under running water; drain well.

Roll half of pastry to ⅛-inch thickness on a lightly floured surface. Place in a 9-inch pie plate; trim off excess pastry along edges. Set aside.

In a large bowl, combine nopalitos, sugar, flour, and cinnamon; mix well by hand. Spoon filling evenly into pastry shell and dot with butter.

Roll remaining pastry to ⅛-inch thickness; cut into ½-inch strips. Arrange strips, lattice fashion, across top of pie. Trim strips even with edges; fold edges under and flute. Bake at 350° for 50 to 60 minutes. Garnish with slice of tuna, if desired. **Yield: One 9-inch pie.**

MARGARITA C. HINOJOSA ∽ MARCH 1998

Texas Buttermilk Pie

Your grandmother probably made a version of this pie; however, she may have called it Chess Pie.

1 c. sugar

¼ c. all-purpose flour

½ c. butter or stick margarine, melted and cooled

3 eggs, beaten

1 c. buttermilk

1 tsp. vanilla

dash of ground nutmeg (optional)

1 unbaked (9-in.) pastry shell

Combine sugar and flour in a medium bowl, stirring well. Add butter, eggs, buttermilk, vanilla, and nutmeg; mix well. Pour into pastry shell and bake at 425° for 15 minutes. Reduce temperature to 325° and continue baking until pie sets (about 25 minutes). Cool completely on a wire rack before slicing. **Yield: One 9-inch pie.**

JANUARY 1984

Alsatian Cheese Tart

Try this dessert when you want to make something unusual for a special occasion.

Sweet Pie Dough (recipe follows)	¾ c. to 1 c. sugar
16 oz. fromage blanc (if necessary, substitute farmer's or ricotta cheese)	½ tsp. cinnamon
	1 tsp. vanilla extract
¾ c. heavy cream	2 T. kirsch (cherry liqueur)
4 large eggs, separated	zest of ½ lemon

Prepare Sweet Pie Dough as directed. After dough has rested, roll it out onto a lightly floured surface and line bottom and sides of a 9-inch pie plate with it. Trim off excess pastry, flute edges, and set aside.

Beat fromage blanc and cream together in a large bowl. Add egg yolks, sugar, cinnamon, vanilla, kirsch, and lemon rind; mix thoroughly until very smooth.

In a separate bowl, beat egg whites until stiff and gently fold into batter. Pour batter into the pastry-lined pan. Bake at 350° for 40 to 45 minutes or until slightly puffed and very brown. Cool tart completely, then chill for several hours before slicing. **Yield: 8 to 10 servings.**

SWEET PIE DOUGH

4 c. cake flour	dash of lemon juice
½ c. plus 2 T. sugar	pinch of fresh vanilla bean seeds, *or* 2 to 3 drops vanilla extract
1¼ c. butter	
1 egg	

Combine all ingredients and mix well, without overworking dough. Allow dough to rest 30 minutes before using. **Yield: Enough pastry for a 9-inch single pie crust.**

MICHEL BERNARD PLATZ ∾ DECEMBER 1992

Almond Mazurek

Often served on Christmas Eve, this traditional Polish dessert can be topped with Almond Glaze or apricot jam or a combination of the two. For the latter option, top crust with apricot jam, make only half the glaze recipe, and then drizzle glaze over jam before sprinkling with toasted almonds.

1 c. unsalted butter	1 c. sugar
¾ c. beaten eggs (about 3 large eggs)	1 tsp. almond extract
2 c. chopped blanched almonds	Almond Glaze (recipe follows), *or* 1 c. apricot jam
1¾ c. all-purpose flour, sifted before measuring	½ c. shaved almonds, toasted dry in a 300° oven

Cream butter and eggs. In another bowl, combine chopped almonds, flour, and sugar. Add slowly to egg mixture, beating after each addition. Stir in almond extract. Pat or roll dough into a greased jelly roll pan. Bake at 350° for 20 minutes or until golden. Spread Almond Glaze or apricot jam over top and sprinkle with shaved, toasted almonds. Cool and cut into 2-inch squares. **Yield: 2½ dozen squares.**

ALMOND GLAZE

2 c. powdered sugar	½ tsp. vanilla
¼ tsp. almond extract	about 2 T. milk

Combine first 3 ingredients and add enough milk to dissolve sugar. **Yield: Enough glaze to top Almond Mazurek.**

RITA MONTGOMERY ～ DECEMBER 1992

Fresh Sweet Potato Bundt Cake

This recipe is adapted from one that appeared in the Golden Sweet Potato Festival cookbook, Country Cookin' with Sweet Potatoes. *You can use baked or microwaved spuds, but sweet potatoes boiled in their skins provide the best flavor.*

4 medium sweet potatoes, unpeeled	1 c. firmly packed brown sugar
3 c. all-purpose flour	1 c. butter or stick margarine, softened
2 tsp. baking soda	4 eggs, beaten
½ tsp. baking powder	2 tsp. grated orange peel
1 tsp. allspice	⅓ c. orange juice
¾ tsp. salt	1 c. chopped pecans
1½ c. sugar	powdered sugar (optional)

Yam Pie (left) and Fresh Sweet Potato Bundt Cake

Scrub sweet potatoes and cook in boiling water for 20 minutes or until soft; drain, cool slightly, and peel. Mash enough to measure 2¾ c. and set aside to cool completely. (Reserve remaining sweet potatoes for another use.)

Sift together next 5 ingredients; set aside.

In a large bowl, combine sugars, butter, and eggs; beat until light and fluffy. Add mashed sweet potatoes and orange peel, mixing well. Add flour mixture alternately with orange juice. Stir in pecans. Pour batter into a greased 12-cup Bundt pan. Bake at 350° for 55 to 60 minutes or until a toothpick inserted in center comes out clean. Cool in pan for 5 minutes. Invert cake onto wire rack and cool thoroughly. Sprinkle with powdered sugar, if desired. **Yield: 1 large Bundt cake.**

JOY SMITH ~ OCTOBER 1997

Rum Cake

Sarah Lively, the wife of former Texas Highways *editor Frank Lively, highly recommends this cake.*

½ c. finely chopped pecans	1 (18.25-oz.) butter cake mix
4 eggs, beaten	1 (3.5-oz.) pkg. vanilla pudding mix (not instant)
½ c. light rum	Rum Glaze (recipe follows)
½ c. vegetable oil	

Grease and flour a 12-cup Bundt pan. Sprinkle pecans in bottom of pan. Set aside.

Combine eggs, rum, oil, and ½ c. water in a large bowl. Add cake and pudding mixes and mix well; pour into pan. Bake at 325° about 1 hour.

While cake is baking, prepare glaze and set aside.

Remove cake from oven, and while cake is still hot, drizzle Rum Glaze over it. Leave cake in pan for at least 30 minutes to allow glaze to soak through. Remove cake from pan, inverting onto serving plate. **Yield: 1 large Bundt cake.**

RUM GLAZE

½ c. butter or stick margarine, melted	¼ c. light rum
1 c. sugar	

Combine ingredients with ¼ c. water in a small saucepan, bring to a boil, and boil 2 to 3 minutes. **Yield: Enough glaze for a large Bundt cake.**

THE FORMER BRENT HOUSE, DALLAS ~ DECEMBER 1980

Tunneling to Fame

Houstonite Ella Rita Helfrich's recipe for Tunnel of Fudge Cake, which won second prize at the 1966 Pillsbury Bake-Off and created a furor across the nation, called for Pillsbury's chocolate dry frosting mix to create the tunnel of fudge. When the company switched to canned frostings, Ella Rita received phone calls from people all over the country trying to find the discontinued product.

The recipe below closely approximates the original. It remains one of Pillsbury's most often requested recipes. In 1999, it was inducted into the Pillsbury Bake-Off Contest Hall of Fame, now a part of the Smithsonian Institution.

TUNNEL OF FUDGE CAKE

Note that nuts are essential to the success of this recipe, as they shore up the tunnel walls. Also, as the recipe can be a little tricky, be sure to check the cake frequently toward the end of the baking time. If the dough near the edge of the pan seems crusty (check with a toothpick), and your finger pushed gently into the dough no longer leaves an imprint, the cake is probably done.

1¾ c. sugar	2¼ c. all-purpose flour
1¾ c. butter or stick margarine, softened	¾ c. unsweetened cocoa
6 eggs	2 c. chopped walnuts or pecans (do not omit)
2 c. powdered sugar	Chocolate Glaze (recipe follows)

Grease and flour a 12-cup Bundt pan or 10-inch tube pan. In a large bowl, combine granulated sugar and butter; beat until light and fluffy. Add eggs one at a time, beating well after each addition. Gradually add 2 c. powdered sugar; blend well. By hand, stir in flour, cocoa, and nuts until well blended. Spoon batter into prepared pan and spread evenly.

Bake at 350° for 45 to 60 minutes or until top is set and edges are beginning to pull away from pan. *Note: Because of the soft filling, an ordinary doneness test won't work. Accurate temperature and baking time are essential.* Cool upright in pan on wire rack 1½ hours. Invert onto serving plate; cool at least 2 more hours.

Spoon glaze over top of cake. Store cake tightly covered. **Yield: 1 large Bundt or tube cake.**

CHOCOLATE GLAZE

¾ c. powdered sugar	¼ c. unsweetened cocoa	4 to 6 tsp. milk

Combine sugar and cocoa in a small bowl; add enough milk for desired drizzling consistency and blend well. **Yield: Enough glaze for a large Bundt or tube cake.**

ELLA RITA HELFRICH ～ NOVEMBER 2002

Red Velvet Cake

This recipe was popularized by a longtime Austin firm, Adams Extract Company, which was known for its flavorings and seasonings. (The company was sold in 2002.) Red Velvet Cake is also known as the $500 Cake and Waldorf-Astoria Cake.

½ c. shortening	1½ oz. red food coloring
1½ c. sugar	2½ c. cake flour, sifted
1 tsp. salt	1 c. buttermilk
2 eggs	1 T. vinegar
1 tsp. vanilla	1 tsp. baking soda
1 tsp. butter flavoring	Vanilla Frosting (recipe follows)
3 T. cocoa	

In a large bowl, cream together shortening, sugar, and salt. Add eggs, one at a time, beating well after each addition. Add vanilla and butter flavoring and mix well. Set aside.

In a small bowl, make a paste of cocoa and food coloring; stir into shortening mixture. Alternately add flour and buttermilk, beating well after each addition. Combine vinegar and soda; add to batter, mixing well.

Pour batter into 3 greased and floured 9-inch or 10-inch round cake pans. Bake at 350° for 20 to 25 minutes or until a toothpick inserted in center comes out clean. Cool in pans 10 minutes; remove from pans and let cool completely on wire racks. Spread Vanilla Frosting between layers and on top and sides of cake. **Yield: One 3-layer cake.**

VANILLA FROSTING

3 T. all-purpose flour	1 c. sugar
½ tsp. salt	2 tsp. vanilla
1 c. milk	¼ tsp. butter flavoring
1 c. shortening	

Place flour and salt in a double boiler or saucepan. Add milk gradually, using a whisk, until mixture is smooth. Cook over low heat, whisking constantly until thickened. Remove from heat and cool.

In a large mixing bowl, cream shortening and sugar thoroughly; add vanilla and butter flavoring, mixing well. Combine with first mixture and beat well. **Yield: Enough frosting for a 3-layer cake.**

ADAMS EXTRACT COMPANY ～ FEBRUARY 1998

Rosemary-Orange Rum Cake

This recipe was adapted from one that appears in Along the Garden Path *(1995) by Bill and Sylvia Varney of Fredericksburg Herb Farm.*

1 (18.25-oz.) pkg. yellow cake mix	½ c. rum
1 (3.4-oz.) pkg. instant vanilla pudding	4 extra-large eggs
1 T. minced fresh rosemary	1 c. chopped pecans or walnuts
zest of 1 orange	Glorious Glaze (recipe follows)
½ c. canola oil	

Combine cake mix, pudding mix, rosemary, and orange peel in a large mixing bowl and blend well with an electric mixer. Add ½ c. water, oil, and rum, mixing well. Beat in eggs one at a time. Stir nuts into batter. Pour mixture into a well-greased and floured 12-cup Bundt pan and bake at 325° about 40 minutes. Cool in pan.

Prepare glaze. Pour hot glaze immediately over cooled cake while cake is still in pan. Let sauce soak completely into cake. Remove cake from pan, inverting onto serving plate. **Yield: 1 large Bundt cake.**

½ c. unsalted butter	¼ c. rum
1 c. sugar	

Combine butter, sugar, ¼ c. water, and rum in a small saucepan and cook over medium heat to soft-ball stage (238°, if using a candy thermometer). **Yield: Enough glaze for 1 large Bundt cake.**

BILL AND SYLVIA VARNEY ～ APRIL 1996

Fresh Apple Cake

This recipe is adapted from one in The Melting Pot: Ethnic Cuisine in Texas *(Institute of Texan Cultures, 1977). Like many German-Texan desserts, it calls for pecans. German immigrants learned quickly to substitute readily available Texas pecans for the walnuts and hazelnuts they had used in Germany.*

1 c. sugar	2 c. chopped apples (2 large apples), unpeeled
½ c. vegetable oil	1 tsp. vanilla
2 eggs	1½ c. chopped pecans, divided
1½ c. all-purpose flour	½ c. firmly packed brown sugar
½ tsp. salt	lady apple (or small apple), sliced in half (optional)
1 tsp. baking soda	grapes (optional)
2 T. hot water	mint leaves (optional)

Combine sugar, oil, and eggs; beat well. Sift together flour, salt, and soda; add to egg mixture along with 2 T. hot water. Mix well. Add chopped apples, vanilla, and 1 c. chopped pecans, and mix well. Pour into two 8-inch greased and floured deep quiche pans or 8-inch round cake pans or one greased and floured 12-cup Bundt pan.

Combine brown sugar and remaining pecans, and sprinkle half the mixture on top of each cake (if using a Bundt pan, sprinkle all on top). Bake at 325° for 30 to 35 minutes (if using a Bundt pan, bake 50 to 60 minutes). Cool in pan 10 minutes; remove from pan, and let cool completely on a wire rack. Garnish with apple halves, grapes, and mint leaves, if desired. **Yield: Two 8-inch cakes or one large Bundt cake.**

MARCH 1996

Opposite page: Fresh Apple Cake

Orange Sponge Cake

You'll need to prepare a filling, a frosting, and a special garnish for this cake, but make the cake first; you'll have time to make the other recipes while it's cooling.

1¼ c. sifted all-purpose flour	1 tsp. vanilla
1½ c. sugar, divided	1 tsp. cream of tartar
½ tsp. baking powder	Orange Curd Filling (recipe follows)
½ tsp. salt	Buttercream Frosting (recipe follows)
6 eggs, separated	Candied Orange Zest (recipe follows)

Sift together flour, 1 c. sugar, baking powder, and salt. Set aside.

In a large bowl, combine egg yolks (reserve whites), ¼ c. water, and vanilla, then add flour mixture. Beat with an electric mixer at medium-high speed for 4 minutes or until mixture is light and fluffy.

In another large mixing bowl, beat reserved egg whites until frothy. Add cream of tartar and beat until soft peaks form. Gradually add ½ c. sugar and beat until whites form stiff, but not dry, peaks. Fold egg-yolk mixture gently into beaten egg whites. Pour into a greased 10-inch tube pan. Bake at 350° for about 45 minutes. Invert pan and cool 1½ hours or until cake is set.

Slice cake into 3 horizontal layers. Spread half of Orange Curd Filling on top of bottom layer. Place second layer on top of filling and spread remaining filling on top. Place third layer on top of other layers. Frost sides and top of cake with Buttercream Icing. Crumble Candied Orange Zest over cake. **Yield: One 10-inch tube cake.**

ORANGE CURD FILLING

5 large eggs	½ c. fresh orange juice
1 c. sugar	zest of 1 orange, minced
½ c. butter or stick margarine, melted	

Beat eggs with an electric mixer until thick and pale. Combine eggs and remaining ingredients in a saucepan; stir until smooth. Cook over low heat, stirring until mixture thickens. Cool before spreading between layers.

BUTTERCREAM ICING

6 c. powdered sugar, sifted	½ tsp. salt
½ c. plus 1 T. butter or stick margarine, softened	1 T. vanilla

In a large mixing bowl, gradually add sugar to butter and mix until creamy. Add salt and vanilla. If icing is too thin, add a little more powdered sugar; if too thick, add a little cream or milk. **Yield: Enough frosting for sides and top of a 3-layer cake.**

CANDIED ORANGE ZEST

Zest of 1 orange	2 T. sugar

Combine orange zest and sugar in a small, heavy saucepan and cook over low heat, stirring, until zest is caramelized. Cool on buttered aluminum foil.

Sue Sims ～ November 1987

Rose Petal Pound Cake

This recipe was adapted from one provided by the Peaceable Kingdom School near Washington. Look for rose water and dried rose petals suitable for cooking at Fiesta grocery stores. Note that the amount of batter in this recipe is too much for a full-size Bundt pan, but the remainder fits perfectly in a half-size Bundt pan. This cake is great for giving away or freezing for later.

½ c. butter or stick margarine	1 tsp. baking powder
⅔ c. shortening	½ tsp. salt
3 c. sugar	1 c. milk
5 eggs	2 T. rose water
3 c. all-purpose flour	2 heaping tsp. minced dried rose petals

Cream butter, shortening, and sugar. Add eggs one at a time, beating after each addition.

Sift flour, baking powder, and salt together, then add to creamed mixture alternately with milk, mixing well after each addition. Fold in rose water and rose petals. Pour about ¾ of batter in a greased and floured 12-cup Bundt pan or 10-inch tube pan. Pour remainder of batter in a greased and floured 6-cup Bundt pan or 9-inch round cake pan. Bake both cakes at 350° and check smaller cake for doneness after 20 minutes. Bake large cake for about 1 hour or until done. **Yield: 1 large Bundt or tube cake, plus 1 half-size Bundt cake or 9-inch cake.**

Peaceable Kingdom School ～ July 1994

Gateau du Sirop (Syrup Cake)

This simple, gingerbread-like dessert was adapted from an old Cajun recipe.

2 tsp. baking soda	2 eggs, beaten
1 c. boiling water	2½ c. all-purpose flour
½ c. sugar	½ tsp. cinnamon
1½ c. vegetable oil	1 tsp. ground ginger
1 c. cane syrup (such as Steen's or Fain's)	½ tsp. ground nutmeg

Combine soda and boiling water in a large bowl. Add sugar, oil, and syrup, mixing well; stir in eggs. Set aside.

Combine flour and spices; add to syrup mixture and mix thoroughly. Pour into a greased and floured 9 x 13–inch pan. Bake at 350° for 30 to 40 minutes. **Yield: 12 servings.**

JEANELLE HEBERT MONTET ~ DECEMBER 1996

Streusel-Filled Coffee Cake

This recipe appears in Texas Morning Glory: Memorable Breakfast Recipes from Lone Star Bed and Breakfast Inns *(Great Texas Lines, 2002) by Barry Shlachter. It's served at the Iron Horse Inn in Granbury.*

3 c. all-purpose flour	2 tsp. vanilla
2 T. baking powder	3 T. butter or stick margarine, melted
½ tsp. salt	¾ c. firmly packed brown sugar
1½ c. sugar	¾ c. chopped pecans
½ c. shortening	3 T. all-purpose flour
2 eggs, lightly beaten	1 T. cinnamon
1 c. milk	

Combine first 4 ingredients in a large bowl and cut in shortening with a pastry blender until mixture has the consistency of cornmeal.

In a separate bowl, combine eggs, milk, and vanilla. Add shortening mixture and blend until just mixed. *Do not overmix.* Spoon half the batter into a well-greased and floured 9 x 13–inch pan, making sure the top of the dough is even and fills corners of the pan.

Combine melted butter and remaining ingredients to make streusel. Sprinkle half of streusel over batter in pan. Spoon remaining batter on top evenly (don't worry if it doesn't cover completely). Sprinkle remaining streusel on top. Bake at 350° for 25 to 30 minutes. Serve immediately. **Yield: 15 to 20 servings.**

NOTE: You can mix up this cake, refrigerate it, and bake it the next morning. Just take it out of the fridge 30 minutes before baking and bake an extra 5 to 10 minutes.

BARRY SHLACHTER ~ JULY 2003

Blueberry Crunch Cake

Not fond of muffins? Here's another way to enjoy fresh blueberries.

1¼ c. all-purpose flour, divided	⅓ c. vegetable oil
⅔ c. sugar, divided	1 T. lemon juice
2 tsp. baking powder	1 c. fresh blueberries
½ tsp. salt	¼ tsp. cinnamon
1 egg	½ c. chopped pecans
½ c. milk	2 T. butter or stick margarine, softened

Combine 1 c. flour, ⅓ c. sugar, baking powder, and salt; set aside.

Combine egg, milk, oil, and lemon juice. Stir into flour mixture, mixing well. Pour batter into a greased 9-inch tart pan or 8-inch square pan. Top with blueberries.

Combine remaining ¼ c. flour and ⅓ c. sugar with remaining ingredients and sprinkle mixture over blueberries. Bake at 350° for 40 minutes. **Yield: 8 servings.**

MAY 1992

Apple-Mincemeat Cobbler

If you like mincemeat pie, then you'll want to try this cobbler.

2 c. apple pie filing	brandy or rum to taste
2 c. mincemeat	⅓ c. butter or stick margarine
¼ c. lemon juice	2 c. biscuit mix
1 c. firmly packed brown sugar	½ c. butter or stick margarine, softened (not melted)
2 tsp. cinnamon	6 T. boiling water
1 tsp. ground nutmeg	

Combine first 7 ingredients and pour into a 9 x 13–inch pan. Dot with ⅓ c. butter and set aside.

Combine biscuit mix with ½ c. softened butter in a medium-size mixing bowl. Pour in boiling water and mix with a fork until mixture forms a ball. Grease hands and pat out dough on a lightly floured surface until it measures roughly 9 x 13 inches. Place crust on top of fruit mixture and bake at 375° for 30 minutes or until hot and bubbly and crust is brown.

THE FORMER BRENT HOUSE, DALLAS ～ DECEMBER 1980

Candy Cane Coffee Cakes

This beautiful dessert makes a wonderful holiday gift for friends and neighbors.

2 c. sour cream	1½ c. finely chopped dried apricots
1 (¼-oz.) pkg. active dry yeast	¾ c. drained, finely chopped maraschino cherries
½ c. warm, but not hot, water	¾ c. candied pineapple
¼ c. butter or stick margarine, softened	⅓ c. melted butter or stick margarine
⅓ c. sugar	Thin Icing (recipe follows)
2 tsp. salt	red and green maraschino cherry halves (optional)
2 eggs	additional chopped dried apricots (optional)
about 6 c. all-purpose flour, divided	mint leaves (optional)

Heat sour cream over low heat just until lukewarm. Dissolve yeast in warm water. Stir in sour cream, ¼ c. softened butter, sugar, salt, eggs, and 2 c. flour. Beat until smooth. Mix in enough remaining flour to make dough easy to handle.

Turn dough onto a well-floured board; knead until smooth (about 10 minutes). Place in a greased bowl; turn greased side up. Cover; let rise in warm place until double (about 1 hour).

Punch down dough; divide into 3 equal parts. Roll each part into a rectangle 15 x 6 inches; place on greased baking sheet. With pizza cutter or scissors, make 2-inch cuts at ½-inch intervals on long sides of rectangles (will resemble fringe). Combine apricots, cherries, and pineapple; spread ⅓ of mixture down center of each rectangle. Starting at the bottom, crisscross strips over filling. Stretch dough to 22 inches; curve to form cane. Bake at 375° for 15 to 20 minutes or until golden brown. While warm, brush with melted butter and drizzle canes with Thin Icing. Decorate with cherry halves, chopped apricots, and mint leaves, if desired. **Yield: 3 coffee cakes.**

THIN ICING

2 c. powdered sugar	2 T. water

Blend ingredients together. If icing is too stiff, stir in a few drops of water. **Yield: Enough icing for 3 coffee cakes.**

NORA GARZA ～ DECEMBER 1999

Opposite page: Candy Cane Coffee Cake

Bizcochitos

You can find versions of these flavorful cookies at panaderías across the state. Try your hand at the following recipe, provided by Mary Rosales of Mi Tierra Café y Panadería in San Antonio. Although the fleur-de-lis shape is traditional for these cookies, many people use cactus, coyote, and other Southwestern motifs.

6 c. sifted all-purpose flour	1¾ c. sugar, divided
1 T. baking powder	2 tsp. aniseed
1 tsp. salt	2 eggs, beaten until light and fluffy
2 c. lard or butter (lard is traditional and makes more tender cookies)	¼ c. brandy, or more as needed
	1 T. cinnamon

Sift flour with baking powder and salt; set aside.

Cream lard with 1½ c. sugar and aniseed by hand or with an electric mixer at medium speed. Add eggs to creamed mixture and mix well. Add flour mixture and brandy; mix until blended. Use only enough brandy to form a stiff dough. Knead dough lightly and pat or roll to ¼-inch to ½-inch thickness. Cut into desired shapes.

Combine remaining ¼ c. sugar with cinnamon and dust tops of cookies. Bake at 350° for 10 minutes or until very lightly browned. **Yield: 6 to 10 dozen cookies (depending on size).**

MARY ROSALES ∽ NOVEMBER 1994

Pepparkakor
(GINGER COOKIES)

These spicy cookies mark the Christmas holidays for many Swedish-Americans. This recipe, from the late Johanna Wimberly of Hutto, is adapted from one brought by a Swedish immigrant to New Sweden, Texas, in 1893.

¾ c. shortening	¼ tsp. salt
½ c. sugar	2 tsp. baking soda
½ c. firmly packed brown sugar	½ tsp. ground cloves
1 egg	1 tsp. cinnamon
¼ c. molasses	1 tsp. ground ginger
2¼ c. all-purpose flour	

Cream shortening with sugars and beat until fluffy. Add egg and molasses and beat well; set aside.

Combine remaining ingredients and gradually add to first mixture, mixing well. Chill dough in refrigerator at least 2 hours.

Working with half the dough at a time (leave rest refrigerated), roll dough to ⅛-inch to ¼-inch thickness on a lightly floured surface and cut into shapes, using heart-shaped and round (with scalloped edges) cookie cutters. (Dipping cookie cutters in flour helps dough to release.)

Place cookies on a lightly greased cookie sheet in the middle of the oven and bake at 350° for 5 to 8 minutes or until lightly browned (watch closely). Cool on wire racks. **Yield: About 4 dozen cookies.**

N O T E : These cookies can also be made without rolling out the dough. Place walnut-size balls of dough on a lightly greased cookie sheet and press each ball firmly with the bottom of a glass that has been dipped in sugar. Follow the same procedure as for rolled cookies, but bake 8 to 12 minutes.

JOHANNA WIMBERLY ⁓ DECEMBER 2002

Jam Cuts

This attractive Swedish cookie adds variety to holiday dessert plates.

1 c. butter or stick margarine, softened	⅓ c. firm, seedless raspberry jam
½ c. sugar	½ c. powdered sugar
2½ c. all-purpose flour	

Using your hands, combine butter, sugar, and flour in a large mixing bowl; work the crumbs between your fingers. After a few minutes, you should have a soft, well-blended dough that holds together. Shape the dough into four 13 x 1½-inch logs and place them on 2 greased baking sheets. Flatten logs slightly and make a shallow depression down the length of each log (a pencil or dowel rod wrapped in waxed paper works well for this.) Fill with jam, using a pastry bag or small spoon. Bake logs at 350° for 15 to 18 minutes or until edges are golden.

While logs are baking, combine powdered sugar and about 1 T. water to make a thin glaze; set aside.

After logs are baked, drip the glaze from a spoon over the jam while logs are still warm. Let logs cool for about 5 minutes. Then slice diagonally in 1½-inch strips, making diamond shapes. **Yield: About 2½ dozen cookies.**

CARRIN PATMAN ⁓ DECEMBER 2002

(Clockwise from left)
Pepparkakor (Ginger Cookies),
Spritsar (Spritz Cookies),
and Jam Cuts

Spritsar

(SPRITZ COOKIES)

Spritz Cookies are another traditional Swedish dessert at Christmas. Donna Olson of Austin makes this recipe with an old-fashioned Swedish cookie press that, along with the recipe, came from her mother-in-law, Myrtle Lundgren Olson.

2 c. butter, softened	red and green sprinkles (optional)
1 c. sugar	candied fruit (optional)
1 egg	maraschino cherries (optional)
¼ tsp. almond or vanilla flavoring	Red Hots candy (optional)
5 c. all-purpose flour	

Cream butter with sugar until smooth. Add egg and flavoring, mixing well. Gradually add flour, mixing thoroughly. Using a cookie press with a star-shaped opening, extrude dough onto an ungreased cookie sheet in long, ridged strips. Cut strips at 3-inch intervals and shape pieces into wreaths. Add sprinkles or decorate with candied fruit or cherries to resemble holly sprigs, if desired. Bake at 350° for 5 to 8 minutes or until edges start turning golden. If using Red Hots for decorations, press them lightly into cookies immediately after removal from the oven. **Yield: About 7½ dozen cookies.**

DONNA OLSON ～ DECEMBER 2002

Spicy Rainforest Chip Cookies

This recipe was adapted from one that appears in Along the Garden Path *(1995) by Bill and Sylvia Varney of the Fredericksburg Herb Farm.*

½ c. unsalted butter, softened	½ c. roasted peanuts, slightly crushed
¼ c. sugar	½ c. golden raisins
½ c. firmly packed brown sugar	1 c. semisweet chocolate chips
1 large egg	½ c. plus 2 T. unbleached flour
1 T. warm water	½ tsp. salt
½ tsp. vanilla	½ tsp. baking soda
1½ c. old-fashioned rolled oats	½ tsp. cinnamon
½ c. sweetened flaked coconut	

Cream butter; gradually add sugars, beating well at medium speed with an electric mixer. Add egg, water, and vanilla, beating well. Stir in oats, coconut, peanuts, raisins, and chocolate chips.

In another bowl, combine flour, salt, baking soda, and cinnamon. Add to first mixture and mix well. Drop dough by tablespoonfuls onto greased cookie sheets. Bake at 350° for about 14 minutes or until golden. Cool on a wire rack. **Yield: 3 dozen cookies.**

BILL AND SYLVIA VARNEY ～ APRIL 1996

Apple Dumplings

This recipe is adapted from one that appears in Love Creek Orchards'
Adams Apple Cookbook (Morris Press, 1994 and 2001). Note: Instead of making
the dough from scratch, you can buy ready-made pie crust or puff pastry.

2 c. sugar	4 to 5 T. sugar
1 tsp. cinnamon	6 to 8 tsp. butter or stick margarine
1 tsp. ground nutmeg	additional sugar
¼ c. butter or stick margarine	mint leaves (optional)
6 to 8 medium apples	raspberries (optional)
Dumpling Dough (see recipe below)	

Combine first 4 ingredients and 2 c. water in a medium saucepan. Cook 5 minutes over medium heat; set aside.

Core and peel apples (and slice, if desired). Roll Dumpling Dough to ⅛-inch thickness and cut into squares large enough to cover each apple or mound of apple slices. Place apple in center of each pastry square; sprinkle each apple with about 2 tsp. sugar and dot with 1 tsp. butter. Bring all 4 corners to the top of the apples and crimp together. Place dumplings in a 9 x 13–inch baking dish. Sprinkle with sugar. Pour butter-sugar mixture around dumplings. Bake at 375° for 1 hour. Garnish with mint leaves and raspberries, if desired. **Yield: 6 to 8 servings.**

DUMPLING DOUGH

2 c. all-purpose flour	3¾ c. shortening
1 tsp. salt	½ c. milk
2 tsp. baking powder	

Sift together flour, salt, and baking powder. Cut in shortening and add milk, mixing well. **Yield: Enough dough to make 6 to 8 apple dumplings.**

JUNE 1995

Opposite page: Apple Blossom Ice Soda (left), Apple Cooler, and Apple Dumpling

Bread Pudding with Lemon Sauce

Many diners at the Village Bakery Café in Amarillo make it a point to save room for this finale.

1 lb. day-old French bread, cubed	2 T. pure vanilla
1 qt. whole milk, scalded	½ c. heavy cream
3 eggs, beaten	1 c. currants
2 c. sugar	1 c. pecan halves
1 tsp. cinnamon	Lemon Sauce (recipe follows)
¼ c. butter or stick margarine, melted	

Combine bread and milk in a greased 3-qt. baking dish and set aside.

Combine eggs, sugar, cinnamon, butter, and vanilla; beat well. Blend in cream and stir in currants and pecans. Combine with bread mixture. Bake at 350° for about 45 minutes. Serve warm or at room temperature with Lemon Sauce. **Yield: 10 to 12 servings.**

LEMON SAUCE

1 c. sugar	4 egg yolks
¼ c. cornstarch	⅓ c. lemon juice
dash of salt	3 T. butter or stick margarine
2 c. milk	heavy cream (optional)

Combine dry ingredients in a heavy saucepan. Gradually add milk, stirring until blended. Cook over medium heat, stirring constantly, until mixture thickens and comes to a boil; remove from heat and set aside.

Beat egg yolks until thick in a medium bowl. Gradually stir ¼ hot mixture into yolks; add back to remaining hot mixture and cook over medium heat, stirring constantly, for 2 to 3 minutes. Remove from heat and stir in lemon juice and butter. Cover top of pan with plastic wrap or waxed paper. Cool. Thin with heavy cream, if desired. **Yield: Enough sauce for Bread Pudding.**

CINDY LEE ～ FEBRUARY 2000

Sweet Tamales

Adapted from a recipe that appears in Mexico's Feast of Life *(1989) by Patricia Quintana, this version of sweet tamales was developed by Miguel Ravago, co-owner and executive chef at Fonda San Miguel in Austin. Miguel says the recipe is based on one his grandmother used. If you've never made tamales before, see "Tamale Tips" on page 132.*

3 c. sugar	red food coloring as desired
1½ c. to 2 c. candied fruit, finely chopped	Sweet Tamale Dough (see recipe below)
1½ c. raisins	1 (8-oz.) pkg. corn husks, washed, soaked in warm water for several hours or until very pliable, drained, and patted dry
1½ c. almonds, finely chopped	

Combine first 5 ingredients, mixing well; set aside.

To assemble tamales, spread about 1 T. of dough over the center of each corn husk, leaving husk bare at the top, bottom, and sides. Spread about 1 T. of sweet filling over the dough. Fold sides of husk inward to center, lengthwise, so that they overlap. Fold pointed end toward center and fold wider end down over pointed end, completely enclosing filling. Continue procedure until all dough is used.

To steam tamales, use a steamer or large pot with a rack or metal colander placed inside on top of a layer of clean corn shucks. Add enough water to fill pot below rack level and keep tamales above water. Place tamales upright on rack (see photograph on page 135) and cover with another layer of shucks. Bring water to a boil. Cover and steam for 1 hour or until tamale dough pulls away from husk; add more boiling water as necessary. Yield: 2½ dozen tamales.

SWEET TAMALE DOUGH

2¼ lb. freshly prepared masa	½ c. cornstarch
1½ c. water	1½ to 2 T. salt, or to taste
1½ tsp. baking powder	½ lb. lard

Place masa in a large bowl. Add 1½ c. water gradually and knead until smooth and no longer sticky. Combine baking powder, cornstarch, and salt; knead into the masa. Set aside. In a separate bowl, beat the lard with an electric mixer or food processor until it is fluffy (about 5 minutes). Work the lard into the masa gradually, kneading thoroughly until mixture is smooth and stiff or until a spoonful floats in a glass of cold water. Yield: Enough dough for 2½ dozen tamales.

MIGUEL RAVAGO ∼ DECEMBER 1995

Pumpkin Cake Roll

This attractive dessert has a cream cheese filling.

3 eggs	1 tsp. ground ginger
1 c. sugar	½ tsp. ground nutmeg
⅔ c. cooked or canned pumpkin	½ tsp. salt
1 tsp. lemon juice	1 c. chopped pecans or walnuts
¾ c. all-purpose flour	Cream Cheese Filling (recipe follows)
1 tsp. baking powder	additional powdered sugar
2 tsp. cinnamon	

Beat eggs at high speed with electric mixer for 5 minutes. Gradually beat in sugar, pumpkin, and lemon juice.

Sift together flour, baking powder, cinnamon, ginger, nutmeg, and salt. Add to other mixture and stir until evenly combined. Spread batter in greased and parchment-lined or floured 10 x 15–inch jelly-roll pan. Sprinkle with nuts. Bake at 375° for 15 minutes or until cake is done. Turn out immediately onto a smooth cotton tea towel sprinkled with powdered sugar. (If parchment sticks to cake, leave it in place until filling is added.) Starting with narrow end, roll towel and cake together.

Unroll cake, remove parchment, and spread filling on inside of cake. Reroll cake (without towel). Sprinkle with powdered sugar. Cover; chill thoroughly. Slice like a jelly roll to serve. **Yield: 1 cake roll.**

CREAM CHEESE FILLING

2 (3-oz.) pkg. cream cheese, softened	1 c. powdered sugar
¼ c. butter or stick margarine, softened	½ tsp. vanilla

Beat together cream cheese and butter. Add powdered sugar and vanilla and blend well.

PUNKIN DAYS FESTIVAL ～ OCTOBER 1993

Buñuelos

Mi Tierra Café y Panadería in San Antonio provided this recipe.

4 c. all-purpose flour	½ c. orange juice
2 tsp. baking powder	warm water
3 T. shortening	vegetable oil
1 egg	sugar
1 T. white vinegar	cinnamon

Combine first 6 ingredients and mix well. Add enough warm water to make a dough. Divide dough into 12 portions and roll very thin into 12 tortilla-size rounds.

Heat oil in a skillet large enough to hold dough rounds without bending them. Drop rounds, one at a time, into hot oil and fry until crisp. Drain on paper towels and sprinkle with sugar and cinnamon. **Yield: About 1 dozen.**

MARY ROSALES ∽ NOVEMBER 1994

Cranberry-Pear Crisp

Cathy Barber, food editor of The Dallas Morning News, *credits this recipe to the USA Rice Federation in Houston. Cathy sometimes serves it warm, with a little ice cream or whipped cream.*

3 c. cooked brown rice	¼ c. rolled oats
2 c. peeled and diced pears	3 T. butter or stick margarine
1 c. fresh or frozen chopped cranberries	¼ c. chopped pecans
½ c. firmly packed dark brown sugar, divided	¼ c. flaked coconut
⅓ c. all-purpose flour, divided	pear slices (optional)

Combine rice, pears, and cranberries, ⅓ c. brown sugar, and 2 T. flour; place mixture in a well-greased 2-qt. baking dish and set aside.

Combine remaining sugar, remaining flour, and oats in a small bowl. Cut in butter with a pastry blender until mixture resembles coarse meal. Add pecans and coconut; blend well. Sprinkle over rice mixture. Bake, uncovered, in a 375° oven for 25 minutes or until thoroughly heated. Garnish with pear slices, if desired. **Yield: 8 servings.**

CATHY BARBER ∽ DECEMBER 1999

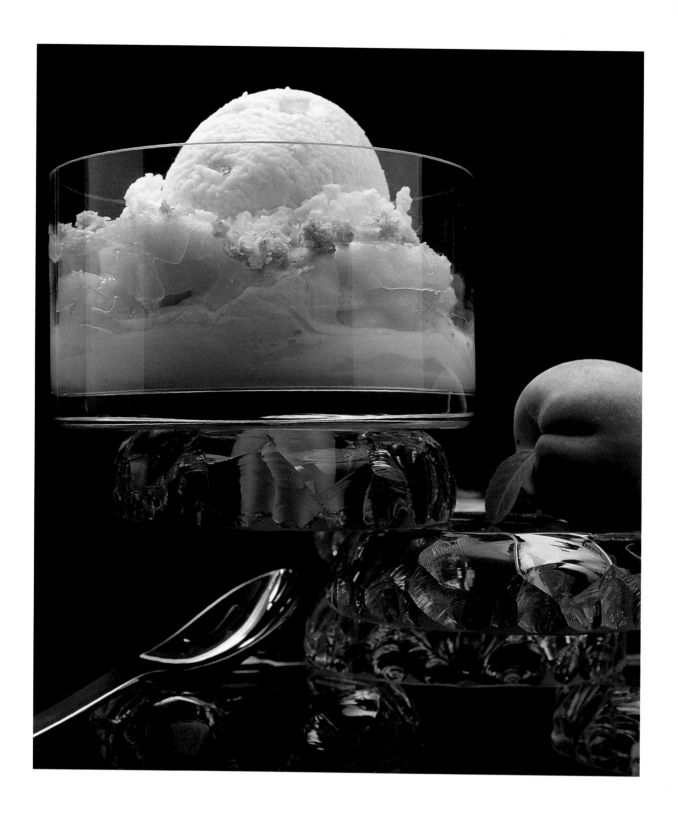

Mrs. Lyndon B. Johnson's Peach Ice Cream

Mrs. Lyndon B. Johnson's Peach Ice Cream

Here's an easy way to peel all those peaches: Bring a pot of water to a boil, add peaches, and leave for 1 minute. Rinse fruit under cold water; skins should slip off easily.

3 eggs	1 qt. whipping cream
1 c. sugar	½ gal. soft peaches, peeled, mashed, and sweetened to taste
1 pt. milk	

Beat eggs in a heavy saucepan until thick. Gradually add sugar, beating well. Add milk and whipping cream; mix well. Bring to a boil, stirring constantly. Reduce heat to low; continue cooking and stirring until mixture thickens and coats a metal spoon. Let cool.

Stir in peaches and pour into freezer can of a 1-gal. ice cream freezer. Freeze according to manufacturer's instructions. **Yield: 1 gallon.**

MRS. LYNDON B. JOHNSON ✒ JULY 1994

Raspberry Salsa over Ice Cream

The chefs who created this dish for Texas Highways *readers say you can also use the salsa as a sauce for meat or fish. Now that's versatile!*

2 dried chipotle chiles	1 T. ground oregano
6 serrano chiles, finely chopped	½ c. water
1 c. sugar	12 oz. fresh or frozen raspberries
½ c. firmly packed brown sugar	3 T. chocolate syrup
½ tsp. salt	2 c. chopped pecans, toasted
1 T. cinnamon	chocolate ice cream

Place chipotles in a saucepan, cover with water, and bring to a boil. Cover and boil until tender (about 15 minutes); drain. Set aside to cool.

Dice rehydrated chipotles and combine with serranos, sugars, salt, cinnamon, oregano, and ½ c. water in a medium saucepan. Bring mixture to a low boil. Cook until thickened slightly (about 7 to 8 minutes), stirring frequently. Add raspberries and cook until they start to break up but not disintegrate. (You want the salsa to have a chunky texture.) Remove mixture from heat and stir in chocolate syrup and pecans. Chill thoroughly.

Spoon ice cream into clear dessert dishes and top with chilled salsa. **Yield: 6 to 8 servings.**

MARK LASHLEY AND RICHARD WHEATLEY ✒ JANUARY 1998

Apple Blossom Ice Cream Soda

This recipe is adapted from one that appears in Love Creek Orchards'
Adams Apple Cookbook *(Morris Press, 1994 and 2001).*

2 c. apple cider	chilled ginger ale
1 pt. peach ice cream	

Pour ½ c. apple cider in each of 4 tall glasses. Divide ice cream equally among glasses. Fill glasses with ginger ale. Stir gently to mix. **Yield: 4 servings.**

LOVE CREEK ORCHARDS ∼ JUNE 1995

Pecan Pralines

A touch of cinnamon gives these pralines a distinctive taste, reminiscent of the pralines found in many Mexican restaurants.

2 c. firmly packed brown sugar	1½ c. pecan pieces
1 c. sugar	1 T. butter
¾ c. milk	1 tsp. vanilla
pinch of salt	½ tsp. cinnamon

Combine sugars, milk, and salt in a heavy saucepan; bring to a boil and continue boiling for 5 minutes, stirring constantly. Add pecans, stir, and boil for 5 more minutes. Remove from heat and add butter, vanilla, and cinnamon. Stir for 2 minutes or until mixture begins to thicken. Using a large spoon, drop by spoonfuls onto waxed paper; let stand until firm. **Yield: 1½ to 2 dozen pralines.**

MRS. IO BRIGGS ∼ DECEMBER 1982

Dutch-Oven Dishes

When the term *Dutch oven* comes up in most recipes, it's usually in reference to a large, deep pot with handles on both sides and a domed lid. However, in this section, it refers to the *original* Dutch oven (sometimes called a camp oven), a heavy cast-iron pot that sits on three legs and has a flanged lid for holding hot coals.

Why a special section on Dutch-oven dishes? Two reasons. One, because there are so many Dutch-oven enthusiasts in Texas. The Lone Star Dutch Oven Society is one of the largest such societies in the world, with more than a dozen chapters scattered across the state. (At one point, the organization even had a member in Japan.) Chuck-wagon cooking groups also abound, and, of course, use the same venerable black pots. Charles Goodnight, who invented the chuck wagon, supposedly took one along on Texas' first trail drive.

Of course, you don't have to belong to any special group to enjoy Dutch-oven cooking. Which brings us to the second reason we decided to include this category: Dutchin', as it's affectionately called, goes hand-in-hand with Texans' love of the outdoors. Campers discovered the versatility of this durable container long ago. You can use it for baking and roasting, just like a conventional oven. You can also use it as a stewpot, a frying pan, a deep fryer, a slow-cooker, or a steamer. If that list sounds like a stretch, see our recipe for Black Forest Icebox Pie, made in—what else?—a Dutch oven.

Some of our other recipes may also surprise you. Check out Nutty Chicken and Sassy Meat Loaf Ring, for example, entrées with unusual flavor combinations. And Brie with Toasted Pecans is downright elegant, even if it is made in a plain-Jane pot.

We've also included some of the old standards, from *pan de campo* (camp bread) and vinegar cobbler to a recipe for sourdough starter, which you can use to make both sourdough biscuits and sourdough flapjacks. What to do with your extra starter? Give some to a friend and introduce that person to the art of Dutch-oven cooking. It's a passion easily shared. But be sure to give fair warning: Once bitten by the black-pot bug, you're usually hooked for life.

Going Dutch

An experienced Dutcher, Texas Highways *photo editor Mike Murphy not only shot the story we ran on Dutch-oven cooking in November 2000, he also tested the recipes and wrote up these helpful tips for novices.*

Hankering to break into the art of Dutch-oven cooking? Working on our story rekindled my interest in Dutchin', and I've compiled a few observations and tips that might make your start a little easier.

If you're going to get only one oven at first, my recommendation is to go with a 10-inch oven from Lodge Manufacturing. This size allows you to test and improve your skills without using too much food. Several of the recipes we've included in this section work perfectly in this size oven, and will make a meal for a family of four just fine.

After buying a new oven, wash it with soap and hot water to remove the manufacturer's protective film, dry it completely, and season it immediately. To do this in a conventional home oven, warm the pot slightly, wipe it and its lid inside and out with a good vegetable oil or shortening (I use Crisco), and place both the pot and the lid (turn the pot upside down) in a 350° oven for an hour. When the hour is up, turn the stove off. Let the pot and lid cool completely before removing them. Your Dutch oven is now ready to use.

If you have, find, or buy an old oven that's rusted, use steel wool or emery paper to remove the rust, then wash and season it as described earlier. If the oven's gunked up with old grease, boil some water in it for a while to loosen the residue, clean it, and re-season it.

When your oven is ready to use, gather up these tools (see page 228) before you fire up the coals:

- Long-handled tongs, for handling hot charcoal briquettes
- A lid-lifter, which you can buy or make. (Caution: You can get by with pliers, but if you do, you won't want to dally while picking up a lid full of coals unless you like toasted knuckles! I plopped down $15 for a lid-lifter, which gives you a good grip on most any lid.)
- Lid stand, for setting lids on when you're preparing or checking the food
- Thick potholders and/or welder's gloves
- Charcoal briquettes
- A charcoal chimney starter for lighting briquettes. (If you cook outdoors at all, you should have one of these anyway—they're much more environmentally friendly than lighter fluid.)

The last thing you need is a place to cook. This can be a patch of dirt in your backyard—you just want a spot where you can have a small ring of coals without setting your place ablaze. (I cut an old 55-gallon drum in thirds, discarded the middle portion, and used one of the two ends, filled with 1 to 2 inches of sand, as a Dutch-oven firebox. You can give the other end to another Dutch-oven enthusiast or cook with two ovens simultaneously.)

Gather the ingredients for the recipe you want and get started. Keep in mind that the recipes are starting points; you can adjust the seasoning at any time to tailor the taste to your druthers.

Light the briquettes in the charcoal chimney, and while they're heating up (this takes 15 to 20 minutes), prepare the dish for the oven. Use the number of briquettes called for in the recipe as a beginning point. If the top of the meal isn't browning properly, add more briquettes from the chimney to the lid. Occasionally rotating the oven, and the lid, helps keep the heat even. When lifting the lid to check for doneness, be sure to keep it downwind of the oven, or a small breeze may coat your food with ashes! Using briquettes makes controlling the overall heat easier than cooking with the coals from various woods. (Once you're experienced with briquettes, feel free to experiment with wood coals.)

When your meal is done, you can either remove the oven from the heat entirely or leave a few briquettes underneath and on top to keep it warm.

After you and your guests, *con mucho gusto*, have emptied the oven of its contents, let it cool before washing it. Scrape out all the remaining contents and use hot water and a pad or brush to clean it. Dry it completely, then re-coat it with oil before putting it away. Storing the oven with the lid slightly ajar, or with a paper towel inside, will help prevent rust formation. In any case, if you have to use lots of soap and/or a wire brush to clean your oven, you'd better re-season it, and you might want to heat it with a little less enthusiasm next time around.

New Lodge ovens come with a pamphlet covering the care of ovens in more detail, and the brochure also has a handy chart for converting conventional cooking temperatures to number of briquettes for the size oven you're using. Some cookbooks also have similar charts and other methods for gauging the heat. The bottom line, though, is that your skill will improve with experience, and, as with most endeavors, patience is usually rewarded more deliciously than haste.

Charcoal & Temperature Control

Longtime members of the Lone Star Dutch Oven Society, Duane and Sandy Dinwiddie enjoy showing novice cooks the ropes. Here are some of Duane's tips for controlling the heat when cooking in a Dutch oven.

Beginners frequently over-start their charcoal, or leave it in the charcoal chimney too long before they use it. It should take only 10 to 15 minutes to start charcoal in a chimney starter. It may not look lit in the starter, but if it has flames coming out the top and no smoke, it is ready. Dump out the coals and use the fully lit ones first. Charcoal that has been started for 30 minutes before it is put on a pot will be half burned away and will not produce as much heat per briquette. It will also not provide heat long enough to finish some recipes.

Always start more charcoal than you need, so you can add the extra later to maintain heat if necessary, especially if it is windy. A few lit coals in a chimney will light new charcoal put on top.

Freshly lit charcoal will burn for about an hour when placed on/under a pot, unless it is very windy. Wind makes it burn faster and "blows" the heat downwind. Turn the pot 180° two or three times while cooking to even out this effect.

All recipes assume that you use fresh, properly lit charcoal. (I use Kingsford charcoal briquettes or the equivalent.)

When I first started this Dutch-oven thing, I tried to count out the number of charcoal briquettes called for in the Dutch-oven recipe books. I rapidly found this to be less than satisfactory for me, and decided to measure quantities of hot charcoal by geometric patterns. Today, all of my recipes are based on the following "ring" method of temperature control. The following definitions apply:

- 1 ring: A circle of hot charcoal with all of the briquettes lying flat and sides touching (leave three spaces in a bottom ring for the oven's legs). The *outside edge of the ring* is lined up with the *outside edge of the oven,* top or bottom.
- ½ ring: The same size circle, but with every other briquette missing.
- 2 rings: A second ring just inside the first, with the rings touching.
- Full spread: The briquettes are spread (one layer deep, lying flat with sides touching) either under (very rare, except in frying) or on top of the pot.

This ring technique is somewhat self-correcting for the size of the briquettes used. If your charcoal has been burning for a while, the pieces will be smaller and will put out less heat. But it will take more of them to make a ring, so you still get about the same temperature. Of course they won't last as long and the comparison is rough, but it's better than counting briquettes.

Dutch ovens were designed hundreds of years ago to cook food using coals from wood fires. Experienced cooks can gauge correctly how many coals to use on top and bottom, but the ring method proves easier for beginning cooks.

The temperature of your oven depends on the size and brand of your charcoal, how long it has been lit, the wind, and even whether it is sunny or shady (a black pot will cook 25° hotter in the summer sun than in the shade). I have been able to cook almost everything there is to cook with just four temperatures—slow, medium, hot, and very hot. For a 12-inch oven, *slow* will have 1 ring under the pot and 1 ring on top and will be 300° F. +/- 25°. *Medium* will have 1 ring under and 1½ rings on top and will be 350° +/- 25°. *Hot* will have 1 ring under and 2 rings on top and will be 400° +/- 25°, and *very hot* will have 1 ring under and 2½ rings on top and will be 450° to 500°.

One advantage of this method is that you never change the number of rings *under* the pot. The exception is for frying or boiling, where I start with a full spread under the pot, and cook with the lid on with a few coals on top just to keep the heat in. Once the contents are frying or boiling briskly, take a few coals out from under the pot until it is cooking properly. Add some back if it slows down too much.

Note that you will need more charcoal on top for ovens larger than 12 inches and less for smaller ones. Temperature is controlled partly by what percentage of the lid is covered with charcoal. A 10-inch pot with 2 rings on top will be considerably hotter than a 14-inch pot with 2 rings on top. This is because two rings on top of a 10-inch oven will cover a lot more of the lid than two rings on a 14-inch pot.

Learn to "feel" how much charcoal is right for a particular dish. I don't mean feel with your hands, but look inside the pot to see if your food is simmering or baking properly or browning properly, etc., and then add or take away charcoal as needed. You will rapidly learn how much charcoal it takes to make your pot do what you want it to. My motto is to err on the hot side, as it is really hard to burn something in these pots!

NOTE: Not all the recipes that follow use the ring method to describe the amount of heat needed, but with a bit of practice, you'll be able to make the necessary conversions.

A chuck-wagon cook for nearly half a century, the late Richard Bolt made a lasting contribution to Dutch-oven cooking when he published a collection of his recipes in 1974. Called Forty Years behind the Lid, *the little book remains a standard reference for serious Dutchers. It devotes six pages to sourdough baking alone and contains this warning:* "Sourdough starter is as temperamental as a woman so treat it like your wife—with tender loving care." *The context may be politically incorrect, but the cooking advice is still sound.*

Dutch-oven cooking tools include (from left) a lid-lifter, tongs, a lid stand, a charcoal chimney starter, a cast-iron Dutch oven, and a metal work table.

Richard Bolt's Sourdough Biscuits

If you have sourdough starter on hand, this recipe doesn't take long to make. Since these biscuits don't have to rise before baking, they're a bit denser than most, but still tasty.

2 c. sifted all-purpose flour	1 T. sugar
2 c. Sourdough Starter (recipe follows)	2 heaping tsp. baking powder
1 tsp. salt	3 T. shortening

Place flour in a large bowl and make a hollow in the flour. Add 2 c. Sourdough Starter and remaining ingredients. Mix well into a soft dough. Pinch off egg-size pieces of dough and place close together in a greased 12-inch Dutch oven. Place hot lid on oven, set oven on coals, and place coals on lid. Cook 5 to 8 minutes or until biscuits brown. **Yield: 10 to 12 biscuits.**

RICHARD BOLT ⟿ OCTOBER 1982 AND SEPTEMBER 1994

SOURDOUGH STARTER

You can order sourdough starter from the Baker's Catalogue (800/827-6836 or www.kingarthurflour.com), but it's more fun to make your own. Here is Richard Bolt's recipe.

1 cake yeast *or* 1 pkg. dry yeast	4 c. unbleached flour
4 c. warm, nonchlorinated water	1 raw potato, quartered
2 T. sugar	

Dissolve yeast in warm water, then mix all ingredients in a 1-gal. crock or other nonmetallic container. Cover with a close-fitting lid and let starter rise until light and bubbly on top (12 hours in warm weather, longer in cool weather).

Each time you use starter, replace the amount used with a half-and-half measure of flour and water plus 1 tsp. sugar. Add more potato occasionally as food for the yeast (when the original potato is used up), but don't add more yeast. For best results, use starter daily; if not used often, it will die. Never let starter get cold. Starter improves with age.

NOTE: Our resident Dutch-oven expert, photo editor Mike Murphy, differs with Richard on one point. He says you can refrigerate the starter if you don't intend to use it for some time. One year he put his starter in the fridge in June and took it out in September; it still worked fine. Unless you bake every day, Mike also suggests that you begin your starter in a large container and then transfer it to a quart-size crock later. The starter will conform to the size of its container, and a quart of starter is adequate for most home bakers.

RICHARD BOLT ⟿ OCTOBER 1982

Dutch-oven enthusiasts are fond of saying, "The Colt wasn't the only iron that won the West."

Cowboy Morning Sourdough Biscuits

Ranchers Tom and Anne Christian have hosted Cowboy Morning Breakfasts on their Figure 3 Ranch, near Amarillo, since 1981. Besides a great breakfast, guests are treated to a spectacular view of Palo Duro Canyon. Although the Christians use their own sourdough starter, Richard Bolt's starter works fine in this recipe. Note that the biscuits need to rise for an hour or two before baking, so the cook has to plan on getting up early.

5 c. all-purpose flour	1 tsp. baking soda
2½ c. sourdough starter (if you don't already have starter, use recipe on page 229)	½ tsp. salt
1 tsp. sugar	¼ c. vegetable oil

Place flour in a large bowl and make a well in the flour. Place starter in the well and add remaining ingredients. Stir until mixture no longer picks up flour. Cover and let rise 3 to 4 hours or overnight.

Place dough on floured board and roll to ½-inch thickness. Cut out biscuits and place in a greased 14-inch Dutch oven. Set by the campfire to rise for 1 to 2 hours.
Place hot lid on oven, set oven on coals, and place coals on lid. Cook 10 to 20 minutes or until brown. **Yield: 20 to 26 biscuits.**

ANNE CHRISTIAN ～ JUNE 1989

Opposite page: Biscuits

*T*he Lone Star Dutch Oven Society,
a statewide organization "dedicated to
preserving the art of Black Pot Cooking
throughout the State of Texas,"
maintains a Web site (www.lsdos.com)
that offers recipes, cooking tips, and
other useful information for both
novice and seasoned Dutchers.

Fluffy Sourdough Biscuits

Note that this recipe needs to be started the night before (unless you like a late breakfast), and if you don't have sourdough starter on hand, two nights before. If you like, you can use honey instead of sugar in the recipe; just add it when you mix in the starter.

1 c. sourdough starter (if you don't already have starter, use recipe on page 229)

3 c. all-purpose flour, divided

1 c. milk

½ tsp. salt

½ tsp. cream of tartar

2 heaping tsp. baking powder

1 T. sugar or honey

⅓ c. shortening

½ tsp. baking soda

2 oz. warm water

3 T. butter or stick margarine

Before turning in for the night, mix sourdough starter, 1 c. flour, and milk together in a nonmetallic container, cover, and let stand in a warm place overnight. (Alternatively, mix in the morning and put in a warm location to rise 4 to 6 hours.)

In a large mixing bowl, sift together remaining 2 c. flour, salt, cream of tartar, baking powder, and sugar (if using honey, add later, as instructed); blend in shortening.

Combine baking soda with 2 oz. warm water and mix this with the now bubbly starter mix. (Add honey now if you're using that instead of sugar.) Add to dry ingredients and mix well. If dough seems dry, add a teaspoon or two of water; if too wet, add a little flour. Knead dough gently for a bit, then roll dough out on a flat surface until ½ to 1 inch thick. Cut with a biscuit cutter.

Place butter in a 12-inch Dutch oven; heat oven just enough to melt the butter and then remove it from coals. Dip each biscuit in melted butter so that both top and bottom are coated. Place biscuits in Dutch oven and cover. (If you have time, place oven close to the fire and let biscuits rise for 20 to 30 minutes at this point.)

Place Dutch oven over 1 ring of hot briquettes and place 2 rings of hot briquettes on lid. *Be sure not to overheat the bottom part of the oven; you want more coals on the lid (⅓ on bottom, ⅔ on lid).* Rotate the lid often; check biscuits once or twice to ensure they're cooking evenly. If the bottom looks done, but the top isn't, take the oven off the bottom coals, leaving the lid coals to finish the tops. **Yield: About 1 dozen.**

NOTE: This recipe will also work in a regular home oven. Preheat a 12-inch cast-iron skillet just enough to melt the butter. Turn heat off, then dip each biscuit in melted butter so that both top and bottom are coated. The biscuits should nicely fill the skillet. If you have time, cover and let rise for 20 to 30 minutes; otherwise, bake at 375° for 16 to 20 minutes.

MICHAEL A. MURPHY ～ 2003

Sourdough Flapjacks

Richard Bolt credited his flapjacks with having almost magical properties. In his words, "If you do not believe these help cowboys work better, ask Tone 'Flapjack' Sparks. He failed to eat his usual six flapjacks for breakfast one morning and had trouble all day trying to flank calves. He was very upset about his many fumbles on the job, and I told him it was purely a dietary problem. The next day Tony indulged in his usual number of flapjacks and was able to flank calves like a good cowboy is suppose to [sic]."

2 eggs	2 tsp. baking powder
1½ c. milk	1 tsp. salt
4½ c. sourdough starter (see recipe on page 229)	3 T. sugar
1½ T. melted shortening	dash of cinnamon
½ tsp. vanilla	2 to 2¼ c. all-purpose flour

Beat eggs slightly; add other ingredients except flour, mixing well. Add sufficient flour to make batter the desired thickness. (Some like their hotcake batter thicker than others. I use about 2 c. flour.) Cook on a lightly greased griddle, pan, or inverted Dutch-oven lid. Turn flapjacks *one* time only. Turning more than once will make the flapjack tough. Yield: 6 to 10 servings.

Richard Bolt ~ September 1994

Award-Winning Pan de Campo

Long a favorite of South Texas cowboys, pan de campo *(camp bread) has become a trademark of outdoor chef Ruben Hinojosa, who has garnered top prizes in several competitions with this recipe. Ruben notes that some cooks prefer shortening to oil in their pan de campo; others use water instead of milk. He suggests experimenting to find the version that suits your taste. He cautions not to knead the dough too much. He says, "Dough that's been overworked becomes tough."*

2 c. all-purpose flour	1 tsp. sugar
2 tsp. baking powder	⅜ c. vegetable oil
1 tsp. salt	½ c. cold milk

Combine all ingredients, mixing well, but knead dough only slightly. If dough feels dry, add a few more drops of milk.

Roll dough into a circle about ½ inch thick. (Roll thinner if you want a crisper loaf.) Place in a preheated 12-inch Dutch oven. With a fork, poke holes in the dough to allow steam to escape. Place Dutch oven over 1 ring of hot briquettes. Place lid on oven and place 1½ rings on the lid. Bake about 6 minutes and turn bread over. Continue baking 5 to 10 minutes or until done. Remove bread from pan and serve hot. **Yield: 1 round loaf.**

RUBEN HINOJOSA ⁓ AUGUST 1992

Brie with Toasted Pecans

It's hard to believe that such an elegant appetizer can be made in a plain-Jane black pot.

1 c. coarsely chopped pecans	1 to 2 wedges Brie cheese, at room temperature
¼ c. butter or stick margarine, or less to taste	assorted crackers

Lightly toast pecans in (any size) Dutch oven placed over 1 ring of hot briquettes. Add butter and simmer with pecans for 2 to 3 minutes. Add Brie and quickly baste cheese with pecans and butter. Allow Brie to warm and soften for 1 to 2 minutes. With a spatula, transfer Brie to a serving platter, then pour pecans and butter on top. Serve with assorted crackers. **Yield: About 12 appetizer servings.**

BETH HAYNIE ⁓ NOVEMBER 2000

Opposite page: Brie with Toasted Pecans

Texas Hill Country Breakfast

Experienced Dutchers often keep a spray bottle of vegetable oil handy;
it works like no-stick cooking spray and is less expensive.

vegetable oil or no-stick cooking spray	8 to 12 large eggs, beaten well
1 lb. light pork sausage	1 lb. grated cheddar cheese
1 medium onion, diced	1 (8-oz.) jar thick-and-chunky salsa
1 tomato, chopped	avocado slices (optional)
2 lb. frozen hash-brown potatoes, thawed	

Preheat a 12-inch Dutch oven over a full spread of hot briquettes. Spray inside of oven with vegetable oil or no-stick cooking spray. Brown sausage, breaking it into small bits. Stir in onion and tomato; cook until onion is translucent. Remove sausage mixture and drain on paper towels.

Add hash browns to Dutch oven; fry until golden brown, stirring constantly. Add drained sausage mixture and mix well. Pour beaten eggs over sausage mixture and place lid on oven. Remove briquettes from the bottom, placing them on top of the lid, until you have 1 ring; add enough fresh hot briquettes to make 1½ rings total on top of the lid. Cook 8 to 10 minutes or until eggs are almost set. Sprinkle cheese on top and continue cooking until eggs are set and cheese is melted. Spread salsa on top, garnish with avocado slices, if desired, and serve. **Yield: 6 to 8 servings.**

BILL BRUMMEL　～　NOVEMBER 2000

Nutty Chicken

Pecans add crunch to this unusual entrée.

1 to 1½ c. chopped pecans	½ tsp. poultry seasoning
vegetable oil or no-stick cooking spray	salt and pepper to taste
2 to 3 lb. chicken tenders or chicken breasts, cut into bite-size pieces	8 oz. grated sharp cheddar cheese
1 c. chopped onion or green onion	3 (5-oz.) bags fresh mixed salad greens *or* 1 lb. washed fresh spinach
½ tsp. ground thyme	2 T. balsamic vinegar

Lightly toast pecans in a 12-inch Dutch oven placed over 1 ring of hot briquettes, then remove pecans. Spray inside of oven with oil and add chicken. Sprinkle onion, thyme, and poultry seasoning over top; lightly salt and pepper. Top with toasted pecans and bake for 30 minutes, with 1 ring of hot briquettes under oven and 2 rings on top. Top with cheese and cook until melted. Add salad greens; cover and cook until greens are wilted (about 3 to 5 minutes). Sprinkle with vinegar. **Yield: 4 to 6 servings.**

BETH HAYNIE ～ NOVEMBER 2000

Dutch-Oven Potatoes

James Stuart, owner of J-S Chuckwagon, says one of the secrets of successful Dutch-oven cooking is to keep less heat under the bottom of the pot than you do on the top.

1½ lb. thick-sliced bacon, cut into 1-inch squares	2 (8-oz.) jars Cheez Whiz *or* 16 oz. grated cheddar cheese
4 medium onions, sliced	6 to 8 slices American cheese
2 cloves elephant garlic, crushed	paprika
10 lb. potatoes, peeled and sliced ⅛ inch thick	
1 c. milk (if needed)	

Place bacon, onion, and garlic in a 14-inch Dutch oven and stir-fry over hot coals until bacon is done. Remove from heat. Add potatoes to mixture and stir gently until potatoes are coated with bacon fat.

Place lid on oven and place hot coals on lid. Cook over hot coals 15 to 20 minutes. Add Cheez Whiz (and milk, if potatoes seem dry); stir gently. Heat thoroughly. Add layer of cheese slices on top and heat until cheese is melted and lightly browned. Sprinkle with paprika. **Yield: 20 to 25 servings.**

JAMES STUART ～ SEPTEMBER 1994

Dutch-oven cooks delight in mastering the challenges of cooking outdoors. Shirley's Peach Cobbler (left) and Dutch-Oven Potatoes are two crowd-pleasers.

Easy Chicken Pot Pie

It takes only five ingredients to make this dish—an important factor to consider when you're cooking outdoors and have to pack your kitchen to go.

2 (9-in.) unbaked flat pie crusts

1 (10¾-oz.) can cream of celery soup

1 (10-oz.) can cooked chicken, drained

1 (20-oz.) can large-cut mixed vegetables, drained

1½ tsp. poultry seasoning

Place one pie crust inside a 10-inch Dutch oven. Combine remaining ingredients and pour mixture into pie crust. Cover mixture with remaining pie crust. Crimp edges of crusts together and cut 2 or 3 slits in top crust. Bake over 1 ring of hot briquettes, with 1½ rings on top, for 20 minutes or until top crust is golden brown. **Yield: 4 to 5 servings.**

WAYNE SWITZER AND JAY SWITZER ∼ NOVEMBER 2000

Sassy Meat Loaf Ring

Longtime Dutch-oven cook Bill Brummel turns ordinary ground beef into a masterpiece meatloaf.

2 large eggs, beaten

¼ c. nonfat dry milk powder

½ c. unseasoned fine, dry breadcrumbs

¼ c. finely chopped onion

2 T. dried parsley flakes

1 tsp. salt

½ tsp. pepper

½ tsp. garlic salt

½ c. thick-and-chunky salsa

1 T. Worcestershire sauce

2 lb. lean ground beef

vegetable oil or no-stick cooking spray

¼ c. ketchup

2 T. firmly packed brown sugar

1¼ tsp. ground mustard

½ tsp. concentrated lemon juice

mashed potatoes (optional)

Combine eggs and milk powder in a large bowl. Stir in next 8 ingredients, mixing well. Add ground beef and mix thoroughly. Set aside.

Spray a 5½-cup gelatin ring mold with oil. Spoon mixture into it, packing down firmly. Lightly spray the inside of a 10-inch Dutch oven with oil. Carefully unmold meat mixture into the Dutch oven. Place oven on top of 1 ring of hot briquettes; place 1½ rings on the lid. Bake for 50 minutes. Near the end of baking, use a turkey baster or spoon to remove any excess liquid from pot.

When meat is nearly done, combine ketchup and next 3 ingredients to make a glaze. Heat several minutes and then spread over top. Replace lid and continue cooking for 10 to 15 minutes. Fill center with mashed potatoes and add a garnish, if desired. Let ring set; cool about 5 minutes before slicing. **Yield: 6 to 8 servings.**

BILL BRUMMEL ∼ 2000

Our Dutch-Oven Heritage

Dutch ovens came to America on the Mayflower more than 375 years ago. Silversmith Paul Revere supposedly added the three stubby legs to give the oven more stability in an open hearth and developed the flanged lid to hold coals on top. The pots were so treasured that Mary Washington, George's mother, listed her "cast-iron kitchen furniture" in her will.

When Americans headed west, they took their indispensable black pots with them. Lewis and Clark lugged a Dutch oven along on their Northwest Expedition. Mountain men favored a lighter kettle while they were on the move, but they used Dutch ovens when they dug in for the winter at their base camps. Pioneers considered the cast-iron pots essential, no matter which frontier they were pushing. They used them on their westward journeys and, once they were settled, continued to cook with them—in many cases, long after they had cast-iron stoves.

With the beginning of the cattle drives after the Civil War, Dutch ovens saw duty as cooking pots for hungry cowboys on the trail. Chuck wagons even had a special compartment for "skillets and lids," as the pots were often known in ranch country. But cowboys weren't the only nineteenth-century travelers who cooked with Dutch ovens—sheepherders, miners, lumbermen, and military units also relied on them. Even today, you'd be hard-pressed to find a more practical piece of camping equipment.

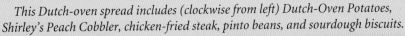

This Dutch-oven spread includes (clockwise from left) Dutch-Oven Potatoes, Shirley's Peach Cobbler, chicken-fried steak, pinto beans, and sourdough biscuits.

The design of Dutch ovens hasn't changed much since they came to America on the Mayflower almost four centuries ago.

Black Forest Icebox Pie

Believe it or not, you really can make an icebox pie in a Dutch oven!

½ c. butter or stick margarine, melted	16 oz. whipped topping, divided
1 c. all-purpose flour	1 (5.1-oz.) pkg. chocolate instant pudding mix
2 c. chopped pecans, divided	1 (5.1-oz.) pkg. vanilla instant pudding mix
1 c. powdered sugar	6 c. milk, divided
8 oz. cream cheese, softened	

To make crust, combine butter, flour, and 1 c. pecans; spread mixture evenly over bottom of a 12-inch Dutch oven. Place oven over 1½ rings of hot briquettes; cover and place a like amount of briquettes on lid. (Rotate oven once or twice during cooking to keep the heat even.) After browning crust (about 5 to 10 minutes), set oven aside to cool.

Mix powdered sugar, cream cheese, and 8 oz. whipped topping; spread mixture over bottom of cooled crust.

In 2 separate bowls, mix chocolate and vanilla pudding mixes and milk according to package directions. Spread vanilla pudding mixture evenly over cream cheese mixture in Dutch oven; repeat with chocolate pudding mixture. To set the pie, place the 12-inch oven inside a 14-inch oven and fill the space between them with ice; cool for 15 to 30 minutes.

Top pie with remaining whipped topping. Sprinkle remaining pecans on top. **Yield: 8 to 10 servings.**

WAYNE SWITZER AND JAY SWITZER ∞ NOVEMBER 2000

Sunday Cobbler

To make this recipe in a conventional home oven, assemble cobbler in a 2- to 3-qt. baking dish and bake at 375° about 25 to 35 minutes.

2 c. plus 2 T. granulated sugar, divided	½ tsp. cinnamon
1 c. all-purpose flour, divided	½ c. butter or stick margarine
1 (15-oz.) can water-packed cherries or other canned berries	½ c. chopped pecans
½ c. firmly packed brown sugar	½ c. sourdough starter (see recipe on page 229)

Combine 1½ c. sugar and ¼ c. flour in a 10-inch Dutch oven. Stir in cherries and mix well. Cook over live coals, stirring occasionally, until juice is thick and cherries are hot. Set aside.

In a separate bowl, combine remaining flour, ½ c. granulated sugar, brown sugar, and cinnamon. Cut in butter. Stir in pecans and ½ c. sourdough starter. Spread mixture over cherries and place oven back on coals. Cover with lid and place hot coals on the lid to bake. After top begins to brown, lift lid, and with a sharp knife, cut holes in the top so juice can bubble up through. Replace lid and continue baking a few more minutes. When top crust is golden brown, sprinkle with remaining 2 T. sugar, replace lid, and bake 1 more minute. **Yield: 6 to 8 servings.**

RICHARD BOLT ⌇ OCTOBER 1982

Vinegar Cobbler

To make this recipe in a conventional home oven, follow the same directions, assembling cobbler in a 2- to 3-qt. baking dish, and then bake at 375° for 15 to 20 minutes or until top is brown.

1¼ c. all-purpose flour	¼ c. apple vinegar
½ tsp. salt	1 c. sugar
½ c. shortening	1 tsp. vanilla
2½ c. water, divided	2 T. butter or stick margarine

Combine flour and salt; cut in shortening. Stir ¼ c. water into dough. Divide dough into 3 equal parts; roll each into a sheet ½ inch thick. Cut into strips 1 inch wide and break into short lengths.

Mix remaining ingredients except butter in a 10-inch Dutch oven and bring to a boil. Drop strips of pastry into boiling mixture until two-thirds of them are used. Remove Dutch oven from heat and use the last third of pastry strips to crisscross over top. Dot with butter and bake about 15 to 20 minutes or until top is brown. **Yield: 4 to 6 servings.**

RICHARD BOLT ⌇ OCTOBER 1982

Shirley's Peach Cobbler

Chuck-wagon cook James Stuart credits his wife, Shirley, with developing this recipe. Over the years, James has won more than twenty-five first-place awards with this cobbler.

1 recipe Vinegar Pie Crust (recipe follows), divided	1 c. all-purpose flour
1 (6-lb. 10-oz.) can sliced peaches in light syrup	3 c. sugar
⅔ c. butter or stick margarine	½ tsp. cinnamon
1 c. water	½ tsp. ground nutmeg
2 tsp. vanilla	

Grease bottom and sides of a 16-inch Dutch oven and dust lightly with flour. Roll out half of pie-crust dough to ⅛-inch thickness. Line bottom of Dutch oven with pie crust and set aside.

In a separate pot, heat peaches, butter, water, and vanilla. Combine dry ingredients and stir slowly into peach mixture, mixing well. Cook until hot. Remove from heat and pour into pie crust inside Dutch oven. Set aside.

Roll out remaining pie crust dough to ⅛-inch thickness and place on top of peach mixture. Place lid on Dutch oven and put hot coals on lid. Bake 15 to 20 minutes or until top is golden brown, making sure to rotate Dutch oven often. (Baking time varies according to the amount of wind.) **Yield: 40 servings.**

VINEGAR PIE CRUST

4 c. all-purpose flour	½ c. water
⅓ c. sugar	2 T. cider vinegar
2 tsp. salt	1 egg
1¾ c. shortening	

Combine flour, sugar, and salt. Cut in shortening until mixture is crumbly. Combine water, vinegar, and egg; beat well with a fork. Add to shortening mixture and mix well. Chill at least 2 hours before using. **Yield: Enough crust for one Peach Cobbler or two 9-inch double-crust pies.**

SHIRLEY STUART ～ SEPTEMBER 1994

Bumblebee Cobbler

Michele Castleberry made this cobbler for the 1999 Colonel Charles Goodnight Chuckwagon Cookoff in Clarendon. She notes that it can also be baked in a conventional home oven. After assembling the dish in a Dutch oven, put the lid on top, place it inside your conventional oven, and bake at 375° for 25 to 35 minutes.

enough pastry for sides, bottom, and top of a 14-inch Dutch oven, divided (the Vinegar Pie Crust recipe on page 242 works well)	1 (15-oz.) can sliced peaches
	1 c. sugar
1 (15-oz.) can blackberries	1 c. pecan halves or pieces, divided
1 (15-oz.) can blueberries	additional sugar
1 (20-oz.) can sliced apples	cinnamon
	½ c. butter or stick margarine, cut into pats

Line bottom and sides of a 14-inch Dutch oven with half of pastry; set aside.

Drain canned fruit well, reserving juice. Combine fruit juices in a small container and set aside 2 c. (reserve remaining juice for another use).

Combine fruit, 2 c. juice, and 1 c. sugar in a medium-size bowl and mix gently. Pour mixture into the pastry-lined Dutch oven. Top with ½ c. pecans and sprinkle with sugar and cinnamon to taste.

Roll out remaining pie crust and cut into strips. Crisscross dough over top of cobbler, making a basket weave. Sprinkle with more cinnamon and remaining pecans, then dust with sugar. Place butter pats on top evenly.

Cover and cook over 1 ring of hot briquettes, with 2 rings on top, for 20 to 30 minutes. **Yield: 15 to 20 servings.**

MICHELE CASTLEBERRY ~ 1999

*D*utchin' is an art, not a science; learning to do it well takes a while.

Index